GREAT CATHOLIC WRITINGS

THOUGHT, LITERATURE,

GREAT CATHOLIC WRITINGS

SPIRITUALITY, SOCIAL ACTION

Robert Feduccia Jr., editor
with Jerry Windley-Daoust;
Michael C. Jordan, PhD; and J. D. Childs

SAINT MARY'S PRESS®

Genuine recycled paper with 10% post-consumer waste. 1352

The publishing team included Robert Feduccia Jr., development editor; Jerry Windley-Daoust, writer; Michael C. Jordan, PhD, and J. D. Childs, consultants; Lorraine Kilmartin, reviewer; Mary Koehler, permissions editor; prepress and manufacturing coordinated by the prepublication and production services departments of Saint Mary's Press.

Printed in the United States of America

ISBN 978-0-88489-672-2 (perfectbound)

The Library of Congress has cataloged the hardcover edition as follows:

Great Catholic writings : thought, literature, spirituality, social action / Robert Feduccia Jr., editor ; with Jerry Windley-Daoust, Michael C. Jordan, and J. D. Childs.
    p. cm.
ISBN 978-0-88489-887-0 (hardbound)
    1. Catholic Church—Doctrines—History. 2. Catholic literature—History and criticism. 3. Catholics—Biography. 4. Catholic youth—Religious life. I. Feduccia, Robert. II. Windley-Daoust, Jerry. III. Jordan, Michael C., 1952– IV. Childs, J. D. (James Donald), 1968–
BX1751.3.G74 2006
282—dc22

2005030191

Contents

PART 4:
GREAT CATHOLIC WRITINGS ON SOCIAL ACTION

Introduction

Great Catholic Writings:
Thought, Literature, Spirituality, Social Action

Seeing with God-soaked Eyes

> And all of us, with unveiled faces, seeing the glory of the Lord as
> though reflected in a mirror, are being transformed into the same
> image from one degree of glory to another; for this comes from
> the Lord, the Spirit. (2 Corinthians 3:18)

Catholics believe that the world — all of material reality — is absolutely
soaked with the presence of God. The world is a place of infinite possibility for encountering God. This is the principle of sacramentality.
Grace, or God's presence, permeates all of reality.

The Catholic worldview lies in seeing the world sacramentally — with
God-soaked eyes. A Catholic vision celebrates the fact that the world is a
place of infinite possibility for encountering God. God's presence absolutely penetrates all of reality; he has even joined our world as a human
being, Jesus of Nazareth. Throughout the centuries, people who have
viewed the world with eyes such as these have written, and written
greatly. This book contains but a handful of such compositions — great,
Catholic writings.

These writings from the Roman Catholic Tradition are essentially
a dialogue; they contain the capacity for conversation. These essays,
speeches, stories, reflections, and dissertations speak out to us: sometimes they whisper, sometimes they shout, but they always provoke an
encounter of some sort. They place us in a vulnerable position when
they speak to us. A great story, poem, or essay can capture your imagination. When a writing you encounter really speaks to you, it impacts your
world. Perhaps it echoes or challenges your view of the world or your
hopes for what the world could be. Such an experience can be continued
as you and your friends discuss the story, poem, or essay. Something
exciting is happening. Real learning is taking place. These writings are a
form of art, and you learn about yourself, and your own journey, both
through art that captures your imagination and in conversations with
your friends. This book is different from other books you may have used
in school. It contains great writings that will echo, challenge, and provide hope.

This book marks a decisive shift in the way teachers might approach religious topics with you. The new emphasis allows you an opportunity to encounter classic expressions of thought in order to form *and inform* your imagination. This approach seeks to engage you in the whole context of your life. It seeks to bridge the gap between your experiences and the weight and richness of the Catholic tradition. It is our hope to foster a Catholic imagination both in your mind and heart so that it may be enfleshed in the choices you make and in the *person you become*.

Consider a 3-D movie, a special kind of film that makes images jump out at the viewers; movement and action on the screen seem to fill the theatre. Necessary for this effect, however, are the special red- and green-lensed glasses that we put on for watching. Without the glasses, we are largely incapable of receiving the effect the 3-D film provides. Similarly, if we wear the glasses when we watch a normal movie, there is no effect and our ability to see clearly is diminished (not to mention, we look foolish!). We get the full effect of the 3-D show only when we wear the glasses and are watching a movie that has been formatted for this purpose. When we come to the theatre anticipating that we will enjoy the full impact of the 3-D production, and we watch it while *engaged*, with our eyes wide open, we are in for a treat!

Grace works like that. God's world is like the screen that shows the special three-dimensionally formatted film. Our faith, our relationship with God whereby we are engaged actively with love and devotion, is how we put on the special glasses that enable us to see. With the glasses and the potential for 3-D effects, we can look at reality in a way that sees God in an infinite variety of situations. God's very Self, the dynamic life of the Holy Trinity into which we are invited through love, is the effect of the movie we participate in: God's grace *is* the special effect! For in each moment of our lives, God plants seeds in the soil of our freedom, enabling spontaneity, engagement, and love—God's very Self. We are capable of encountering God in many ways within every moment of every day of our lives, if we are looking through the right lenses. This is a sacramental worldview—to see with God-soaked eyes. It is to perceive and realize God's profound presence everywhere in everything. It is how Catholicism teaches us to see—to look and act as a saint.

PART ONE
GREAT CATHOLIC THOUGHT

Pope John Paul II

Blaise Pascal

Saint Thomas Aquinas

"The Five Ways"

SAINT THOMAS AQUINAS

Introduction

Saint Thomas Aquinas was so quiet and so large that his fellow university students nicknamed him the Dumb (mute) Ox. But his teacher, Albert the Great, predicted that one day the bellow of that "dumb ox" would be heard around the world. He was right.

Saint Thomas Aquinas was born in 1225 to a wealthy noble family in southern Italy. His family sent him to live with Benedictine monks so that he would eventually become the abbot at the monastery. Instead, Aquinas announced that he wanted to join the recently created Order of Preachers, the Dominicans. The Dominicans' mission was to combat ignorance of the faith by preaching and teaching wherever they went.

When he joined the Dominicans, Saint Thomas was sent to the University of Paris, where he received a doctorate in theology. He quickly became a popular preacher whose passionate sermons frequently moved people to tears and applause. But Saint Thomas was to become best known for his innovative theology. His groundbreaking work was made possible not only by his genius, but by the scholarly renewal that was sweeping Europe. Expanding trade, along with the Crusades, had brought western Europe into contact with Eastern Christianity and the Arab world, both of which reintroduced the West to classic texts from the early Church fathers and Greek philosophers. The work of Aristotle (384–322 BCE) especially challenged and intrigued scholars. For centuries, the great thinkers of western Europe had drawn primarily on divine revelation to answer questions about the world, but Aristotle described the world through the use of reason alone. Scholars began to use Aristotle's logic to debate disputed questions in every field, including theology. The attempt to integrate faith with reason became known as Scholasticism, with Saint Thomas Aquinas as the greatest of the Schoolmen, as these new theologians were called.

Saint Thomas began his work with the assumption that faith cannot contradict reason when they are both properly understood. Truth's single source is God. Saint Thomas's attempt to explore the truths of faith resulted in his greatest work, the *Summa Theologica*. This great effort attempted to summarize all aspects of Christian faith in an integrated, logical way. Even though he never finished it, this "summary" runs more than three thousand pages long. "The Five Ways" comes from the part of the *Summa Theologica* in which Saint Thomas responds to the question of the existence of God.

Aquinas is well known for his sharp intellect, but he was also a passionately prayerful person. During Mass on the feast of Saint Nicholas in 1273, he had an experience in which he was overwhelmed by the power and presence of God. He quit writing the *Summa Theologica* after that, saying that compared to what God had revealed to him, everything he had written was as insignificant as straw. He died a few months later, on March 7, 1274. He was canonized a saint in 1323, and declared a Doctor of the Church in 1567.

GREAT CATHOLIC THOUGHT
"The Five Ways"

The existence of God can be proved in five ways.

The first and more manifest way is the argument from motion. It is certain, and evident to our senses, that in the world some things are in motion. Now whatever is moved is moved by another, for nothing can be moved except it is in potentiality to that towards which it is moved; whereas a thing moves inasmuch as it is in act. For motion is nothing else than the reduction of something from potentiality to actuality. But nothing can be reduced from potentiality to actuality, except by something in a state of actuality. Thus that which is actually hot, as fire makes wood, which is potentially hot, to be actually hot, and thereby moves and changes it. Now it is not possible that the same thing should be at once in actuality and potentiality in the same respect, but only in different respects. For what is actually hot cannot simultaneously be potentially hot; but it is simultaneously potentially cold. It is therefore impossible that in the same respect and in the same way a thing should be both mover and moved, *i.e.*, that it should move itself. Therefore, whatever is moved must be moved by another. If that by which it is moved be itself moved, then this also must needs be moved by another, and that by another again. But this cannot go on to infinity, because then there would be no first mover, and, consequently, no other mover; seeing that subsequent movers move only inasmuch as they are moved by the first mover, as the staff moves only because it is moved by the hand. Therefore it is necessary to arrive at a first mover, put in motion by no other; and this everyone understands to be God.

THE CAUSES

- Efficient Cause — That which causes something else to exist. It can also be called the first cause.

- Intermediate Cause — Something used by the first cause to accomplish a particular goal.

- Ultimate Cause — The goal or destination intended by the first cause.

The second way is from the nature of the efficient cause. In the world of sensible things we find there is an order of efficient causes. There is no case known (neither is it, indeed, possible) in which a thing is found to be the efficient cause of itself; for so it would be prior to itself, which is impossible. Now in efficient causes it is not possible to go on to infinity, because in all efficient causes following in order, the first is the cause of the intermediate cause, and the intermediate is the cause of the ultimate cause, whether the intermediate cause be several, or only one. Now to take away the cause is to take away the effect. Therefore, if there be no first cause among efficient causes, there will be no ultimate, nor any intermediate, cause. But if in efficient causes it is possible to go on to infinity, there will be no first efficient cause, neither will there be an ultimate effect, nor any intermediate efficient causes; all of which is plainly false. Therefore it is necessary to admit a first efficient cause, to which everyone gives the name of God.

The third way is taken from possibility and necessity, and runs thus. We find in nature things that are possible to be and not to be, since they are found to be generated, and to be corrupted, and consequently, it is possible for them to be and not to be. But it is impossible for these always to exist, for that which can not-be at some time is not. Therefore, if everything can not-be, then at one time there was nothing in existence. Now if this were true, even now there would be nothing in existence, because that which does not exist begins to exist only through something already existing. Therefore, if at one time nothing was in existence, it would have been impossible for anything to have begun to exist; and thus even now nothing would be in existence — which is absurd. Therefore, not all beings are merely possible, but there must exist something the existence of which is necessary. But every necessary thing either has its necessity caused by another, or not. Now it is impossible to go on to infinity in necessary things which have their necessity caused by another, as has been already proved in regard to efficient causes. Therefore we cannot but admit the existence of some being having of itself its own necessity, and not receiving it from another, but rather causing in others their necessity. This all men speak of as God.

The fourth way is taken from the gradation to be found in things. Among beings there are some more and some less good, true, noble, and the like. But *more* and *less* are predicated of different things according as they resemble in their different ways something which is the maximum, as a thing is said to be hotter according as it more nearly resembles that which is hottest; so that there is something which is truest, something best, something noblest, and, consequently, something which is most being, for those things that are greatest in truth are greatest in being, as it is written in *Metaph. ii.* Now the maximum in any genus is the cause of all in that genus, as fire, which is the maximum of heat, is the cause of all hot things as is said in the same book. Therefore there must also be something which is to all beings the cause of their being, goodness, and every other perfection; and this we call God.

The fifth way is taken from the governance of the world. We see that things which lack knowledge, such as natural bodies, act for an end, and this is evident from their acting always, or nearly always, in the same way, so as to obtain the best result. Hence it is plain that they achieve their end, not fortuitously, but designedly. Now whatever lacks knowledge cannot move towards an end, unless it be directed by some being endowed with knowledge and intelligence; as the arrow is directed by the archer. Therefore some intelligent being exists by whom all natural things are directed to their end; and this being we call God.

Review Questions

1. How does Saint Thomas Aquinas define "motion"?

2. What does Saint Thomas Aquinas have to say about the possibility of a thing bringing itself into existence?

3. What does Saint Thomas Aquinas have to say about the possibility that nothing necessary exists?

4. What is meant by "the graduation to be found in things"?

5. How does Saint Thomas Aquinas think things without intelligence are moved?

In-depth Questions

1. Of the Five Ways, which one do you think is best proof that God exists? Please explain.

2. If you were asked to add a sixth proof to the Five Ways, what would you add?

3. What do you think this quote means: "There is a difference between belief in God and believing in God."

4. The Catholic Church has long held that faith and reason cannot contradict each other. Why do you think it is important for belief in God to be rational and logical?

From *Pensées* (Pascal's Wager)

BLAISE PASCAL

Introduction

Blaise Pascal lived in a period when Europeans began using logic and reason to develop modern philosophy, science, and mathematics. Some also began using reason to explore—and challenge—the foundations of Christian faith. As a groundbreaking mathematician and scientist, Pascal joined such figures as Descartes and Fermat as one of the leading lights of this "Age of Reason." But before his short life was over, he became convinced that reason alone fails to fully grasp the heart of reality; his unfinished defense of Christianity, the *Pensées* (or "thoughts") remains one of the classics of Christian literature.

Pascal was born in 1623 in Claremont, France, and demonstrated his genius for mathematics when he taught himself geometry at the age of twelve. Throughout his teens, his reputation as a mathematical genius was known throughout Europe. He would go on to establish the modern theory of probability with Pierre Fermat, prove the existence of a vacuum, conduct experiments on barometric pressure, and contribute to the development of differential calculus.

As a young man, Pascal was Catholic in name only. That began to change in 1646, when two religious brothers caring for Pascal's injured father introduced the young man to Jansenism, a heresy that believed humans were so damaged by Original Sin that they lost their free will. They preached a need for very rigorous penance that struck a chord with Pascal. His contact with them led to his first religious conversion. Then in 1654, he narrowly escaped death when his horses bolted, leaving his carriage hanging on the edge of a bridge over the river Seine. Fifteen days later he had an intense mystical experience of God's presence that left him full of peace and joy. He recorded the experience on a piece of parchment that he sewed into his coat next to his heart.

Having given himself completely over to God, he gave up his work in science and mathematics and moved to Port Royal, the center of Jansenism. From there he turned his formidable mind to writing a systematic defense of Christianity. In these writings he addressed the skeptical intellectuals of the time—friends and colleagues he knew well.

Perhaps the most famous of his writings is known as Pascal's wager. In an imaginary conversation with a friend, there is a debate about whether it is more reasonable to believe in God or not. He frames the question in terms of gambling (a favorite pastime of his youth); his seemingly strange references to wagering two or three lives reflect his use of probability theory and decision theory, both of which he pioneered, to provide an answer in favor of belief in God.

As he wrote, he suffered enormously from a chronic illness that ultimately took his life in 1662, at the age of 39. Although he never finished his greatest project, his notes (basically scraps of paper covered in rough scribbles) were published after his death as the *Pensées*.

GREAT CATHOLIC THOUGHT
From *Pensées* (Pascal's Wager)

If there is a God, He is infinitely incomprehensible, since, having neither parts nor limits, He has no affinity to us. We are then incapable of knowing either what He is or if He is. This being so, who will dare to undertake the decision of the question? Not we, who have no affinity to Him.

Who then will blame Christians for not being able to give a reason for their belief, since they profess a religion for which they cannot give a reason? They declare, in expounding it to the world, that it is a foolishness, *stultitiam*; and then you complain that they do not prove it! If they proved it, they would not keep their word; it is in lacking proofs, that they are not lacking in sense. "Yes, but although this excuses those who offer it as such, and takes away from them the blame of putting it forward without reason, it does not excuse those who receive it." Let us then examine this point, and say, "God is, or He is not." But to which side shall we incline? Reason can decide nothing here. There is an infinite chaos which separated us. A game is being played at the extremity of this infinite distance where heads or tails will turn up. What will you wager? According to reason, you can do neither the one thing nor the other; according to reason, you can defend neither of the propositions.

Do not then reprove for error those who have made a choice; for you know nothing about it. "No, but I blame them for having made, not this choice, but a choice; for again both he who chooses heads and he who chooses tails are equally at fault, they are both in the wrong. The true course is not to wager at all."

Yes; but you must wager. It is not optional. You are embarked. Which will you choose then? Let us see. Since you must choose, let us see which interests you least. You have two things to lose, the true and the good; and two things to stake, your reason and your will, your knowledge and your happiness; and your nature has two things to shun, error and misery. Your reason is no more shocked in choosing one rather than the other, since you must of necessity choose. This is one point settled. But your happiness? Let us weigh the gain and the loss in wagering that God is. Let us estimate these two chances. If you gain, you gain all; if you lose, you lose nothing. Wager, then, without hesitation that He is. — "That is very fine. Yes, I must wager; but I may perhaps wager too much." — Let us see. Since there is an equal risk of gain and of loss, if you had only to gain two lives, instead of one, you might still wager. But if there were three lives to gain, you would have to play (since you are under the necessity of playing), and you would be imprudent, when you are forced to play, not to chance your life to gain three at a game where there is an equal risk of loss and gain. But there is an eternity of life and happiness. And this being so, if there were an infinity of chances, of which one only would be for you, you would still be right in wagering one to win two, and you would act stupidly, being obliged to play, by refusing to stake one life against three at a game in which out of an infinity of chances there is one for you, if there were an infinity of an infinitely happy life to gain. But there is here an infinity of an infinitely happy life to gain, a chance of gain against a finite number of chances of loss, and what you stake is finite. It is all divided; wherever the infinite is and there is not an infinity of chances of loss against that of gain, there is no time to hesitate, you must give all. And thus, when one is forced to play, he must renounce reason to preserve his life, rather than risk it for infinite gain, as likely to happen as the loss of nothingness.

For it is no use to say it is uncertain if we will gain, and it is certain that we risk, and that the infinite distance between the *certainty* of what is staked and the *uncertainty* of what will be gained, equals the finite good which is certainly staked against the uncertain infinite. It is not so, as every player stakes a certainty to gain an uncertainty, and yet he stakes a finite certainty to gain a finite uncertainty, without transgressing against reason. There is not an infinite distance between the certainty staked and the uncertainty of the gain; that is untrue. In truth, there is an infinity between the certainty of gain and the certainty of loss. But the uncertainty of the gain is proportioned to the certainty of the stake according to the proportion of the chances of gain and loss. Hence it comes that, if there are as many risks on one side as on the other, the course is to play even; and then the certainty of the stake is equal to the uncertainty of the gain, so far is it from fact that there is an infinite distance between them. And so our proposition is of infinite force, when there is the finite to stake in a game where there are equal risks of gain and of loss, and the infinite to gain. This is demonstrable; and if men are capable of any truths, this is one.

"I confess it, I admit it. But, still, is there no means of seeing the faces of the cards?" — Yes, Scripture and the rest, etc. "Yes, but I have my hands tied and my mouth closed; I am forced to wager, and am not free. I am not released, and am so made that I cannot believe. What, then, would you have me do?"

True. But at least learn your inability to believe, since reason brings you to this, and yet you cannot believe. Endeavour then to convince yourself, not by increase of proofs of God, but by the abatement of your passions. You would like to attain faith, and do not know the way; you would like to cure yourself of unbelief, and ask the remedy for it. Learn of those who have been bound like you, and who now stake all their possessions. These are people who know the way which you would follow, and who are cured of an ill of which you would be cured. Follow the way by which they began; by acting as if they believed, taking the holy water, having masses said, etc. Even this will naturally make you believe, and deaden your acuteness. —"But this is what I am afraid of." — And why? What have you to lose?

But to show you that this leads you there, it is this which will lessen the passions, which are your stumbling-blocks.

The end of this discourse. — Now, what harm will befall you in taking this side? You will be faithful, honest, humble, grateful, generous, a sincere friend, truthful. Certainly you will not have those poisonous pleasures, glory and luxury; but will you not have others? I will tell you that you will thereby gain in this life, and that at each step you take on this road, you will see so great certainty of gain, so much nothingness in what you risk, that you will at last recognise that you have wagered for something certain and infinite, for which you have given nothing.

"Ah! This discourse transports me, charms me," etc.

If this discourse pleases you and seems impressive, know that it is made by a man who has knelt, both before and after it, in prayer to that Being, infinite and without parts, before whom he lays all he has, for you also to lay before Him all you have for your own good and for His glory, that so strength may be given to lowliness.

Review Questions

1. In this mock conversation between Pascal and his friend, the friend says it is best that one not place a wager on God's existence. How does Pascal respond?

2. What could be won or lost if one wagers that God does exist?

3. What advice does Pascal have for those who cannot believe?

4. Rather than harm, what can one expect in this life by wagering that God exists?

In-depth Questions

1. Pascal writes that if a Christian proves that God exists, then the Christian has not kept his word. What do you think he means by that?

2. In any wager or bet, something of value is risked and laid on the line. What do you risk losing by wagering on God's existence?

3. Some have criticized the idea of wagering on God's existence. They say that making a wager is not the same as making an act of faith. Do you think taking Pascal's wager is enough, or does believing in God require something different? Please explain.

4. If a person finds Pascal's wager to be convincing but is still unable to believe in God, what do you think that person should do?

GREAT CATHOLIC THOUGHT: READING 3

"Message to the Pontifical Academy of Sciences: On Evolution"

POPE JOHN PAUL II

Introduction

The Pontifical Academy of Sciences is a nonsectarian group of eighty or so leading scientists who conduct scientific investigations for the Church, and who advise the Pope on scientific matters. As important as its work is, it does not normally make headlines around the world—but it did when Pope John Paul II delivered his message on evolution to the academy on October 22, 1996. Some background on the contentious relationship between religion and science around the subject of evolution will help us understand why it got worldwide publicity.

Before the nineteenth century, most educated people had no reason to doubt that God created the world in seven, 24-hour days, as the Book of Genesis describes. But as scientists learned more about geological processes, they realized that the Earth had to be much older than a literal interpretation of Genesis would indicate. When Charles Darwin published *The Origin of Species* in 1859, the theory of evolution by natural selection became widely accepted.

Many religious people found evolution threatening; the theory of evolution seemed to not only discredit the truth of the Bible, but also the idea that humans hold a unique place in creation because they are created in the image of God. The evolution of species even seemed to suggest that God is unnecessary.

At first, Catholics rejected the theory of evolution too. But with evidence for the theory mounting, Pope Pius XII issued an encyclical in 1950, *Humani Generis,* stating that there is not necessarily a conflict between the theory of evolution and Christian faith. Pope John Paul II's 1996 message on evolution reaffirmed that the theory is not incompatible with Christian faith because it is impossible for scientific truth to contradict truth revealed by God.

Like Pope Pius XII, Pope John Paul II was cautious about how any theory of evolution might be used to describe the nature of the human person. Anthropology — the study of human beings — had long been a concern of the Pope. After earning his doctorate in philosophy, he had spent years reflecting and writing on various aspects of anthropology. He drew on his background in anthropology to help craft the Second Vatican Council's landmark document *Gaudium et Spes (The Church in the Modern World)*, particularly the section on the meaning and purpose of human activity. Having reflected so extensively on human nature, the pope would not casually dismiss concerns about evolution's implications for understanding what it means to be human. How, then, could the Church conclude that the theory of evolution did not necessarily contradict Christian revelation concerning the human person created by God?

The Vatican II document *Dei Verbum* explains that God inspired the human authors of the Bible to write, without error, the truth necessary for salvation. But these human authors used the human knowledge and human images of their time to communicate that truth, including the poetic imagery of Genesis. The metaphors used by the authors of Genesis to describe the creation of the world accurately convey the sacred truth that God has revealed himself as the ultimate source of everything. Humans are created in the image of God and are created to be in an intimate relationship with him.

These are the truths that God revealed for the sake of salvation. As the Pope made clear in his message to the Pontifical Academy of Sciences, the Church rejects any theory of evolution that would deny those essential truths, especially any theory that reduces human beings to a purely biological reality by denying their spiritual dimension.

Seen in this light, the evolution of species does not displace God from his role as Creator. In fact, for Catholic thinkers like Sara Maitland (see pages 91–98), God uses the mechanism of evolution to create, and this idea reveals God to be more generous, playful, and extravagant than anyone had previously imagined.

GREAT CATHOLIC THOUGHT
"Message to the Pontifical Academy of Sciences: On Evolution"

It is with great pleasure that I send my cordial greetings to you, Mr. President, and to all of you who constitute the Pontifical Academy of Sciences, on the occasion of your plenary assembly. I send my particular best wishes to the new members of the Academy, who come to take part in your work for the first time. I also wish to recall the members who have died in the course of the past year; I entrust them to the Maker of all life.

1. In celebrating the 60th anniversary of the re-foundation of the Academy, it gives me pleasure to recall the intentions of my predecessor, Pius XI, who wished to bring together around him a chosen group of scholars who could, working with complete freedom, inform the Holy See about the developments in scientific research and thus provide aid for reflections.

To those whom he enjoyed calling the Scientific Senate of the Church, he asked simply this: that they serve the truth. That is the same invitation which I renew today, with the certainty that we can all draw profit from "the fruitfulness of frank dialogue between the Church and science." (Discourse to the Academy of Sciences, October 28, 1986, #1)

2. I am delighted with the first theme which you have chosen: the origin of life and evolution — an essential theme of lively interest to the Church, since Revelation contains some of its own teachings concerning the nature and origins of man. How should the conclusions reached by the diverse scientific disciplines be brought together with those contained in the message of Revelation? And if at first glance these views seem to clash with each other, where should we look for a solution? We know that the truth cannot contradict the truth. (Leo XIII, *Providentissimus Deus*) However, in order better to understand historical reality, your research into the relationships between the Church and the scientific community between the 16th and 18th centuries will have a great deal of importance.

In the course of this plenary session, you will be undertaking a "reflection on science in the shadow of the third millennium," and beginning to determine the principal problems which the sciences face, which have an influence on the future of humanity. By your efforts, you will mark out the path toward solutions which will benefit all of the human community. In the domain of nature, both living and inanimate, the evolution of science and its applications gives rise to new inquiries. The Church will be better able to expand her work insofar as we understand the essential aspects of these new developments. Thus, following her specific mission, the Church will be able to offer the criteria by which we may discern the moral behavior to which all men are called, in view of their integral salvation.

3. Before offering a few more specific reflections on the theme of the origin of life and evolution, I would remind you that the magisterium of the Church has already made some pronouncements on these matters, within her own proper sphere of competence. I will cite two such interventions here.

In his encyclical *Humani Generis* (1950), my predecessor Pius XII has already affirmed that there is no conflict between evolution and the doctrine of the faith regarding man and his vocation, provided that we do not lose sight of certain fixed points.

MAGISTERIUM

This refers to the authority with which the Catholic Church teaches. When teaching on matters of morality or faith, the Church cannot be in error.

For my part, when I received the participants in the plenary assembly of your Academy on October 31, 1992, I used the occasion —and the example of Gallileo—to draw attention to the necessity of using a rigorous hermeneutical approach in seeking a concrete interpretation of the inspired texts. It is important to set proper limits to the understanding of Scripture, excluding any unseasonable interpretations which would make it mean something which it is not intended

HERMENEUTICS

Hermeneutics is the method one uses to interpret the Bible. For example, one person may interpret the Bible literally, while another interprets the Bible figuratively. These are examples of two different hermeneutics.

to mean. In order to mark out the limits of their own proper fields, theologians and those working on the exegesis of the Scripture need to be well informed regarding the results of the latest scientific research.

4. Taking into account the scientific research of the era, and also the proper requirements of theology, the encyclical *Humani Generis* treated the doctrine of "evolutionism" as a serious hypothesis, worthy of investigation and serious study, alongside the opposite hypothesis. Pius XII added two methodological conditions for this study: one could not adopt this opinion as if it were a certain and demonstrable doctrine, and one could not totally set aside the teaching Revelation on the relevant questions. He also set out the conditions on which this opinion would be compatible with the Christian faith—a point to which I shall return.

Today, more than a half-century after the appearance of that encyclical, some new findings lead us toward the recognition of evolution as more than an hypothesis. In fact it is remarkable that this theory has had progressively greater influence on the spirit of researchers, following a series of discoveries in different scholarly disciplines. The convergence in the results of these independent studies—which was neither planned nor sought—constitutes in itself a significant argument in favor of the theory.

What is the significance of a theory such as this one? To open this question is to enter into the field of epistemology. A theory is a meta-scientific elaboration, which is distinct from, but in harmony with, the results of observation. With the help of such a theory a group of data and independent facts can be related to one another and inter-

EPISTEMOLOGY

Epistemology is a philosophical discipline that studies the source and nature of knowledge. How do we know something is true? Can we know something that we cannot perceive with our five senses? These are questions asked in epistemology.

preted in one comprehensive explanation. The theory proves its validity by the measure to which it can be verified. It is constantly being tested against the facts; when it can no longer explain these facts, it shows its limits and its lack of usefulness, and it must be revised.

Moreover, the elaboration of a theory such as that of evolution, while obedient to the need for consistency with the observed data, must also involve importing some ideas from the philosophy of nature.

And to tell the truth, rather than speaking about the theory of evolution, it is more accurate to speak of the theories of evolution. The use of the plural is required here—in part because of the diversity of explanations regarding the mechanism of evolution, and in part because of the diversity of philosophies involved. There are material-ist and reductionist theories, as well as spiritualist theories. Here the final judgment is within the competence of philosophy and, beyond that, of theology.

5. The magisterium of the Church takes a direct interest in the question of evolution, because it touches on the conception of man, whom Revelation tells us is created in the image and likeness of God. The conciliar constitution *Gaudium et Spes* has given us a magnificent exposition of this doctrine, which is one of the essential elements of Christian thought. The Council recalled that "man is the only crea-ture on earth that God wanted for its own sake." In other words, the human person cannot be subordinated as a means to an end, or as an instrument of either the species or the society; he has a value of his own. He is a person. By this intelligence and his will, he is capable of entering into relationship, of communion, of solidarity, of the gift of himself to others like himself. Saint Thomas observed that man's resemblance to God resides especially in his speculative intellect, because his relationship with the object of his knowledge is like

God's relationship with his creation. (*Summa Theologica* I-II, q 3, a 5, ad 1) But even beyond that, man is called to enter into a loving relationship with God himself, a relationship which will find its full expression at the end of time, in eternity. Within the mystery of the risen Christ the full grandeur of this vocation is revealed to us. (*Gaudium et Spes*, 22) It is by virtue of his eternal soul that the whole person, including his body, possesses such great dignity. Pius XII underlined the essential point: if the origin of the human body comes through living matter which existed previously, the spiritual soul is created directly by God ("animas enim a Deo immediate creari catholica fides non retimere iubet"). (*Humani Generis*)

As a result, the theories of evolution which, because of the philosophies which inspire them, regard the spirit either as emerging from the forces of living matter, or as a simple epiphenomenon of that matter, are incompatible with the truth about man. They are therefore unable to serve as the basis for the dignity of the human person.

6. With man, we find ourselves facing a different ontological order—an ontological leap, we could say. But in posing such a great ontological discontinuity, are we not breaking up the physical conti-

⊙ΠΤΟLOGICAL

Ontology is a philosophical discipline that studies the nature, essence, or being of things. What separates humans from other animals? What comprises a human person: intellect, imagination, will? These are ontological questions.

nuity which seems to be the main line of research about evolution in the fields of physics and chemistry? An appreciation for the different methods used in different fields of scholarship allows us to bring together two points of view which at first might seem irreconcilable. The sciences of observation describe and measure, with ever greater precision, the many manifestations of life, and write them down along the time-line. The moment of passage into the spiritual realm is not something that can be observed in this way—although we can nevertheless discern, through experimental research, a series of very valuable signs of what is specifically human life. But the experience of metaphysical knowledge, of self-consciousness and self-awareness, of moral conscience, of liberty, or of aesthetic and religious experience—these must be analyzed through philosophical reflection, while theology seeks to clarify the ultimate meaning of the Creator's designs.

METAPHYSICS

Literally meaning "beyond the physical," metaphysics is a philosophical discipline that studies the realities that are beyond the experience of our senses.

7. In closing, I would like to call to mind the Gospel truth which can shed a greater light on your researches into the origins and the development of living matter. The Bible, in fact, bears an extraordinary message about life. It shows us life, as it characterizes the highest forms of existence, with a vision of wisdom. That vision guided me in writing the encyclical which I have consecrated to the respect for human life and which I have entitled precisely The Gospel of Life.

It is significant that in the Gospel of St. John, life refers to that divine light which Christ brings to us. We are called to enter into eternal life, which is to say the eternity of divine beatitude.

To set us on guard against the grave temptations which face us, our Lord cites the great words of Deuteronomy: "Man does not live by bread alone, but by every word that comes from the mouth of God." (Deut 8:3; Mt 4:4)

Even more, life is one of the most beautiful titles which the Bible gives to God; he is the living God.

With a full heart, I invoke upon all of you, and all to whom you are close, an abundance of divine blessings.

From the Vatican, October 22, 1996, John Paul II

Review Questions

1. How did Pope Pius XII address the apparent conflict between evolution and the doctrine of faith?

2. Why did Pope John Paul II refer to *theories* of evolution rather than *theory*?

3. What does it mean that a person is created for his or her own sake?

4. Regarding human dignity, what essential point was made by Pope Pius XII?

5. What does Pope John Paul II say is the role of philosophy and theology in studying the human person?

In-depth Questions

1. Saint Thomas Aquinas said that humanity's imagination or speculative intellect made humans unique. Pope John Paul II said humanity's ability to enter into a living relationship with God made humans unique. What do you think makes humans distinct from the other animals?

2. Do you think the theory of evolution poses a threat to Christian faith? Please explain.

3. Do you think scientists and theologians should work together or do you think it is best if they work independently? Please explain.

4. Compare this reading to Saint Thomas Aquinas's "The Five Ways," on pages 14–16. Do you think studying science and observing nature can lead someone to affirm God's existence? Please explain.

"Leisure and Its Threefold Opposition"

JOSEF PIEPER

Introduction

Most people would not find German philosopher Josef Pieper's (PEEP-er) work on topics such as fortitude, love, and leisure to be earth-shaking. But the Nazis considered his work dangerous enough to confiscate during World War II. While the Nazis condemned his work, Pieper's philosophical insights eventually won him a worldwide audience; his more than fifty books have been translated into fifteen languages, collectively selling more than a million copies.

Born on May 4, 1904, in Elte, Germany, Pieper grew up during turbulent times. World War I began when he was ten years old, and the Nazis rose to power just as his career in philosophy was getting underway. He was initially fascinated by the nineteenth-century Danish philosopher Søren Kierkegaard, but after a mentor recommended that he read Saint Thomas Aquinas (see pages 14–16, "The Five Ways"), this great medieval theologian became Pieper's inspiration. In fact, Pieper eventually became a leading Aquinas scholar. Not surprisingly, the classical Greek philosophers who so influenced Aquinas — Plato, Aristotle, Socrates — were also sources for Pieper.

At the end of World War II, he earned a teaching position at the University of Münster, where he taught philosophy for fifty years. As his reputation grew, he was offered more prestigious positions elsewhere in Germany and the United States, but he refused them all because he did not want to abandon the garden he was so fond of tending at his home. Such simplicity demonstrates how he lived what he taught.

"Leisure and Its Threefold Opposition" reflects one of Pieper's perennial concerns: the modern attitude that human beings find their fulfillment primarily through work — that is, through their efforts to change the world around them. Not so, says Pieper. Saint Thomas Aquinas held that humans fulfill their quest for happiness through the beatific vision — the full, direct experience of God. Drawing on that insight, Pieper argues that humans find fulfillment not only by acting on the world but also by realizing God at play in the world around them. Such a realization occurs during authentic leisure, and finds its expression in authentic celebration. That line of reasoning has parallels in the thought of Pope John Paul II, who defined the "culture of death" as one in which people emphasize *having* over *being,* and value human life only in terms of its utility.

Pieper is best known in the United States for the book that he wrote on work and leisure, *Leisure: The Basis of Culture* (1952). That book is probably even more relevant now than it was when it was published, as cell phones and e-mail make it easier for the workplace to follow many workers home. His words are a reminder that life is found in enjoying beauty, not the bottom line.

Pieper died in 1997 at the age of 93.

GREAT CATHOLIC THOUGHT
"Leisure and Its Threefold Opposition"

Whoever advocates leisure nowadays may already be on the defensive. We have to face an opposition that at first seems to prevail. Things are not made easier by the fact that this opposition does not come from "someone else" but indeed springs from a conflict within ourselves. Worse yet, when put on the spot, we are not even able to define exactly what we are trying to defend. For example, when Aristotle says, "We work so we can have leisure," we must admit in all honesty that we do not know what this offensive statement means.

This, I think, is our situation.

The first question, therefore, is: What is leisure? How is this concept defined in our great philosophical tradition?

I deem it advisable to attempt an answer in such a way as to deal first with those opposing forces that could be labeled "overvaluation of work." This is admittedly a tentative expression. For "work" can mean several things, at least three. "Work" can mean "activity as such." Second, "work" can mean "exertion, effort, drudgery." And third is the usage of "work" for all "useful activity", especially in the sense "useful for society." Which of the three concepts do I have in mind when I speak of the "overvaluation of work"? I would say: all three! We encounter overvaluation of activity for its own sake, as well as overvaluation of exertion and drudgery, and—last but not least—overvaluation of the social function of work. This specifically is the three-faced demon everyone has to deal with when setting out to defend leisure.

Overvaluation of activity for its own sake. By this I mean the inability to let something simply happen; the inability to accept a kindness graciously, to be on the receiving end in general. This is the attitude of "absolute activity" that, according to Goethe, always ends bankrupt. The most extreme expression so far of this heresy can be found in a statement by Adolf Hitler: "Any activity is meaningful, even a criminal activity; all passivity, in contrast, is meaningless." This, of course, is an insane formulation, simply absurd. But "milder" forms of such insanity, I surmise, are typical of our contemporary world.

Overvaluation of exertion and drudgery. Strangely enough, this too can be found. Yes, we may even assert that the average ethical understanding of "decent" modern people is to a large extent colored by such an overvaluation of drudgery: goodness is by nature difficult, and whatever is gained without effort cannot have moral value. [The German poet] Friedrich Schiller has ridiculed this attitude in a ditty aimed at Kant:

Readily do I help all my friends —
Too bad, I do so with pleasure;
Much am I grieved that I, with this,
Can gain no virtuous treasure.

The ancients — who are for me the great Greeks Plato and Aristotle but also the famous teachers of Western Christianity — did not hold that goodness is difficult by nature and therefore will always and necessarily be so. They were well aware of the fact that the highest forms of applied goodness are indeed always effortless because they essentially flow from love. In this same way the highest forms of perception — the sudden flash of ingenious insight or true contemplation — do not really require mental labor but come without effort because they are by nature gifts. "Gifts" — this may well be the key concept. If we consider the strange propensity toward hardship that is engraved into the face of our contemporaries as a distinct expectation of suffering (a more typical trait, I believe, than the oft deplored craving for pleasure) — if we consider this, then to our surprise we may face the question: Could perhaps the deepest reason be the people's refusal to accept a gift, no matter where it comes from?

Overvaluation of the social function at work. Not much has to be said to show how this trait dominates contemporary societies. We should, however, think not just of those totalitarian "five-year plans" whose infamy lies not so much in their attempt to order everything as rather in their claim to provide the exclusive value standards for all aspects of life, not only industrial production but the personal life of individuals as well. Oh yes, the nontotalitarian world, too, can effectively be dominated by the dictatorship of "social usefulness."

FIVE-YEAR PLANS

These were plans for economic development in the former Soviet Union and other communist regimes.

At this point we should recall the ancient distinction between *artes liberates* and *artes serviles,* between "free" and "servile" activities. This distinction states that some human activities contain their purpose in themselves and other activities are ordered toward a purpose outside themselves and thus are merely "useful." This idea may at first appear rather outmoded and pedantic. And yet it deals with something of contemporary political relevance. The question, "Are there 'free' activities?" translated into the jargon of totalitarian societies would ask: "Are there human activities that in themselves neither require nor accept any justification based on the provisions of a five-year plan?" The ancients have answered this question with a decisive "yes." The answer in a totalitarian environment would be an equally decisive: "No! Humans are defined by their function. Any 'free' activity that does not serve a socially useful purpose is undesirable and should therefore be liquidated."

If we now direct our attention from the threefold overvaluation of work toward the concept of "leisure," then one thing becomes immediately clear: there is no room for it in such a world. The idea of leisure here is not only preposterous but morally suspect. As a matter of fact, it is absolutely incompatible with the prevailing attitude. The idea of leisure is diametrically opposed to the totalitarian concept of the "worker," and this under each of the three aspects of work we have considered.

Against the idolizing of "activity." Leisure is essentially "nonactivity;" it is a form of silence. Leisure amounts to that precise way of being silent which is a prerequisite for listening in order to hear; for only the listener is able to hear. Leisure implies an attitude of total receptivity toward, and willing immersion in, reality; an openness of the soul, through which alone may come about those great and blessed insights that no amount of "mental labor" can ever achieve.

Against the overvaluation of drudgery. Leisure means an attitude of celebration. And celebration is the opposite of exertion. Those who are basically suspicious of achievement without effort are by the same token as unable to enjoy leisure as they are unable to celebrate a feast. To truly celebrate, however, something else is required; more on this shortly.

Against the overvaluation of social usefulness. Leisure implies that a person is freed for this period of time from any social function. Yet leisure does not mean the same as a "break." A break, whether for an hour or three weeks, is designed to provide a respite from work in anticipation of more work; it finds its justification in relation to work. Leisure is something entirely different. The essence of leisure is not to assure that we may function smoothly but rather to assure that we, embedded in our social function, are enabled to remain fully human. That we may not lose the ability to look beyond the limits of our social and functional station, to contemplate and celebrate the world as such, to become and be that person who is essentially oriented toward the whole of reality. And that all this be achieved through our own free disposition, which contains its own significance and is not "geared toward" anything.

True culture does not flourish except in the soil of leisure—provided we mean by "culture" whatever goes beyond the mere necessities of life yet is nonetheless indispensable for the fullness of human existence. If culture is thus rooted in leisure, where, then, does leisure find its roots? How can we be enabled to "achieve leisure" (as the classical Greeks put it)? What can be done to prevent our becoming mere "workers" who are totally absorbed trying to function properly? I have to admit that I am unable to give a specific and practical answer to this question. The basic difficulty is such that it cannot be remedied with a simple decision, be it ever so well intentioned. Still, we can point out why this is so.

It is well known that physicians for some time now have reminded us how important it is for our health to have leisure—and they are certainly correct. But: it is impossible to "achieve leisure" in order to stay or to become healthy, not even in order to "save our culture"! Some things can be approached only if they are seen as meaningful in and by themselves. They cannot be accomplished "in order to" effect something else. (Thus it is impossible, for example, to love someone "in order to . . ." and "for the purpose of . . ."). The order of certain realities cannot be reversed; to try it anyway is not only inappropriate but simply doomed to failure.

Related to our question, this means: if leisure is not conceived as meaningful in and by itself, then it is plainly impossible to achieve. Here we should once again mention the celebration of a feast. Such a celebration combines all three elements that also constitute leisure: first, non-activity and repose; second, ease and absence of exertion; third, leave from the everyday functions and work. Everybody knows how difficult an endeavor it is for us moderns really to celebrate. Indeed, this difficulty is identical with our inability to achieve leisure. The reason that our celebrations fail is the same reason that we fail to achieve leisure.

At this point there appears an inevitable consideration that to most people, as I have frequently experienced, seems quite uncomfortable. Put in a nutshell, it is this: to celebrate means to proclaim, in a setting different from the ordinary everyday, our approval of the world as such. Those who do not consider reality as fundamentally "good" and "in the right order" are not able to truly celebrate, no more than they are able to "achieve leisure". In other words: leisure depends on the precondition that we find the world and our own selves agreeable. And here follows the offensive but inevitable consequence: the highest conceivable form of approving of the world as such is found in the worship of God, in the praise of the Creator, in the liturgy. With this we have finally identified the deepest root of leisure.

We should expect, I believe, that humanity will make strenuous efforts to escape the consequences of this insight. It may try, for example, to establish "artificial" feast days in order to avoid the ultimate and true approval of reality — while producing a resemblance of genuine celebration through the immense display of outward arrangements supported by the political authorities. In reality, the "organized" recreation of such pseudo celebrations is merely a more hectic form of work.

It would be a misconception to assume that this proposition regarding the cultic essence of all celebration and the cultic roots of leisure and culture would be a specifically Christian thesis. What in our days is called "secularism" represents perhaps not so much the loss of a Christian outlook as rather the loss of some more fundamental insights that have traditionally constituted humanity's patrimony of natural wisdom. I believe that our thesis on leisure and culture is part of this patrimony. It was the Greek Plato, long before Christianity, who in his old age formulated this thesis by employing the

PATRIMONY

Patrimony literally refers to things that have been inherited from one's ancestors. Pieper is using the term to describe the culture, art, wisdom, literature, and so on, that humanity as a whole has inherited.

imagery of a magnificent myth. Plato asks whether there would be no respite for the human race, destined as it seems for labor and suffering. And he replies. Yes indeed, there is a respite: "The gods, out of compassion for us humans who are born into hardship, provided respite by granting periodic cultic celebrations, and by giving us, to join in our feasts, the Muses with their leaders Apollo and Dionysus, so that we may be sustained by joyfully conversing with the gods, and be lifted up and given a sense of direction." And the other great Greek, Aristotle, of a more critical turn of mind than his teacher Plato and, as is well known, less given to images from myth—even Aristotle has expressed the same insight in his usual dispassionate manner. In the same *Nichomachean Ethics* that also contains the sentence quoted at the beginning ("We work so we can have leisure") we read that we cannot achieve leisure insofar as our human nature is concerned but only insofar as we possess the divine spark in us.

Review Questions

1. What are the three meanings of "work"?

2. How do humans attain the highest forms of perception?

3. What kind of an attitude does leisure imply?

4. How does true culture flourish?

5. What are the three elements of leisure embodied in celebration?

6. What is the highest form of approving of the world?

In-depth Questions

1. Most people hope to have a successful career when they begin to work. After reading "Leisure and Its Threefold Opposition," how would you define a successful career for yourself?

2. Pieper talks about false celebrations. In the popular culture of today, what do you categorize as false celebrations?

3. Pieper categorizes worship as an activity of leisure. Do you agree with him? Please explain your answer.

4. "Work should allow us to be more human, not amass material goods." What do you think this quote means? Do you agree with its meaning? Please explain.

"The Prayer of the Church"

SAINT EDITH STEIN

Introduction

The young Edith Stein seemed an unlikely candidate to one day be named a Catholic saint. First, she was a stubborn child who was prone to angry outbursts when she did not get her way. Second, she was born into a devoutly Jewish family. Third, as a teenager she made a conscious decision to abandon her faith. Nonetheless, she was canonized in 1998. How did she arrive at such an unexpected legacy? Her unrelenting quest for the truth, combined with the courage and strength to firmly commit herself to that truth, shaped the course of her life in ways that surprised even her.

Saint Edith Stein was born on October 12, 1891 in Germany, the youngest of her parents' seven surviving children. The day she was born happened to fall on Yom Kippur, the Jewish Day of Atonement, an occurrence that she later regarded as foreshadowing her purpose in life.

Edith was an eager student who excelled in school. In 1911 she became one of the first women to be admitted to a German university. While there, she studied under Edmund Husserl, the founder of phenomenology. Phenomenology is a type of philosophy that emphasizes the importance of human experience and consciousness (as opposed to deductive logic) for describing the meaning of things. Edith so impressed Husserl that he made her his assistant.

Many of Edith's university colleagues were committed Christians who impressed her with the depth of their faith. One evening at a friend's home she picked up a copy of Saint Teresa of Ávila's autobiography. She read the entire book that night. It convinced her of the truth of the Catholic faith, and ultimately led to her baptism just a few months later on January 1, 1922.

For the next eight years, Edith taught German at a Dominican college, continuing her scholarly work in her spare time. She became a leader of the Catholic Women's Movement and lectured throughout Germany on the role of women in society. Her integration of feminism with Catholicism would later influence the teaching of Pope John Paul II.

Edith took a teaching position at the University of Münster in 1932, but was forced to leave within a year because of laws passed by the National Socialists (Nazis) that forbade people of Jewish descent from teaching. With the doors of academia closed to her, she decided to fulfill her dream of becoming a Carmelite nun. She took the name Teresia Benedicta a Cruce—literally, "Teresa Blessed by the Cross." She later explained that the name referred to the cross that was being laid on the backs of the Jewish people through the Nazi persecution. Edith prayed that she would be able to carry that cross for the sake of her people. In her last work, *The Science of the Cross*, she meditated on the power of the cross to transform suffering into joy, and failure into victory.

The Carmelite nuns protected Edith and her sister from the Nazis for nine years, but when Catholic bishops issued a letter condemning the anti-Semitic policies of the Nazis, the Gestapo retaliated by rounding up all Catholics of Jewish descent—including Edith and her sister, who had also converted to Catholicism. Edith and her sister were led on a horrific four-day journey to Auschwitz, where Edith was among those killed on August 9, 1942.

As tragic as her death was, Edith's faith and philosophy held that there is a deeper reality to life. In the days before the Nazis took her away, she insisted that she could not expect to be spared the fate of her fellow Jews because of her baptism; instead, she resolved to stand along-side them in their suffering. In doing so, she made her death a prayer.

GREAT CATHOLIC THOUGHT
"The Prayer of the Church"

"Through him, with him, and in him in the unity of the Holy Spirit, all honor and glory is yours. Almighty Father, for ever and ever." With these solemn words, the priest ends the Eucharistic prayer at the center of which is the mysterious event of the consecration. These words at the same time encapsulate the prayer of the church: honor and glory to the triune God through, with, and in Christ. Although the words are directed to the Father, all glorification of the Father is at the same time glorification of the Son and of the Holy Spirit. Indeed, the prayer extols the majesty that the Father imparts to the Son and that both impart to the Holy Spirit from eternity to eternity.

All praise of God is *through, with,* and *in* Christ. *Through* him, because only through Christ does humanity have access to the Father and because his existence as God-man and his work of salvation are the fullest glorification of the Father; *with* him, because all authentic prayer is the fruit of union with Christ and at the same time buttresses this union, and because in honoring the Son one honors the Father and vice versa; *in* him, because the praying church is Christ himself, with every individual praying member as a part of his Mystical Body, and because the Father is in the Son and the Son the reflection of the Father, who makes his majesty visible. The dual meanings of *through*, *with*, and *in* clearly express the God-man's mediation.

The prayer of the church is the prayer of the ever-living Christ. Its prototype is Christ's prayer during his human life.

THE PRAYER OF THE CHURCH AS LITURGY AND EUCHARIST

The Gospels tell us that Christ prayed the way a devout Jew faithful to the law prayed. Just as he made pilgrimages to Jerusalem at the prescribed times with his parents as a child, so he later journeyed to the temple to celebrate the high feasts there with his disciples. Surely he sang with holy enthusiasm along with his people the exultant hymns in which the pilgrim's joyous anticipation streamed forth: "I rejoiced when I heard them say: Let us go to God's house" (Ps 122:1). From his last supper with his disciples, we know that Jesus said the old blessings over bread, wine, and the fruits of the earth, as they are prayed to this day. So he fulfilled one of the most sacred religious duties: the ceremonial Passover seder to commemorate deliverance from slavery in Egypt. And perhaps this very gathering gives us the most profound glimpse into Christ's prayer and the key to understanding the prayer of the church.

> While they were at supper, he took bread, said the blessing, broke the bread, and gave it to his disciples, saying, "Take this, all of you, and eat it: this is my body which will be given up for you."
> In the same way, he took the cup, filled with wine. He gave you thanks, and giving the cup to his disciples, said, "Take this, all of you, and drink from it: this is the cup of my blood, the blood of the new and everlasting covenant. It will be shed for you and for all so that sins may be forgiven."

Blessing and distributing bread and wine were part of the Passover rite. But here both receive an entirely new meaning. This is where the life of the church begins. Only at Pentecost will it appear publicly as a Spirit-filled and visible community. But here at the Passover meal the seeds of the vineyard are planted that make the outpouring of the Spirit possible. In the mouth of Christ, the old blessings become life-giving words. The fruits of the earth become his body and blood, filled with his life. Visible creation, which he entered when he became a human being, is now united with him in a new, mysterious way. The things that serve to sustain human life are fundamentally transformed, and the people who partake of them in faith are transformed too, drawn into the unity of life with Christ and filled with his divine life. The Word's life-giving power is bound to the sacrifice. The Word became flesh in order to surrender the life he assumed, to offer himself and a creation redeemed by his sacrifice in praise to the Creator. Through the Lord's last supper, the Passover meal of the Old Covenant is converted into the Easter meal of the New Covenant: into the sacrifice on the cross at Golgotha and those joyous meals between Easter and Ascension when the disciples recognized the Lord in the breaking of bread, and into the sacrifice of the Mass with Holy Communion.

As the Lord took the cup, he gave thanks. This recalls the words of blessing thanking the Creator. But we also know that Christ used to give thanks when, prior to a miracle, he raised his eyes to his Father in heaven. He gives thanks because he knows in advance that he will be heard. He gives thanks for the divine power that he carries in himself and by means of which he will demonstrate the omnipotence of the Creator to human eyes. He gives thanks *for* the work of salvation that he is permitted to accomplish, and *through* this work, which is in fact itself the glorification of the triune Godhead, because it restores this Godhead's distorted image to pure beauty. Therefore the whole perpetual sacrificial offering of Christ—at the cross, in the holy Mass, and in the eternal glory of heaven—can be conceived as a single great thanksgiving—as Eucharist: as gratitude for creation, salvation, and consummation. Christ presents himself in the name of all creation, whose prototype he is and to which he descended to renew it from the inside out and lead it to perfection. But he also calls upon the entire created world itself, united with him, to give the Creator the tribute of thanks that is his due. Some understanding of this eucharistic character of prayer had already been revealed under the Old Covenant. The wondrous form of the tent of meeting, and later, of Solomon's temple, erected as it was according to divine specifications, was considered an image of the entire creation, assembled in worship and service around its Lord. The tent around which the people of Israel camped during their wanderings in the wilderness was called the "home of God among us" (Ex 38:21). It was thought of as a "home below," in contrast to a "higher home." "O Lord, I love the house where you dwell, the place where your glory abides," sings the

Psalmist (Ps 26:8), because the tent of meeting is "valued as much as the creation of the world." As the heavens in the creation story were stretched out like a carpet, so carpets were prescribed as walls for the tent. As the waters of the earth were separated from the waters of the heavens, so the curtain separated the Holy of Holies from the outer rooms. The "bronze" sea is modeled after the sea that is contained by its shores. The seven-branched light in the tent stands for the heavenly lights. Lambs and birds stand for the swarms of life teeming in the water, on the earth, and in the air. And as the earth is handed over to people, so in the sanctuary there stands the high priest "who is purified to act and to serve before God." Moses blessed, anointed, and sanctified the completed house as the Lord blessed and sanctified the work of his hands on the seventh day. The Lord's house was to be a witness to God on earth just as heaven and earth are witnesses to him (Dt 30:19).

In place of Solomon's temple, Christ has built a temple of living stones, the communion of saints. At its center, he stands as the eternal high priest; on its altar he is himself the perpetual sacrifice. And, in turn, the whole of creation is drawn into the "liturgy," the ceremonial worship service: the fruits of the earth as the mysterious offerings, the flowers and the lighted candlesticks, the carpets and the curtain, the ordained priest, and the anointing and blessing of God's house. Not even the cherubim are missing. Fashioned by the hand of the artist, the visible forms stand watch beside the Holy of Holies. And, as living copies of them, the "monks resembling angels" surround

---

OPUS DEI; MENOLOGIES OF THE CHURCH

- *Opus Dei* literally means "work of God." In the sense used here, it means that the entirety of one's life, work, and prayer are a conscious gift to God.

- *Menologies of the Church* are the stories of the saints' lives that are read in accordance with the liturgical year.

---

the sacrificial altar and make sure that the praise of God does not cease, as in heaven so on earth. The solemn prayers they recite as the resonant mouth of the church frame the holy sacrifice. They also frame, permeate, and consecrate all other "daily work," so that prayer and work become a single *opus Dei*, a single "liturgy." Their readings from the holy Scriptures and from the fathers, from the menologies of the church and the teachings of its principal pastors, are a great, continually swelling hymn of praise to the rule of providence and to the progressive actualization of the eternal plan of salvation. Their morning hymns of praise call all of creation together to unite once more in praising the Lord: mountains and hills, streams and rivers, seas and lands and all that inhabit them, clouds and winds, rain and snow, all peoples of the earth, every class and race of people, and finally also the inhabitants of heaven, the angels and the saints. Not only in representations giving them human form and made by human hands are they to participate in the great Eucharist of creation, but they are to be involved as personal beings — or better, we are to unite ourselves through our liturgy to their eternal praise of God.

THE PREFACE AND THE SANCTUS

The Sanctus is the prayer at the Eucharistic liturgy that begins with the phrase "Holy, Holy, Holy." This is the prayer of the angels from Isaiah 6:3. Prior to this hymn of worship, the Preface is a prayer that invites the people gathered on earth to join the angels in heaven in worshiping God.

"We" here refers not just to the religious who are called to give solemn praise to God, but to all Christian people. When these stream into cathedrals and chapels on holy days, when they joyously participate daily in worship using the "people's choral Mass" and the new "folk Mass" forms, they show that they are conscious of their calling to praise God. The liturgical unity of the heavenly with the earthly church, both of which thank God "through Christ," finds its most powerful expression in the preface and Sanctus of the Mass. However, the liturgy leaves no doubt that we are not yet full citizens of the heavenly Jerusalem, but pilgrims on the way to our eternal home. We must always prepare ourselves before we may dare to lift our eyes to the luminous heights and to unite our voices with the "holy, holy, holy" of the heavenly chorus. Each created thing to be used in the worship service must be withdrawn from its profane use, must be purified and consecrated. Before the priest climbs the steps to the altar, he must cleanse himself by acknowledging his sins, and the faithful must do so with him. Prior to each step as the offertory continues, he must repeat his plea for the forgiveness of sins — or himself and for those gathered around him as well as for all to whom the fruits of the sacrifice are to flow. The sacrifice itself is a sacrifice of expiation that transforms the faithful as it transforms the gifts, unlocks heaven for them, and enables them to sing a hymn of praise pleasing to God. All that we need to be received into the communion of saints is summed up in the seven petitions of the Our Father, which the Lord did not pray in his own name, but to instruct us. We say it before communion, and when we say it sincerely and from our hearts and receive communion in the proper spirit, it fulfills all our petitions. Communion delivers us from evil, because it cleanses us of sin and gives us peace of heart that takes away the sting of all other "evils." It brings us the forgiveness of past sins and strengthens us in the face of temptations. It is itself the bread of life that we need daily to grow into eternal life. It makes our will into an instrument at God's disposal. Thereby it lays the foundation for the kingdom of God in us and gives us clean lips and a pure heart to glorify God's holy name.

So we see again how the offertory, communion, and praise of God [in the Divine Office] are internally related. Participation in the sacrifice and in the sacrificial meal actually transforms the soul into a living stone in the city of God — in fact, each individual soul into a temple of God.

Review Questions

1. What does Saint Edith Stein mean that all praise of God is *through*, *with*, and *in* Christ?

2. When did the life of the Church begin?

3. How are those who partake of the bread and cup transformed?

4. What symbols were in the tent of meeting for the Old Covenant, and what did they represent?

5. What are the living stones of Christ's temple?

6. What must the faithful do to purify and consecrate themselves for worship at the liturgy?

In-depth Questions

1. At the last supper, Jesus raised the cup and gave thanks to the Creator. Name the three things for which you are most thankful.

2. Saint Edith Stein describes the Eucharist as "gratitude for creation, salvation, and consummation" (the second coming of Jesus). Explain why Christians should be thankful about each of the following events:
   • Creation
   • Salvation
   • Consummation

3. Saint Edith Stein places a great emphasis on the eternal praise of God. What role do you think the Eucharistic liturgy has in this eternal praise?

4. Saint Edith Stein says that participating in the liturgy transforms a person's soul into the temple of God. What do you think it means to be a temple of God?

"Is There Really Hope in the Young?"

Pope John Paul II

Introduction

When Pope John Paul II died in 2005, the world replayed images from his twenty-six-year papacy: kissing the ground of the 129 countries he visited, standing shoulder-to-shoulder with leaders of other faiths, forgiving his would-be assassin, praying at Jerusalem's Western Wall for forgiveness for Christians' persecution of Jews, a triumphant return to Poland that eventually overthrew communism in Eastern Europe without a single gunshot.

The man the world came to know as John Paul II was born as Karol Józef Wojtyla in a small Polish town on May 18, 1920. His mother and older brother died while he was still a boy, leaving him to ponder the meaning of suffering at a young age. He was very talented: athletic, intellectual, friendly, and thoughtful.

He was very devout. Yet, as a young man, Karol felt a greater pull toward the theater than to the priesthood, and devoted his undergraduate university studies to literature and philosophy. Those studies were interrupted as he worked at a rock quarry when the Nazis invaded Poland in 1939. He also joined an underground theater group that illegally performed plays intended to subvert the Nazi regime.

Witnessing so many of his friends and neighbors killed or taken away by the Nazis in the middle of the night changed Karol. He concluded that he had been spared for some higher purpose, and he sought that purpose in the priesthood. He entered an underground seminary and was ordained to the priesthood in 1946. He continued his studies and earned doctorates in philosophy and theology, writing many scholarly papers—although he still indulged his love of literature by writing plays and poetry in his spare time.

In 1958, at the age of thirty-eight, he was ordained a bishop—the youngest in Poland's history. By the time the Second Vatican Council convened in 1962, Bishop Karol Wojtyla had established a reputation as one of the most gifted men in the Church. That talent played a key role in fashioning *Gaudium et Spes*, the Council's landmark document on the

Church's relationship with the modern world. He later helped Pope Paul VI draft *Humanae Vitae*, which addressed issues of human sexuality.

Karol Wojtyla's election as the bishop of Rome on October 16, 1978, shocked the world; he was the first non-Italian pope in more than four centuries. John Paul II was a pope who loved young people. As a parish priest, he often taught and listened to the young people in his care by playing sports with them and taking them to enjoy the outdoors. As Pope, he continued this relationship with young people by establishing World Youth Day. During its festivals he met with millions of youth from around the world.

"Is There Really Hope in the Young?" is taken from the 1994 book *Crossing the Threshold of Hope*, a book containing the Pope's responses to a journalist's questions. In responding to questions about today's young people, the Pope recalls how, in his own youth, he and his peers sought hope in a world gripped by great evil. Times have changed, he says, but young people still have a heroic role to play in today's world.

GREAT CATHOLIC THOUGHT
"Is There Really Hope in the Young?"

[Interviewer]
Young people have a special place in the heart of the Holy Father, who often repeats that the whole Church looks to them with particular hope for a new beginning of evangelization. Your Holiness, is this a realistic hope? Or are we adults only indulging in the illusion that each new generation will be better than ours and all those that came before?

[Pope John Paul II]
Here you open an enormous field for discussion and reflection. *What are young people of today like, what are they looking for?* It could be said that they are the same as ever. There is something in man which never changes, as the Council recalled in *Gaudium et Spes* (10). This is true especially in the young. But today's youth are also different from those who came before. In the past, the younger generations were shaped by the painful experience of war, of concentration camps, of constant danger. This experience allowed young people — I imagine all over the world, although I have Polish youth in mind — to develop *traits of great heroism*.

I think of the Warsaw uprising in 1944 — the desperate revolt of my contemporaries, who sacrificed everything. They laid down their young lives. They wanted to demonstrate that they could live up to their great and demanding heritage. I was a part of that generation and I must say that *the heroism of my contemporaries helped me to define my personal vocation.* Father Konstanty Michalski, one of the great professors at the Jagellonian University in Krakow, wrote the book *Between Heroism and Brutality* after returning from the Sachsenhausen concentration camp. The title of this book captures the climate of the times. Referring to Friar Albert Chmielowski, Michalski recalled the words of the Gospel about the need "to give up one's life" (cf. Jn 15:13). Precisely in that period of absolute contempt for man, when the price of human life had perhaps never been considered so cheap, precisely then each life became precious, acquiring the value of a free gift.

In this regard, *today's young people certainly grow up in a different context.* They do not carry within them the experiences of the Second World War. Furthermore, many of them have not known — or do not remember — the struggle against Communism, against the totalitarian state. They live in freedom, which others have won for them, and have yielded in large part to the consumer culture. This is, in broad terms, the *status of the present situation.*

All the same, it is difficult to say that the young have rejected traditional values, that they have left the Church. The experiences of teachers and pastors *confirm, today no less than yesterday, the idealism present in young people,* even if nowadays it perhaps tends to be expressed mostly in the form of criticism, whereas before it would have translated more simply into duty. In general, the younger generations grow up *in an atmosphere marked by a new positivism,* whereas in Poland, when I was a boy, *romantic traditions* prevailed. The young people with whom I came into contact after I was ordained as a priest believed in these traditions. In the Church and in the Gospel they saw a point of reference which helped them to focus their inner strength, to lead their lives in a way that made sense. I still remember my conversations with those young people who spoke of their relationship with the faith in precisely these terms.

My most memorable experience of that period, when my pastoral activities concentrated above all on the young, was *the discovery of the fundamental importance of youth.* What is youth? It is not only a period of life that corresponds to a certain number of years, it is also *a time given by Providence to every person and given to him as a responsibility.* During that time he searches, like the young man in the Gospel, for answers to basic questions; he searches not only for the meaning of life but also for a concrete way to go about living his life. This is the most fundamental characteristic of youth. Every mentor, beginning with parents, let alone every pastor, must be aware of this characteristic and must know how to identify it in every boy and girl. I will say more: *He must love this fundamental aspect of youth.*

If at every stage of his life man desires to be his own person, to find love, during his youth he desires it even more strongly. The desire to be one's own person, however, must not be understood as a license to do anything, without exception. The young do not want that at all—they are willing to be corrected, they want to be told yes or no. *They need guides,* and they want them close at hand. If they turn to authority figures, they do so because they see in them a wealth of human warmth and a willingness to walk with them along the paths they are following.

Clearly, then, the *fundamental problem of youth is profoundly personal.* In life, youth is when we come to know ourselves. It is also a time of *communion.* Young people, whether boys or girls, know they must live for and with others, they know that their life *has meaning to the extent that it becomes a free gift for others.* Here is the origin of all vocations—whether to priesthood or religious life, or to marriage and family. The call to marriage is also a vocation, a gift from God. I *will never forget a young man, an engineering student in Krakow, who everyone knew aspired with determination to holiness.* This was his life plan. He knew he had been "created for greater things," as Saint Stanislaus Kostka once expressed it. And at the same time, he had no doubt that his vocation was neither to priesthood nor to religious life. He knew he was called to remain in the secular world. Technical work, the study of engineering, was his passion. He sought a companion for his life and sought her on his knees, in prayer. I will never forget the conversation in which, after a special day of retreat, he said to me: "I think that this is the woman who should be my wife, that it is God who has given her to me." It was almost as if he were following not only the voice of his own wishes but above all the voice of God Himself. He knew that all good things come from Him, and he made a good choice. I am speaking of Jerzy Ciesielski, who died in a tragic accident in the Sudan, where he had been invited to teach at the University. The cause for his beatification is already under way.

It is this vocation to love that naturally allows us to draw close to the young. As a priest I realized this very early. I felt almost an inner call in this direction. It is necessary to prepare young people for marriage, it is necessary *to teach them love.* Love is not something that is learned, and yet there is nothing else as important to learn! *As a young priest I learned to love human love.* This has been one of the fundamental themes of my priesthood—my ministry in the pulpit, in the confessional, and also in my writing. If one loves human love, there naturally arises the need to commit oneself completely to the service of "fair love," because love is fair, it is beautiful.

After all, young people are always searching for the beauty in love. They want their love to be beautiful. If they give in to weakness, following models of behavior that can rightly be considered a "scandal in the contemporary world" (and these are, unfortunately, widely diffused models), in the depths of their hearts they still desire a beautiful and pure love. This is as true of boys as it is of girls. Ultimately, they know that only God can give them this love. As a result, they are willing to follow Christ, without caring about the sacrifices this may entail.

As a young priest and pastor I came to this way of looking at young people and at youth, and it has remained constant all these years. It is an outlook which also allows me to meet young people wherever I go. Every parish priest in Rome knows that my visits to the parish must conclude with a meeting between the Bishop of Rome and the young people of the parish. And not only in Rome, but anywhere the Pope goes, *he seeks out the young and the young seek him out. Actually, in truth, it is not the Pope who is being sought out at all. The one being sought out is Christ,* who knows "that which is in every man" (cf. Jn 2:25), especially in a young person, and who can give true answers to his questions! And even if they are demanding answers, the young are not afraid of them; more to the point, they even await them.

This also explains the idea of holding World Youth Days. At the very beginning, during the Jubilee Year of the Redemption, and then again for the International Year of Youth, sponsored by the United Nations (1985), young people were invited to Rome. This was the beginning. *No one invented the World Youth Days. It was the young people themselves who created them.* Those Days, those encounters, then became something desired by young people throughout the world. Most of the time these Days were something of a surprise for priests, and even bishops, in that they surpassed all their expectations.

The World Youth Days have become a great and fascinating witness that young people give of themselves. They have become a powerful means of evangelization. *In the young there is, in fact, an immense potential for good and for creative possibility.* Whenever I meet them in my travels throughout the world, I *wait first of all to hear what they want to tell me about themselves,* about their society, about their Church. And I always point out: "What I am going to say to you is not as important as what you are going to say to me. You will not necessarily say it to me in words; you will say it to me by your presence, by your song, perhaps by your dancing, by your skits, and finally by your enthusiasm."

We need the enthusiasm of the young. We need their *joie de vivre.* In it is reflected something of the original joy God had in creating man. The young experience this same joy within themselves. This joy is the same everywhere, but it is also ever new and original. The young know how to express this joy in their own special way.

It is not true that the Pope brings the young from one end of the world to the other. It is they who bring him. Even though he is getting older, they urge him to be young, they do not permit him to forget his experience, his discovery of youth and its great importance for the life of every man. I believe this explains a great deal.

The very day of the inauguration of my papal ministry, on October 22, 1978, at the conclusion of the liturgy, I said to the young people gathered in St. Peter's Square: "You are the hope of the Church and of the world. You are my hope." I have often repeated these words.

I would like to sum up by stressing that *the young are searching for God,* they are searching for the meaning of life, they are searching for definitive answers: "What must I do to inherit eternal life?" (Lk 10:25). In this search, they cannot help but encounter the Church. *And the Church also cannot help but encounter the young.* The only necessity is that the Church have a profound understanding of what it means to be young, of the importance that youth has for every person. *It is also necessary that the young know the Church, that they perceive Christ in the Church,* Christ who walks through the centuries alongside each generation, alongside every person. He walks alongside each person as a friend. An important day in a young person's life is the day on which he becomes convinced that this is the only Friend who will not disappoint him, on whom he can always count.

Review Questions

1. The Pope says that young people are different today. What does he say is the reason for the difference?

2. What does the Pope say is the most fundamental aspect of youth?

3. What is the origin of a vocation?

4. According to the Pope, why does the Church need the enthusiasm of young people?

5. What does the Pope say is necessary for young people to discover about the Church and Christ?

In-depth Questions

1. The Pope has said that young people today "have yielded in large part to the consumer culture." How would you define "the consumer culture"? Do you think the Pope is right? Why or why not?

2. Do you think young people are driven primarily by a desire for love? Please explain your answer.

3. According to the Pope, the priesthood and religious life are not the only types of vocations. What other types of vocations does he name? What do all these types of vocation have in common?

4. How would you describe the "beautiful" or "pure" love that the Pope talks about?

5. The Pope says that the most important day in a young person's life is the day he or she discovers that Jesus is the only friend that will not disappoint. Do you think you have encountered that day yet? Please explain your answer.

"Things in Their Identity"

THOMAS MERTON

Introduction

Thomas Merton is one of the most compelling Catholics of the twentieth century. He became famous when his autobiography, *The Seven Storey Mountain*, the story of a turbulent young man who eventually converted to Catholicism, was published in 1948. Born in 1915, Merton's childhood was upset at the age of six by the death of his mother, and then at the age of sixteen by the death of his father. Merton was French, but he frequently traveled throughout the world with his father, a painter. After the death of his father, he lived in France and England and attended England's University of Cambridge and then Columbia University in New York. During these years Merton was far from religious — in fact, he even fathered a child out of wedlock.

He also traveled across Europe, visiting old churches along the way. It was during this trip that he began a religious awakening that eventually led to his conversion. He was baptized in 1938. He pursued a career in writing, but his reading of Christianity's spiritual masters stirred a possible call to the priesthood. He answered that call in 1941 by entering the Abbey of Our Lady of Gethsemani, a Trappist monastery near Bardstown, Kentucky.

Merton entered the monastery assuming that he had given up a writing career, but his religious superiors urged him to keep writing. *The Seven Storey Mountain* was only the first of many successful books. Like countless others before him, Thomas Merton entered monastic life to contemplate the mystery of God more deeply. He insisted that the contemplative life is not just for monks and nuns; in fact, for Merton, contemplation is as necessary as breathing for anyone who wants to live fully.

Merton helped Christians broaden and deepen their understanding of contemplative prayer through his writing, especially in *New Seeds of Contemplation* (1961). In that book, he described the contemplative life as one that is fully awake to the reality of God's presence in all things. Although generations of Catholics often viewed the contemplative life as isolating, Merton came to see contemplative prayer as raising one's awareness of the interconnectedness of all God's creation. Consequently, contemplation has a social dimension that cannot be ignored — an insight that profoundly affected a generation of monks and nuns. In the fifth chapter of *New Seeds of Contemplation*, titled "Things in Their Identity," Merton reflects on a critical task of the contemplative life — refusing the false identities that we create for ourselves, and thus finding our true identity by finding God.

GREAT CATHOLIC THOUGHT
"Things in Their Identity"

A tree gives glory to God by being a tree. For in being what God means it to be it is obeying Him. It "consents," so to speak, to His creative love. It is expressing an idea which is in God and which is not distinct from the essence of God, and therefore a tree imitates God by being a tree.

The more a tree is like itself, the more it is like Him. If it tried to be like something else which it was never intended to be, it would be less like God and therefore it would give Him less glory.

No two created beings are exactly alike. And their individuality is no imperfection. On the contrary, the perfection of each created thing is not merely in its conformity to an abstract type but in its own individual identity with itself. This particular tree will give glory to God by spreading out its roots in the earth and raising its branches into the air and the light in a way that no other tree before or after it ever did or will do.

Do you imagine that the individual created things in the world are imperfect attempts at reproducing an ideal type which the Creator never quite succeeded in actualizing on earth? If that is so they do not give Him glory but proclaim that He is not a perfect Creator.

Therefore each particular being, in its individuality, its concrete nature and entity, with all its own characteristics and its private qualities and its own inviolable identity, gives glory to God by being precisely what He wants it to be here and now, in the circumstances ordained for it by His Love and His infinite Art.

The forms and individual characters of living and growing things, of inanimate beings, of animals and flowers and all nature, constitute their holiness in the sight of God.

Their inscape is their sanctity. It is the imprint of His wisdom and His reality in them. The special clumsy beauty of this particular colt on this April day in this field under these clouds is a holiness consecrated to God by His own creative wisdom and it declares the glory of God.

The pale flowers of the dogwood outside this window are saints. The little yellow flowers that nobody notices on the edge of that road are saints looking up into the face of God.

This leaf has its own texture and its own patter of veins and its own holy shape, and the bass and trout hiding in the deep pools of the river are canonized by their beauty and their strength.

The lakes hidden among the hills are saints, and the sea too is a saint who praises God without interruption in her majestic dance.

The great, gashed, half-naked mountain is another of God's saints. There is no other like him. He is alone in his own character; nothing else in the world ever did or ever will imitate God in quite the same way. That is his sanctity.

But what about you? What about me?

Unlike the animals and the trees, it is not enough for us to be what our nature intends. It is not enough for us to be individual men. For us, holiness is more than humanity. If we are never anything but men, never anything but people, we will not be saints and we will not be able to offer to God the worship of our imitation, which is sanctity.

It is true to say that for me sanctity consists in being myself and for you sanctity consists in being *your* self and that, in the last analysis, your sanctity will never be mine and mine will never be yours, except in the communism of charity and grace.

For me to be a saint means to be myself. Therefore the problem of sanctity and salvation is in fact the problem of finding out who I am and of discovering my true self.

Trees and animals have no problem. God makes them what they are without consulting them, and they are perfectly satisfied.

With us it is different. God leaves us free to be whatever we like. We can be ourselves or not, as we please. We are at liberty to be real, or to be unreal. We may be true or false, the choice is ours. We may wear now one mask and now another, and never, if we so desire, appear with our own true face. But we cannot make these choices with impunity. Causes have effects, and if we lie to ourselves and to others, then we cannot expect to find truth and reality whenever we happen to want them. If we have chosen the way of falsity we must not be surprised that truth eludes us when we finally come to need it!

Our vocation is not simply to *be*, but to work together with God in the creation of our own life, our own identity, our own destiny. We are free beings and sons of God. This means to say that we should not passively exist, but actively participate in His creative freedom, in our own lives, and in the lives of others, by choosing the truth. To put it better, we are even called to share with God the work of *creating* the truth of our identity. We can evade this responsibility by playing with masks, and this pleases us because it can appear at times to be a free and creative way of living. It is quite easy, it seems to please everyone. But in the long run the cost and the sorrow come very high. To work out our own identity in God, which the Bible calls "working out our salvation," is a labor that requires sacrifice and anguish, risk and many tears. It demands close attention to reality at every moment, and great fidelity to God as He reveals Himself, obscurely, in the mystery of each new situation. We do not know clearly beforehand what the result of this work will be. The secret of my full identity is hidden in Him. He alone can make me who I am, or rather who I will be when at last I fully begin to be. But unless I desire this identity and work to find it with Him and in Him, the work will never be done. The way of doing it is a secret I can learn from no one else but Him. There is no way of attaining to the secret without faith. But contemplation is the greater and more precious gift, for it enables me to see and understand the work that He wants done.

The seeds that are planted in my liberty at every moment, by God's will, are the seeds of my own identity, my own reality, my own happiness, my own sanctity.

To refuse them is to refuse everything; it is the refusal of my own existence and being: of my identity, my very self.

Not to accept and love and do God's will, is to refuse the fullness of my existence.

If I never become what I am meant to be, but always remain what I am not, I shall spend eternity contradicting myself by being at once something and nothing, a life that wants to live and is dead, a death that wants to be dead and cannot quite achieve its own death because it still has to exist.

To say I was born in sin is to say I came into the world with a false self. I was born in a mask. I came into existence under a sign of contradiction, being someone that I was never intended to be and therefore a denial of what I am supposed to be. And thus I came into existence and nonexistence at the same time because from the very start I was something that I was not.

To say the same thing without paradox: as long as I am no longer anybody else than the thing that was born of my mother, I am so far short of being the person I ought to be that I might as well not exist at all. In fact, it were better for me that I had not been born.

Every one of us is shadowed by an illusory person: a false self.

This is the man that I want myself to be but who cannot exist, because God does not know anything about him. And to be unknown of God is altogether too much privacy.

My false and private self is the one who wants, to exist outside the reach of God's will and God's love — outside of reality and out-side of life. And such a self cannot help but be an illusion.

We are not very good at recognizing illusions, least of all the ones we cherish about ourselves — the ones we are born with and which feed the roots of sin. For most of the people in the world, there is no greater subjective reality than this false self of theirs, which cannot exist. A life devoted to the cult of this shadow is what is called a life of sin.

All sin starts from the assumption that my false self, the self that exists only in my own egocentric desires, is the fundamental reality of life to which everything else in the universe is ordered. Thus I use up my life in the desire for pleasures and the thirst for experiences, for power, honor, knowledge and love, to clothe this false self and construct its nothingness into something objectively real. And I wind experiences around myself and cover myself with pleasures and glory like bandages in order to make myself perceptible to myself and to the world, as if I were an invisible body that could only become visible when something visible covered its surface.

But there is no substance under the things with which I am clothed. I am hollow, and my structure of pleasures and ambitions has no foundation. I am objectified in them. But they are all destined by their very contingency to be destroyed. And when they are gone there will be nothing left of me but my own nakedness and emptiness and hollowness, to tell me that I am my own mistake.

The secret of my identity is hidden in the love and mercy of God.

But whatever is in God is really identical with Him, for His infinite simplicity admits no division and no distinction. Therefore I cannot hope to find myself anywhere except in Him.

Ultimately the only way that I can be myself is to become identified with Him in Whom is hidden the reason and fulfillment of my existence.

Therefore there is only one problem on which all my existence, my peace and my happiness depend: to discover myself in discovering God. If I find Him I will find myself and if I find my true self I will find Him.

But although this looks simple, it is in reality immensely difficult. In fact, if I am left to myself it will be utterly impossible. For although I can know something of God's existence and nature by my own reason, there is no human and rational way in which I can arrive at that contact, that possession of Him, which will be the discovery of Who He really is and of Who I am in Him.

That is something that no man can ever do alone.

Nor can all the men and all the created things in the universe help him in this work.

The only One Who can teach me to find God is God, Himself, Alone.

Review Questions

1. How does Merton describe the problem of sanctity and salvation?

2. What is our vocation?

3. What is demanded of us if we are to work out our salvation?

4. Where does one go to discover the secret of one's identity?

5. How does one come to be one's true self?

In-depth Questions

1. Merton describes how different things in creation, such as hills, colts, flowers, and so on, are saints and are holy. What are some things found in nature that you find to be particularly holy? Please explain.

2. Merton says humans use masks to cover their true selves. Can you identify any masks that you have used to cover yourself?

3. Imagine you are a very old person at the end of your life and someone is giving a speech in honor of you. If you have become your true self, what three things will be included in the speech?

4. Colossians 3:3 reads, "Your life is hidden with Christ in God." Do you think you can become your true self without an intimate and personal relationship with God? Please explain.

PART TWO
GREAT CATHOLIC
LITERATURE

GRAHAM GREENE

SARA MAITLAND

OSCAR WILDE

"The Selfish Giant"

OSCAR WILDE

Introduction

Oscar Wilde is largely remembered for his masterful writing, his outrageous wit, and his sensational trial and conviction for homosexual acts. Less well known, though, is the life-long search for Christ that influenced his art and eventually resulted in his deathbed conversion to Catholicism.

Wilde was born in 1854 in Dublin, Ireland, to Anglican parents; his father was a doctor, and his mother was a journalist and poet. He excelled in school, winning a scholarship to Oxford. After his graduation in 1878 he moved to London, where he became popular for his flamboyant lifestyle and outrageous wit. His first book of poetry was published in 1881 to mixed reviews, but his work as an art reviewer soon established him as one of the leading figures of the aesthetic (the study of beauty) movement. Wilde spent a year giving lectures on aesthetics all across North America; the lectures were a huge success, and offered him the opportunity to meet such literary greats as Henry Wadsworth Longfellow, Oliver Wendell Holmes, Walt Whitman, Louisa May Alcott, and Henry James.

On his return to Britain he married Constance Lloyd, with whom he had two sons. The stories and fables he wrote for their amusement were collected in two books, one of which, *The Happy Prince and Other Stories* (1888), included "The Selfish Giant." His first and only novel, *The Picture of Dorian Gray* (1890), was hugely popular, and success followed upon success with the plays he wrote over the next few years: *Lady Windermere's Fan* (1892), *A Woman of No Importance* (1893), *An Ideal Husband* (1895), and *The Importance of Being Earnest* (1895).

Everything changed for Wilde in 1895 when he was arrested on charges of performing homosexual acts, based on his long and increasingly public affair with a young aristocrat. He was sentenced to two years of hard labor in prison, and after his release in 1897 he briefly reunited with his lover, but then spent the next three years wandering Europe. He died of meningitis on November 30, 1900.

Publicly, Wilde was known as an artist and something of a comedian. But he also had a spiritual side that often revealed itself in his work. Friends at Oxford sparked his interest in Roman Catholicism; he even traveled to Rome (twice) for an audience with the Pope, and attended Mass regularly. At first, his fascination with the Church was largely aesthetic—he loved the beauty of its architecture and traditions, and found its outcast status in Protestant Britain to be attractive. Over time, though, his work reflected an increasingly sophisticated concern with Catholic themes. The image of Christ as a suffering outcast appears frequently in his early poetry and again in his children's stories, many of which revolve around love, redemption, and acts of selfless sacrifice.

In prison, Wilde read works by Saint Augustine, Dante, and John Henry Newman (the famous Anglican convert to Catholicism), and his last works reflected that reading. *De Profundis*, the autobiographical letter to his lover explaining why their relationship had to end, contains an extensive commentary on Christ's relationship with the human person.

Upon his release from prison in 1897, he begged the Jesuits to let him make a six-month retreat with them; when they refused, he wept. Despite his attraction to Catholicism, Wilde—by his own admission— had preferred other gods for most of his life, even as many of his friends in the aesthetic movement became Catholics. But as he lay dying in a shabby Paris hotel, a longtime friend brought him a priest, and Wilde, barely able to speak, made clear his desire to enter the Church. He received the sacraments of Baptism, Penance, and the Anointing of the Sick just hours before his death and was welcomed into the universal body of Christ.

GREAT CATHOLIC LITERATURE
"The Selfish Giant"

Every afternoon, as they were coming from school, the children used to go and play in the Giant's garden.

It was a large lovely garden, with soft green grass. Here and there over the grass stood beautiful flowers like stars, and there were twelve peach-trees that in the spring-time broke out into delicate blossoms of pink and pearl, and in the autumn bore rich fruit. The birds sat on the trees and sang so sweetly that the children used to stop their games in order to listen to them. "How happy we are here!" they cried to each other.

One day the Giant came back. He had been to visit his friend the Cornish ogre, and had stayed with him for seven years. After the seven years were over he had said all that he had to say, for his conversation was limited, and he determined to return to his own castle. When he arrived he saw the children playing the in garden.

"What are you doing here?" he cried in a very gruff voice, and the children ran away.

"My own garden is my own garden," said the Giant; "any one can understand that, and I will allow nobody to play in it but myself." So he built a high wall all round it, and put up a notice-board.

TREPASSERS
WILL BE
PROSECUTED

He was a very selfish Giant.

The poor children had now nowhere to play. They tried to play on the road, but the road was very dusty and full of hard stones, and they did not like it. They used to wander round the high walls when their lessons were over, and talk about the beautiful garden inside. "How happy we were there!" they said to each other.

Then the Spring came, and all over the country there were little blossoms and little birds. Only in the garden of the Selfish Giant it was still winter. The birds did not care to sing in it as there were no children, and the trees forgot to blossom. Once a beautiful flower put its head out from the grass, but when it saw the notice-board it was so sorry for the children that it slipped back into the ground again, and went off to sleep. The only people who were pleased were the Snow and the Frost. "Spring has forgotten this garden," they cried, "so we will live here all the year round." The Snow covered up the grass with her great white cloak, and the Frost painted all the trees silver. Then they invited the North Wind to stay with them, and he came. He was wrapped in furs, and he roared all day about the gar-den, and blew the chimney-pots down. "This is a delightful spot," he said, "We must ask the Hail on a visit." So the Hail came. Every day for three hours he rattled on the roof of the castle till he broke most of the slates, and then he ran round and round the garden as fast as he could go. He was dressed in grey, and his breath was like ice.

"I cannot understand why the Spring is so late in coming," said the Selfish Giant, as he sat at the window and looked out at his cold, white garden; "I hope there will be a change in the weather."

But the Spring never came, nor the Summer. The Autumn gave golden fruit to every garden, but to the Giant's garden she gave none. "He is too selfish," she said. So it was always Winter there, and the North Wind and the Hail, and the Frost, and the Snow danced about through the trees.

One morning the Giant was lying awake in bed when he heard some lovely music. It sounded so sweet to his ears that he thought it must be the King's musicians passing by. It was really only a little linnet singing outside his window, but it was so long since he had heard a bird sing in his garden that it seemed to him to be the most beautiful music in the world. Then the Hail stopped dancing over his head, and the North Wind ceased roaring, and a delicious perfume came to him through the open casement. "I believe the Spring has come at last," said the Giant; and he jumped out of bed and looked out.

What did he see?

He saw a most wonderful sight. Through a little hole in the wall the children had crept in, and they were sitting in the branches of the trees. In every tree that he could see there was a little child. And the trees were so glad to have the children back again that they had covered themselves with blossoms, and were waving their arms gently above the children's heads. The birds were flying about and twittering with delight, and the flowers were looking up through the green grass and laughing. It was a lovely scene, only in one corner it was still winter. It was the farthest corner of the garden, and in it was standing a little boy. He was so small that he could not reach up to the branches of the tree, and he was wandering all round it, crying bitterly. The poor tree was still covered with frost and snow, and the North Wind was blowing and roaring above it. "Climb up! Little boy," said the Tree, and it bent its branches down as low as it could; but the boy was too tiny.

And the Giant's heart melted as he looked out. "How selfish I have been!" he said; "now I know why the Spring would not come here. I will put that poor little boy on the top of the tree, and then I will knock down the wall, and my garden shall be the children's playground for ever and ever." He was really very sorry for what he had done.

So he crept downstairs and opened the front door quite softly, and went out into the garden. But when the children saw him they were so frightened that they all ran away, and the garden became winter again. Only the little boy did not run, for his eyes were so full of tears that he did not see the Giant coming. And the Giant stole up behind him and took him gently in his hand, and put him up into the tree. And the tree broke at once into blossom, and the birds came and sang on it, and the little boy stretched out his two arms and flung them round the Giant's neck, and kissed him. And the other children when they saw that the Giant was not wicked any longer, came running back, and with them came the Spring. "It is your garden now, little children," said the Giant, and he took a great axe and knocked down the wall. And when the people were going to market at twelve o'clock they found the Giant playing with the children in the most beautiful garden they had ever seen.

All day long they played, and in the evening they came to the Giant to bid him good-bye.

"But where is your little companion?" he said: "the boy I put into the tree." The Giant loved him the best because he had kissed him.

"We don't know," answered the children: "he has gone away."

"You must tell him to be sure and come to-morrow," said the Giant. But the children said that they did not know where he lived, and had never seen him before; and the Giant felt very sad.

Every afternoon, when school was over, the children came and played with the Giant. But the little boy whom the Giant loved was never seen again. The Giant was very kind to all the children, yet he longed for his first little friend, and often spoke of him. "How I would like to see him!" he used to say.

Years went over, and the Giant grew very old and feeble. He could not play about any more, so he sat in a huge arm-chair, and watched the children at their games, and admired his garden. "I have many beautiful flowers," he said; "but the children are the most beautiful flowers of all."

One winter morning he looked out of his window as he was dressing. He did not hate the Winter now, for he knew that it was merely the Spring asleep, and that the flowers were resting.

Suddenly he rubbed his eyes in wonder and looked and looked. It certainly was a marvelous sight. In the farthest corner of the garden was a tree quite covered with lovely white blossoms. Its branches were golden, and silver fruit hung down from them, and underneath it stood the little boy he had loved.

Downstairs ran the Giant in great joy, and out into the garden. He hastened across the grass, and came near to the child. And when he came quite close his face grew red with anger, and he said, "Who hath dared to wound thee?" For on the palms of the child's hands were the prints of two nails, and the prints of two nails were on the little feet.

"Who hath dared to wound thee?" cried the Giant; "tell me, that I may take my big sword and slay him."

"Nay!" answered the child: "but these are the wounds of Love."

"Who art thou?" said the Giant, and a strange awe fell on him, and he knelt before the little child.

And the child smiled on the Giant, and said to him, "You let me play once in your garden, to-day you shall come with me to my garden, which is Paradise."

And when the children ran in that afternoon, they found the Giant lying dead under the tree, all covered with white blossoms.

Review Questions

1. At the beginning of the story, why had the Selfish Giant been absent from the garden, and for how long was he gone?

2. As spring approached throughout the country, what happened in the Selfish Giant's garden?

3. How did the children enter back into the garden?

4. After the little boy's long absence from the garden, what was it about the little boy that angered the Selfish Giant?

In-depth Questions

1. Name what you think each of the following represents in the story:
   - The children
   - The garden
   - The seasons
   - The Selfish Giant
   - The little boy

2. The story describes selfishness as being bleak and despairing. How have you experienced the effects of another's selfishness? How have you experienced the effects of your own selfishness?

3. Why do you think the little boy described his wounds as wounds of love?

4. The Giant received the promise that he will go to Paradise. What do you believe Paradise will be like? How would you describe the Church's teaching on Paradise? Does anything differ between these two understandings?

"The Hint of an Explanation"

GRAHAM GREENE

Introduction

Graham Greene did not like to be narrowly labeled as a "Catholic novel-ist" — he thought of himself as a novelist who just happened to be Catholic. Although his early work was criticized for being too Catholic, in the end he seems to have gotten his wish. Today, Greene is remem-bered primarily for the skillful storytelling that made him one of the most popular writers of the twentieth century — his stories and novels were made into dozens of movies, including *The Quiet American*, *The End of the Affair*, *This Gun for Hire*, and *The Orient Express*.

Greene was born into a large middle-class family in Berkhamsted, England, near London, in 1904. As a teen, he attended the boarding school where his father was headmaster. Although his family's house was attached to the school, he lived in the dorms with the other boys. Being the son of the headmaster frequently put him in the position of choosing between loyalty to his peers or loyalty to his father, a situation that led to depression and suicide attempts. Such childhood experiences deeply influenced much of his work: the choice between loyalty and betrayal is a persistent theme in his writing, as is the importance of childhood experience. These themes are clearly present in "The Hint of an Explanation."

Greene graduated from Oxford in 1925 and worked as a newspaper journalist for five years, primarily with the London *Times*. Around this time he met the woman he would marry; a devout Catholic, she helped to rekindle the interest in Catholicism he had as a teenager. He entered the Church in 1926.

Other than a stint with M16 (the counterintelligence arm of the British Secret Service) during World War II, Greene spent much of his life writing novels, articles, movie reviews, the occasional screenplay, and short stories such as "The Hint of an Explanation" (1948). The difficulty he had selling his early novels drove him to write what he called "enter-tainments," novels driven by suspense and intrigue such as *The Orient Express*, *This Gun for Hire*, and *The Confidential Agent*. Throughout his career, such popular successes made it possible for him to write the morally complex novels for which he is critically acclaimed.

Greene was no saint—he had numerous affairs, sympathized with communism, and was often at odds with the Church. His life would certainly not be upheld as an example to imitate. However, his writings reveal the biblical cry, the Catholic cry, and the cry of Jesus: "Be not afraid." While his characters are not pious Catholics either, they always inhabit a moral universe. Without a moral context, Greene argued, any novel would be lifeless and two-dimensional. His characters may be deeply flawed, mired in sin, despair, and evil circumstances, but even in this condition—and perhaps *especially* in this condition—they are still capable of heroic acts of love and self-sacrifice. Such acts of love open us to redemption despite our sinfulness, Greene seems to say: in the final act, grace triumphs even over evil. In "The Hint of an Explanation," the triumph over evil is both complete and surprising.

GREAT CATHOLIC LITERATURE
"The Hint of an Explanation"

A long train journey on a late December evening, in this new version of peace, is a dreary experience. I suppose that my fellow traveler and I could consider ourselves lucky to have a compartment to ourselves, even though the heating apparatus was not working, even though the lights went out entirely in the frequent Pennine tunnels and were too dim anyway for us to read our books without straining the eyes, and though there was no restaurant car to give at least a change of scene. It was when we were trying simultaneously to chew the same kind of dry bun bought at the same station buffet that my companion and I came together. Before that, we had sat at opposite ends of the carriage, both muffled to the chin in overcoats, both bent low over type we could barely make out, but as I threw the remains of my cake under the seat our eyes met, and he laid his book down.

By the time we were halfway to Bedwell Junction we had found an enormous range of subjects for discussion; starting with buns and the weather, we had gone on to politics, the Government, foreign affairs, the atom bomb, and by an inevitable progression, God. We had not, however, become either shrill or acid. My companion, who now sat opposite me, leaning a little forward, so that our knees nearly touched, gave such an impression of serenity that it would have been impossible to quarrel with him, however much our views differed, and differ they did profoundly.

I had soon realized I was speaking to a Roman Catholic—to someone who believed—how do they put it?—in an omnipotent and omniscient Deity, while I am what is loosely called an agnostic. I

Agnostic

Generally speaking, agnostics are people who can neither affirm nor deny the existence of God. They might believe that God is ultimately unknowable.

have a certain intuition (which I do not trust, founded as it may well be on childish experienced needs) that a God exists, and I am surprised occasionally into belief by the extraordinary coincidences that beset our path like the traps set for leopards in the jungle, but intellectually I am revolted at the whole notion of such a God who can so abandon his creatures to the enormities of Free Will. I found myself expressing this view to my companion who listened quietly and with respect. He made no attempt to interrupt—he showed none of the impatience or the intellectual arrogance I have grown to expect from Catholics; when the lights of a wayside station flashed across his face which had escaped hitherto the rays of the one globe working in the compartment, I caught a glimpse suddenly of—what? I stopped speaking, so strong was the impression. I was carried back ten years, to the other side of the great useless conflict, to a small town, Gisors in Normandy. I was again, for a moment, walking on the ancient battlements and looking down across the grey roofs, until my eyes for some reason lit on one stony back out of the many where the face of a middle-aged man was pressed against a window pane (I suppose that face has ceased to exist now, just as perhaps the whole town with its medieval memories have been reduced to rubble). I remembered saying to myself with astonishment, "that man is happy—completely happy." I looked across the compartment at my fellow traveler, but his face was already again in shadow. I said weakly, "When you think what God—if there is a God—allows. It's not merely the physical agonies, but think of the corruption, even of children. . . ."

He said, "Our view is so limited," and I was disappointed at the conventionality of his reply. He must have been aware of my disappointment (it was as though our thoughts were huddled as closely as ourselves for warmth), for he went on. "Of course there is no answer here. We catch hints. . . ." and then the train roared into another tunnel and the lights again went out. It was the longest tunnel yet; we went rocking down it and the cold seemed to become more intense with the darkness, like an icy fog (when one sense—of sight—is robbed, the others grow more acute). When we emerged into the mere grey of night and the globe lit up once more, I could see that my companion was leaning back on his seat.

I repeated his last word as a question, "Hints?"

"Oh, they mean very little in cold print—or cold speech," he said, shivering in his overcoat. "And they mean nothing at all to another human being than the man who catches them. They are not scientific evidence—or evidence at all for that matter. Events that don't, somehow, turn out as they were intended—by the human actors, I mean, or by the thing behind the human actors."

"The thing?"

Anthropomorphic

Anthropomorphism is giving human attributes to nonhuman objects or beings.

"The word Satan is so anthropomorphic." I had to lean forward now: I wanted to hear what he had to say. I am—I really am, God knows—open to conviction. He said, "One's words are so crude, but I sometimes feel pity for that thing. It is so continually finding the right weapon to use against its Enemy and the weapon breaks in its own breast. It sometimes seems to me so—powerless. You said something just now about the corruption of children. It reminded me of something in my own childhood. You are the first person—except for one—that I have thought of telling it to, perhaps because you are anonymous. It's not a very long story, and in a way it's relevant."

I said, "I'd like to hear it."

"You mustn't expect too much meaning. But to me there seems to be a hint. That's all. A hint."

He went slowly on turning his face to the pane, though he could have seen nothing in the whirling world outside except an occasional signal lamp, a light in a window, a small country station torn backwards by our rush, picking his words with precision. He said, "When I was a child they taught me to serve at Mass. The church was a small one, for there were very few Catholics where I lived. It was a

East Anglia

East Anglia is an area on the eastern side of England.

market town in East Anglia, surrounded by flat chalk fields and ditches—so many ditches. I don't suppose there were fifty Catholics all told, and for some reason there was a tradition of hostility to us. Perhaps it went back to the burning of a Protestant martyr in the sixteenth century—there was a stone marking the place near where the meat stalls stood on Wednesdays. I was only half aware of the enmity, though I knew that my school nickname of Popey Martin had something to do with my religion and I had heard that my father was very nearly excluded from the Constitutional Club when he first came to the town."

"Every Sunday I had to dress up in my surplice and serve Mass. I hated it—I have always hated dressing up in any way (which is funny when you come to think of it), and I never ceased to be afraid of losing my place in the service and doing something which would put me to ridicule. Our services were at a different hour from the Anglican, and as our small, far-from-select band trudged out of the hideous chapel the whole of the townsfolk seemed to be on the way past to the proper church—I always thought of it as the proper church. We had to pass the parade of their eyes—indifferent, supercilious, mocking; you can't imagine how seriously religion can be taken in a small town—if only for social reasons."

"There was one man in particular; he was one of the two bakers in the town, the one my family did not patronize. I don't think any of the Catholics patronized him because he was called a free-thinker—an odd title, for, poor man, no one's thoughts were less free than his. He was hemmed in by his hatred—his hatred of us. He was very ugly to look at, with one wall-eye and a head the shape of a turnip, with the hair gone on the crown, and he was unmarried. He had no interests, apparently, but his baking and his hatred, though now that I am older I begin to see other sides of his nature—it did contain, perhaps, a certain furtive love. One would come across him suddenly, sometimes, on a country walk, especially if one was alone and it was Sunday. It was as though he rose from the ditches and the chalk smear on his clothes reminded one of the flour on his working overalls. He would have a stick in his hand and stab at the hedges, and if his mood were very black he would call out after you strange abrupt words that were like a foreign tongue—I know the meaning of those words, of course, now. Once the police went to his house because of what a boy said he had seen, but nothing came of it except that the hate shackled him closer. His name was Blacker, and he terrified me."

"I think he had a particular hatred of my father—I don't know why. My father was manager of the Midland Bank, and it's possible that at some time Blacker may have had unsatisfactory dealings with the bank—my father was a very cautious man who suffered all his life from anxiety about money—his own and other people's. If I try to picture Blacker now, I see him walking along a narrowing path between high windowless walls, and at the end of the path stands a small boy of ten—me. I don't know whether it's a symbolic picture or the memory of one of our encounters—our encounters somehow got more and more frequent. You talked just now about the corruption of children. That poor man was preparing to revenge himself on everything he hated — my father, the Catholics, the God whom people persisted in crediting — by corrupting me. He had evolved a horrible and ingenious plan."

"I remember the first time I had a friendly word from him. I was passing his shop as rapidly as I could when I heard his voice call out with a kind of sly subservience as though he were an under-servant. 'Master David,' he called, 'Master David,' and I hurried on. But the next time I passed that way he was at his door (he must have seen me coming), with one of those curly cakes in his hand that we called Chelsea buns. I didn't want to take it, but he made me, and then I couldn't be other than polite when he asked me to come into his parlor behind the shop and see something very special."

"It was a small electric railway — a rare sight in those days, and he insisted on showing me how it worked. He made me turn the switches and stop and start it, and he told me that I could come in any morning and have a game with it. He used the word 'game' as though it were something secret, and it's true that I never told my family of this invitation and of how, perhaps twice a week those holidays, the desire to control that little railway became overpowering, and looking up and down the street to see if I were observed. I would dive into the shop."

Our larger, dirtier, adult train drove into a tunnel and the light went out. We sat in darkness and silence, with the noise of the train blocking our ears like wax. When we were through we didn't speak at once and I had to prick him into continuing.

"An elaborate seduction," I said.

"Don't think his plans were as simple as that," my companion said, "or as crude. There was much more hate than love, poor man in his makeup. Can you hate something you don't believe in? And yet he called himself a free-thinker. What an impossible paradox, to be free and to be so obsessed. Day by day all through those holidays his obsession must have grown, but he kept a grip; he bided his time. Perhaps that thing I spoke of gave him the strength and the wisdom. It was only a week from the end of the holidays that he spoke to me of what concerned him so deeply."

"I heard him behind me as I knelt on the floor, coupling two coaches. He said, 'You won't be able to do this, Master David, when school starts.' "It wasn't a sentence that needed any comment from me any more than the one that followed. 'You ought to have it for your own, you ought,' but how skillfully and un-emphatically he had sowed the longing, the idea of a possibility. . . . I was coming to his parlor every day now, you see I had to cram every opportunity in before the hated term started again, and I suppose I was becoming accustomed to Blacker, to that wall-eye, that turnip head, that nause-ating subservience. The Pope, you know, describes himself as 'the servant of the servants of God,' and Blacker—I sometimes think that Blacker was 'the servant of the servants of . . .', well, let it be."

"The very next day, standing in the doorway watching me play, he began to talk to me about religion. He said with what untruth even I recognized, how much he admired the Catholics; he wished he could believe like that, but how could a baker believe? He accented 'a baker' as one might say a biologist. And the tiny train spun round the gauge 0 track. He said; 'I can bake the things you eat just as well as any Catholic can,' and disappeared into his shop. I hadn't the faintest idea what he meant. Presently he emerged again, holding in his hand a little wafer. 'Here,' he said, 'eat that and tell me. . . .' When I put it in my mouth I could tell that it was made in the same way as our wafers for communion—he had got the shape a little wrong, that was all, and I felt guilty and irrationally scared. 'Tell me,' he said, 'what's the difference?'"

"'Difference?' I asked."

"'Isn't that just the same as you eat in church?'"

"I said smugly, 'It hasn't been consecrated.'"

"He said, 'Do you think if I put the two of them under a micro-scope, you could tell the difference?' But even at ten I had the answer to that question. 'No,' I said. 'The—accidents don't change,' stum-bling a little on the word 'accidents' which had suddenly conveyed to me the idea of death and wounds."

"Blacker said with sudden intensity, 'How I'd like to get one of yours in my mouth—just to see. . . .'"

"It may seem odd to you, but this was the first time that the idea of transubstantiation really lodged in my mind. I had learnt it all by rote; I had grown up with the idea. The Mass was as lifeless to me as the sentences in *De Bello Gallico*, communion a routine like drill in the schoolyard, but here suddenly I was in the presence of a man who took it seriously, as seriously as the priest whom naturally one didn't count—it was his job. I felt more scared than ever."

"He said, 'It's all nonsense, but I'd just like to have it in my mouth.'"

"'You could if you were a Catholic,' I said naïvely. He gazed at me with his one good eye like a Cyclops. He said, 'You serve at Mass, don't you? It would be easy for you to get one of those things. I tell you what I'd do—I'd swap this electric train set for one of your wafers—consecrated, mind. It's got to be consecrated.'"

"'I could get you one out of the box,' I said. I think I still imag-ined that his interest was a baker's interest—to see how they were made."

"'Oh, no,' he said, 'I want to see what your God tastes like.'"

"'I couldn't do that.'"

"'Not for a whole electric train, just for yourself? You wouldn't have any trouble at home. I'd pack it up and put a label inside that your Dad could see — "For my bank manager's little boy from a grateful client." He'd be pleased as Punch with that.'"

"Now that we are grown men it seems a trivial temptation, does not it? But try to think back to your own childhood. There was a whole circuit of rails on the floor at our feet, straight rails and curved rails, and a little station with porter and passengers, a tunnel, a foot-bridge, a level crossing, two signals, buffers, of course — and above all, a turntable. The tears of longing came into my eyes when I looked at the turntable. It was my favourite piece — it looked so ugly and practical and true." "I said weakly. 'I wouldn't know how.'"

"How carefully he had been studying the ground. He must have slipped several times into Mass at the back of the church. It would have been no good, you understand, in a little town like that, pre-senting himself for communion. Everybody there knew him for what he was. He said to me, 'When you've been given communion you could just put it under your tongue a moment. He serves you and the other boy first, and I saw you once go out behind the curtain straight afterwards. You'd forgotten one of those little bottles.'"

"'The cruet,' I said."

"'Pepper and salt.' He grinned at me jovially, and I — well, I look-ed at the little railway which I could no longer come and play with when term started. I said, 'You'd just swallow it, wouldn't you?'"

"'Oh, yes,' he said, 'I'd just swallow it.'"

"Somehow I didn't want to play with the train any more that day. I got up and made for the door, but he detained me, gripping my lapel. He said, 'This will be a secret between you and me. Tomorrow's Sunday. You come along here in the afternoon. Put it in an envelope and post it in. Monday morning the train will be delivered bright and early.'"

"'Not tomorrow,' I implored him."

"'I'm not interested in any other Sunday.' he said. 'It's your only chance.'" He shook me gently backwards and forwards. 'It will always have to be a secret between you and me,' he said. 'Why, if anyone knew they'd take away the train and there'd be me to reckon with. I'd bleed you something awful. You know how I'm always about on Sunday walks. You can't avoid a man like me. I crop up. You would not even be safe in your own house. I know ways to get into houses when people are asleep.' He pulled me into the shop after him and opened a drawer. In the drawer was an odd-looking key and a cut-throat razor. He said, 'That's a master key that opens all locks and that—that's what I bleed people with.' Then he patted my cheek with his plump floury fingers and said. "Forget it. You and me are friends.'"

"That Sunday Mass stays in my head, every detail of it, as though it had happened only a week ago. From the moment of the Confession to the moment of Consecration it had a terrible importance; only one other Mass has ever been so important to me—perhaps not even one, for this was a solitary Mass which could never happen again. It seemed as final as the last Sacrament, when the priest bent down and put the wafer in my mouth where I knelt before the altar with my fellow server."

"I suppose I had made up my mind to commit this awful act for, you know, to us it must always seem an awful act—from the moment when I saw Blacker watching from the back of the church. He had put on his best Sunday clothes, and as though he could never quite escape the smear of his profession, he had a dab of dried talcum on his cheek, which he had presumably applied after using that cut-throat razor of his. He was watching me closely all the time, and I think it was fear—fear of that terrible undefined thing called bleeding—as much as covetousness that drove me to carry out my instructions."

"My fellow server got briskly up and taking the communion plate preceded Father Carey to the altar rail where the other Communicants knelt. I had the Host lodged under my tongue; it felt like a blister. I got up and made for the curtain to get the cruet that I had purposely left in the sacristy. When I was there I looked quickly round for a hiding-place and saw an old copy of the *Universe* lying on a chair. I took the Host from my mouth and inserted it between two sheets—a little damp mess of pulp. Then I thought: perhaps Father Carey has put the paper out for a particular purpose and he will find the Host before I have time to remove it, and the enormity of my act began to come home to me when I tried to imagine what punishment I should incur. Murder is sufficiently trivial to have its appropriate punishment, but for this act the mind boggled at the thought of any retribution at all. I tried to remove the Host, but it had stuck clammily between the pages and in desperation I tore out a piece of the newspaper and screwing the whole thing up, stuck it in my trouser pocket. When I came back through the curtain carrying the cruet, my eyes met Blacker's. He gave me a grin of encouragement and unhappiness—yes, I am sure, unhappiness. Was it perhaps that the poor man was all the time seeking something incorruptible?"

"I can remember little more of that day. I think my mind was shocked and stunned and I was caught up too in the family bustle of Sunday. Sunday in a provincial town is the day for relations. All the family are at home and unfamiliar cousins and uncles are apt to arrive packed in the back seats of other people's cars. I remember that some crowd of that kind descended on us and pushed Blacker temporarily out of the foreground of my mind. There was somebody called Aunt Lucy with a loud hollow laugh that filled the house with mechanical merriment like the sound of recorded laughter from inside a hall of mirrors, and I had no opportunity to go out alone even if I had wished to. When six o'clock came and Aunt Lucy and the cousins departed and peace returned, it was too late to go to Blacker's and at eight it was my own bedtime."

"I think I had half forgotten what I had in my pocket. As I emptied my pocket, the little screw of newspaper brought quickly back the Mass, the priest bending over me, Blacker's grin. I laid the packet on the chair by my bed and tried to go to sleep, but I was haunted by the shadows on the wall where the curtains blew, the squeak of furniture, the rustle in the chimney, haunted by the presence of God there on the chair. The Host had always been to me — well, the Host I knew theoretically, as I have said, what I had to believe, but suddenly, as someone whistled in the road outside, whistled secretively, knowingly, to me, I knew that this which I had beside my bed was something of infinite value — something a man would pay for with his whole peace of mind, something that was so hated one could love it as one loves an outcast or a bullied child. These are adult words and it was a child often who lay scared in bed, listening to the whistle from the road, Blacker's whistle, but I think he felt fairly clearly what I am describing now. That is what I meant when I said this Thing, whatever it is, that seizes every possible weapon against God, is always, everywhere, disappointed at the moment of success. It must have felt as certain of me as Blacker did. It must have felt certain, too, of Blacker. But I wonder, if one knew what happened later to that poor man, whether one would not find again that the weapon had been turned against its own breast."

"At last I couldn't bear that whistle any more and got out of bed. I opened the curtains a little way; and there right under my window, the moonlight on his face was Blacker. I had stretched my hand down, his fingers reaching up could almost have touched mine. He looked up at me, flashing the one good eye with hunger — I realize now that near-success must have developed his obsession almost to the point of madness. Desperation had driven him to the house. He whispered up at me. 'David, where is it?'"

"I jerked my head back at the room. 'Give it me,' he said, 'quick. You shall have the train in the morning.'"

"I shook my head. He said, 'I've got the bleeder here, and the key. You'd better toss it down.'"

"'Go away,' I said. But I could hardly speak with fear."

"'I'll bleed you first and then I'll have it just the same.'"

"'Oh no, you won't,' I said. I went to the chair and picked it — Him — up. There was only one place where He was safe. I couldn't separate the Host from the paper, so I swallowed both. The newsprint stuck like a prune to the back of my throat, but I rinsed it down with water from the ewer. Then I went back to the window and looked down at Blacker. He began to wheedle me. 'What have you done with it, David? What's the fuss? It's only a bit of bread,' looking so longingly and pleadingly up at me that even as a child I wondered whether he could really think that, and yet desire it so much."

"'I swallowed it.' I said."

"'Swallowed it?'"

"'Yes,' I said, 'Go away.' Then something happened, which seems to me now more terrible than his desire to corrupt or my thoughtless act: he began to weep — the tears ran lopsidedly out of the one good eye and his shoulders shook. I only saw his face for a moment before he bent his head and strode off, the bald turnip head shaking, into the dark. When I think of it now, it's almost as if I had seen that Thing weeping for its inevitable defeat. It had tried to use me as a weapon and now I had broken in its hands and it wept its hopeless tears through one of Blacker's eyes."

The black furnaces of Bedwell Junction gathered around the line. The points switched and we were tossed from one set of rails to another. A spray of sparks, a signal light changed to red, tall chimneys jetting into the grey night sky, the fumes of steam from stationary engines — half the cold journey was over and now remained the long wait for the slow cross-country train. I said, "It's an interesting story. I think, should I have given Blacker what he wanted, I wonder what he would have done with it?"

"I really believe," my companion said, "that he would first of all have put it under his microscope — before he did all the other things I expect he had planned."

"And the hint?" I said. "I don't quite see what you mean by that."

"Oh, well," he said vaguely, "you know for me it was an odd beginning, that affair, when you come to think of it," but I should never have known what he meant had not his coat, when he rose to take his bag from the rack, come open and disclosed the collar of a priest.

I said, "I suppose you think you owe a lot to Blacker."

"Yes," he said. "You see, I am a very happy man."

Review Questions

1. How did the passenger define the term *hint*?

2. How many Catholics lived in the passenger's hometown and what were the attitudes of the townspeople toward Catholics?

3. How did Blacker keep the young boy coming back to the bakery day after day?

4. What reason did Blacker provide to the boy for wanting communion?

5. When the boy told Blacker that he swallowed communion, how did Blacker react?

In-depth Questions

1. The narrator of the story claims to be an agnostic but is "surprised occasionally into belief by the extraordinary coincidences." Have you experienced coincidences that have affirmed your belief in God?

2. The corruption of children is used as a proof, not of God, but of evil. Why do you think the corruption of children holds such an important place in the story?

3. In describing Blacker, the story says: "What an impossible paradox, to be free and to be so obsessed." Why are obsession and freedom opposed to each other? How would you describe true freedom?

4. The story is filled with irony. What would you say are some of the most ironic parts of the story?

5. Why do you think the experience with Blacker set the passenger on the path to the priesthood?

GREAT CATHOLIC LITERATURE: READING 3

"God's Breath"

JAMES A. CONNOR

Introduction

James A. Connor had been a Jesuit priest for only six months when he met the couple whose grief shook his faith to the core. The husband and wife had been traveling to a family celebration of their baby's birth; along the way, a boulder had dislodged from a cliff and struck the car, killing the baby. As he sat with the couple, Connor wondered what he could possibly say — everything he thought to say seemed inappropriate, even absurd, in the face of such suffering. In the end he said nothing, because he could think of nothing to make sense of the situation, and the room filled with an awful silence. That silence drove him to leave his parish two days later. He retreated to an isolated cabin in the mountain wilderness of British Columbia, not to escape the silence of the hospital room, but to enter it more deeply. Eccentric neighbors and the natural world kept him company, along with the writings of Thomas Merton, the Desert Fathers, and other spiritual masters.

He emerged from that late 1970s retreat with a stronger faith. Over the next eighteen years, Connor taught, worked in parishes, and ministered to Native Americans. He eventually left active priestly ministry, not because of a lack of faith, but out of a concern that he had not had the right motives for becoming a priest.

He became an English professor and devoted himself to writing. He had already published a collection of short stories in 1988, *God's Breath*. Then, in 2002, he returned to the subject of the retreat he had taken at the beginning of his priesthood. In *Silent Fire: Bringing the Spirituality of Silence to Everyday Life,* he described the holy silence he entered on that retreat as a kind of purifying fire. It was through silent contemplation that he was able to confront his deepest fears, including his inability to make sense of tragic human suffering. Like fire, the silence eventually burned away his anger, shame, and fear; and just as a fire illuminates the darkness, the silence illuminated for him the holiness of everyday life.

"God's Breath"

In the summer after my father had died—his car jumped the railing on the dam and slipped into the lake—my brother and I stood at the entrance of the Magdalena mine and heaved stones at the dark. The mine never paid well; it had opened at the turn of the century, but soon after the First World War it was abandoned. People in town will tell you right off it was named for Magdalena Gomez Alvarado, the founder of the first sporting house in New Mexico. The entrance where we stood was one of the oldest, burrowed into the mountain about a thousand feet above the valley, with a clear view of the dam and the soundless lake behind it. In the library, we have an old photograph of Magdalena Gomez Alvarado, beefy and dark, surrounded by solemn miners the day the mine was dedicated, the tunnel behind her a perfect oh in the rocks as if the mountains were weeping. A priest stood beside her with a cross and a prayer book in his hand. In the photograph, Magdalena is in her wedding dress, and is smiling, though her back is stiff and her hands are held nervously in front of her. Some of the old people remember what Magdalena used to say about the mine, that God wouldn't live there, and that it was not a good place to die.

We went up there in August 1959. Johnny was older than I, and what he was truly like as a boy has been obscured by my childhood sentiments, part adulation and part envy. Even though these days he's grown bald and lies awake nights under an ancient, nameless apprehension of the future, as a child he seemed to me empowered with immense freedom. In his room, he had collected mementos from all his wanderings: a cow's vertebrae, a fossil snail shell, feathers, a piston from a John Deere tractor, a rail spike from the mine. When Dad was alive, he would open the door to Johnny's room, shake his head, and then call him Johnny the Junkman.

The spike had been taken from the tunnel where we threw stones and counted. The one who threw the straightest and farthest into the tunnel before the stone hit a wall or fell to the floor had the highest count.

"Not so fast," Johnny said.

"Six!"

"It was really four. Hey, Leon. Four, right?"

Johnny's friend Leon had followed us out that day, but refused to throw stones. He was a bony fellow with a droopy Adam's apple and thick glasses, and as a consequence he had few friends other than Johnny. That afternoon, he was standing off to the right where the trickle of water from the mine pooled against the rock wall of the mountain. Leon was doing his little dance. *"Oola, oola, oola,"* he said and swung his hips like a hootchie kooch dancer. His reflection in the water followed him. I was no more than eight and thought that doing the hootchie kooch would have been fun, but even though Johnny didn't mind this kind of behavior from Leon, as if he expected it, he would have been embarrassed if I had gotten involved. So I threw rocks as if they were hand grenades and listened as they rattled down the tunnel and disappeared.

I had been left on my own prematurely that year because Mama was working day and night at the Newberry's and Johnny was left to look after me. Johnny was twelve, and every morning, Mama gave him his instructions: "Be careful, watch for snakes, guard your brother, and don't go near the mine."

I wasn't aware of it at the time, but we were throwing stones that afternoon because Johnny needed to work up the courage to disobey Mama and lead us inside. We'd packed a few peanut butter sandwiches into paper bags and stuffed them into our packs, grabbed Daddy's old flashlight, the one that had been sitting on the shelf with the paint and the screwdrivers for at least a year, and then slid down

ARR⊙Y⊙

An arroyo is a water channel or creek bed that runs through a dry or desert area.

the long arroyo and up the mine road, where the rusted machinery lay discarded around open shafts, partly hidden by mesquite. There were shafts all around, one about a hundred feet down the road from the tunnel. At first, Leon had suggested we shinny down the cable hanging from a wooden derrick, but Johnny said it would be better to walk in through the tunnel. That was when Leon started to ignore us and did his hootchie kooch.

Just after three, Johnny switched on the flashlight and played it around the opening of the tunnel; the batteries were low, the light dull orange, flickering as Johnny moved it. I looked at the thin beam, afraid. Leon stopped his dancing long enough to laugh at me, told me to go home if I wanted, I was just a kid anyway. I was fierce to go after that.

It was a sunny afternoon. The desert pavement was cream colored with stones washed out of the mountains. When we entered the mine, it was cold and dark, and though I listened hard, the only sound I could hear was the trickle of water. Just across the threshold, I turned to look at the valley one more time—puffy clouds gathered in white columns over the cliffs. The sky was startlingly blue behind them.

Skidding down the inclined tunnel, our sneakers slid out of control on the hard dirt. Johnny led the way, Leon took up the rear. The darkness surrounded us so fast it caught my breath. It was all around, pressing on me like water at the bottom of the sea. I was afraid to open my mouth too wide for fear I would drown. Leon laughed again nervously. Turning, I saw the whole world outside, with all its noise and motion, shrink to a single white point. Inside, the mine was silent except for the soft crunching of our sneakers on the floor. Leon pushed me on, but I could no longer see the back of Johnny's head. I reached for him.

"Johnny?" I said.

He turned on the light and held it under his chin, his face yellow, without expression, his eyes hidden in the shadows.

"Stick close," he said.

I grabbed his belt, and followed him deeper. The flashlight reflected off a vein of white rock, and then disappeared at a place where the walls receded. We were in a wide room, with tunnels running off in four different directions. Stacked along the right hand wall was the head of an old pickax and three spikes. Nearby lay an empty tobacco tin with the face of an Indian on the front.

"Look at this," Johnny said. We gathered around the tin, which he cleaned with spit, swirling the dirt with the ball of his thumb. "1898."

"Indians don't look like that," Leon said.

"They could've. Back then."

"They didn't. I've got Indian blood."

"Then why don't you live on the Reservation?"

Leon looked away. "I don't. That's all."

Johnny took one of the spikes and the tobacco tin and stuffed them in his pack. Then standing in the middle of the room, he aimed the beam into each tunnel, but we couldn't tell where any of them went. We took the one in the middle, because it seemed to be an extension of the tunnel we came in on.

Soon the floor dipped. Old orecart tracks were spiked into the rock, so we could climb down, holding onto the wooden ties like the rungs of a ladder. Johnny went first to catch me if I fell. We climbed for hours, it seemed. Each time I hoped to see the bottom reflecting in the flashlight beam, the darkness rolled over and covered it. Finally, Johnny stopped and played the beam around the tunnel, flashed it from side to side.

"Why are we stopping, Johnny?"

He didn't answer for a long time. Instead, he picked up a stone and tossed it underhand into the darkness in front of him. We started counting, and got to eight when we heard the rock splash into a pool of water.

"Shaft."

"Can't go through here," Leon said.

"Maybe there's a way around."

"Do you see anything on the other side?"

"A wall."

"Shouldn't we go back now?" I said.

"I don't know. You want to go home, Leon?"

Leon hesitated. "Naw," he said. "Don't be chicken. We shouldn't have brought Sammy along in the first place."

"He'll be ok. Won't you?"

I nodded in the dark, even though Johnny couldn't see me. "Yeah," I said.

"There's another tunnel off this track somewhere down here," Johnny said. He climbed down a few more steps, reached to his right and felt the wall. A space opened there. "Here it is."

We traversed into the new tunnel and sat with our backs against the rock wall to eat our sandwiches. Johnny switched off the light to save batteries while we ate—there was nothing but darkness. It was blacker than the black behind your eyelids when you press your palms against your face. I tried to see something, any single thing, but there was no moonlight, no starlight, not even the shine off your skin. The walls of the tunnel seemed to fall back, to melt away until we were on an empty plain a million miles across, with nothing in it but darkness. All that was left was the smell of dust. I felt abandoned.

"It's dark," Leon said.

"Sure is thick, isn't it?" Johnny said, his voice shaking a little.

The quaver in my brother's voice upset me. The darkness had frightened even Johnny. I began to wonder if I got lost, would anyone be able to find me? Could God see me in the dark? I didn't think so. I didn't think even God could see in this place. There never was a dark like this—it was a force, something alive, like the shadows in fever dreams. The dark breathed in and out—I felt it breathing against my cheek. Johnny moved to my right, and the flashlight came on. The tunnel walls reappeared.

"This way," he said, and pointed deeper into the mine. I didn't want to go that way. I wanted to go home. I wanted to see my mother, to see the sun in the sky and the birds in the trees. I wouldn't have thought this at the time, but as I remember, from inside the tunnel, the world of light and water and trees seemed unreal, as if the tunnel was where I had been born and I had only dreamed there were ever white clouds rising over red cliffs. The darkness was all there was.

"I wonder if this is what it's like being dead," Johnny said.

We walked on. Leon made ghost noises all the way down the tunnel. All I could see were dead people lying in boxes.

"I'm not going to die," I said.

"Everybody dies, stupid," said Leon.

"Leave him alone," Johnny said.

"Not me," I said.

"Even you."

Not me, I thought. God wouldn't let me. The nuns had told us God was everywhere. I tried to think of God being everywhere, but couldn't. All I could see was an old man with a beard running fast from one place to the next. If He was everywhere, I thought, then, he was down here too in the rocks and in the dark. Not much comfort.

A few minutes later, we came to a room with a vertical shaft in the middle of the floor. On the far wall some miner hand carved three letters: M G A. Magdalena's name was even here, in the depths of the mine she had never entered. Johnny took the spike out of his pack and scratched JUNKMAN underneath. Then we lay on our backs and looked up at the rough ceiling as if it were the sky.

"I've been here before," Johnny said. "With Remo and my Dad. Dad promised me some Smithsonite. There's good stuff lower down. We went from here to the next level on ropes. Remo went first, and then Dad lowered me, real slow so I could walk down the side with my feet. Then he came down afterward. There's a tunnel down there, real low, where we crawled for a quarter of a mile on our stomachs. There was water in it too. For two hours I was sure I was going to get stuck and die. Dad said he'd never take me down that far again."

I had never known these things about my father, never known that he and my brother had a life I didn't share. Envious, I wanted to look down the shaft they had gone. The three of us crept to the edge and peered over the side. A draught of air rose from the depths, and down below we heard it blowing through the tunnels. Even deeper, water from an underground river splashed into pools. The air and the water blended together as if a giant were asleep underground. I knew then. This was God under the mountain, his breath sucking and blowing as he snored in his dreams.

Johnny decided this would be a good place to eat the cookies, so we crawled to the cavern wall and rested our backs against it. Sitting between Leon and myself, he stuck the flashlight between his thighs so the beam splayed against the rock ceiling. I sat as close to Johnny as I could, in a place where the air brushed my face as it passed into the tunnel.

How nice it was that God was asleep, I thought. The darkness of death seemed thicker than the darkness of sleep. The thought of God snoring under the mountain the way Dad had done on the living room couch made God seem almost pleasant.

The air brushed my face. I listened to the sound of God's tongue against the back of his throat, and wanted to ask Johnny about God.

I had my mouth open to speak when the flashlight between Johnny's thighs flickered and went out. The spot of light on the ceiling collapsed, turning purple to black. The darkness rushed over us like a wave. Because my mouth was open, the darkness rushed inside me. It was inside and out now—everything about me was dark. Johnny swore. I heard him tap the flashlight against the floor of the mine. He tapped, swore, tapped, swore. In the middle of his swearing, he began to cry.

Somehow we climbed to our feet, shuffled along the wall of the mine, terrified of falling headlong into the shaft. Even though the shaft was in the middle of the room and we hugged the walls, we felt certain that the hole could grow in the dark, grow until it spread from wall to wall.

Now Leon was crying. I felt him shaking behind me and didn't know if I wanted to cry too. I was too frightened to cry, too deep-down terrified. Finally, Johnny tugged my arm. "Let's get out of here," he said. We followed the tunnel out and kept the blowing air at our backs.

Leon whined. "Hurry up, Johnny. I want to get out of here, now."

"Shut up. We can't go any faster."

I heard Johnny's foot shuffle in front of me as if his toes reached out along the floor and felt for sudden holes in the rock. We crawled along this way until we came to a place where the right wall of the tunnel opened up. The air turned in that direction, out of the tunnel we were in, so we followed it.

"Oh God, oh God," Leon said.

"How much farther, Johnny?" I said.

"Be quiet."

Johnny's foot moved. We grabbed onto each other's belts for safety and wormed through the dark tunnel. The air was always at our backs. Finally, we started climbing. There were no orecart tracks here, but the floor wasn't as steep as on our way down. At the top, we came to a place where we felt the walls open again on both sides, probably another chamber. We heard water splash in the distance.

"Careful," Johnny said. "There's a shaft here somewhere." Another stream of air joined the one we followed; it carried the smell of water and mud, of lichens, and of deep, sodden earth.

"What's that smell?" Leon said. "Do you think something *died* down here?"

I didn't want to think about anything dead, about anything at all. I closed my eyes with the hope that the darkness behind my eyelids would be more comfortable that the darkness outside, but it didn't help. We scuttled around the edge of the chamber till we came to another tunnel. The breeze was stronger here, thicker, like streams converging on the sea. The floor of the tunnel rose slightly. Little by little, a white spot of light grew in the distance, took on color and form. The world outside opened.

We staggered out of the mouth of the tunnel. Leon wept. The three of us stood on the top of a hill far from where we entered, and gaped at the sun as it fell behind the mountains. The clouds shimmered with color — white, pink, orange, and purple. The sky, blue at the horizon, shaded to indigo higher up. Stars popped into view one at a time. In the middle of the valley lights of our town were shining. We were infants again, as if seeing the hills and the trees for the first time.

Review Questions

1. Why was Johnny taking care of Sammy, the narrator?

2. How did Sammy describe the darkness of the mine shaft when Johnny switched off the flashlight?

3. Why did Sammy think that he was not going to die?

4. What did Sammy describe as God's breath?

5. What did the boys see as they emerged from the mine shaft?

In-depth Questions

1. In Baptism, a person joins Jesus's death and new life as they enter into and emerge from the water. How do you think that "God's Breath" is an allegory to Baptism?

2. How do you think the three characters changed through their experience in the mine shaft?
   • Sammy
   • Johnny
   • Leon

3. While the boys were in the mine shaft they ate their sandwiches together. Do you see any symbolism or significant meaning in this? Please explain.

4. Have you ever had a frightening experience that compares to Sammy's? Did you rely on God during the experience? How do you think you changed because of that experience?

"Bad Friday"

Sara Maitland

Introduction

Sara Maitland's life has been marked by a series of religious and political conversions. She was born in Scotland in 1950 and was raised in the Scottish Presbyterian church. As a teenager she attended an all-girls boarding school. Although she disliked the school, she made good friends while she was there, and they sparked her interest in socialist politics and societal change. She soon shed her religious beliefs and declared herself an existentialist—one who believes that people are entirely free and therefore responsible for what they make of themselves.

She attended university at Oxford, where she joined protests for political and social change. It was also during this period that she encountered feminist thought about God. This encounter had a profound effect on her. She felt free to once again believe in God—not the God of her childhood, but the "big-enough" God she experienced in courses on science and religion. These became the subject of *A Big-Enough God: A Feminist's Search for a Joyful Theology,* a book which explores recent scientific discoveries' implications about the nature of God.

In 1972 she became an Anglican, and married an American who eventually became an Anglican priest. But she became attracted to the universal nature of the Catholic Church, and became a Catholic in 1993.

Over the years she wrote dozens of short stories and novels and is noted for a confident, inventive writing style in which she convincingly employs a wide range of voices—she is just as comfortable portraying a young girl growing up in Edwardian England as she is giving voice to a Chinese princess or a contemporary feminist. She is also known for taking risks in her writing; for instance, she is fond of interrupting her stories to comment on her own storytelling. "Bad Friday" offers an example of how she uses this technique.

"Bad Friday" is from *Angel & Me,* a collection of short stories published in 1995. Most of the stories in that collection are told from the perspective of well-known biblical women and saints—Sarah, Martha, Mary, Pilate's wife Claudia, the martyrs Perpetua and Felicity, and so on—but five of the stories are about the narrator's somewhat rocky relationship with her guardian angel. Each of the women in these stories finds herself transformed by faith—sometimes comically—in the ordinary circumstances of her life.

GREAT CATHOLIC LITERATURE
"Bad Friday"

I have a bit of a problem with this story. It's not really like some of the other stories about my somewhat tiresome guardian angel.

For one thing it happened in the night.

Oddly enough—well it does seem odd to me—my guardian angel does not often appear in the night. As a matter of fact, I strongly suspect that this is because she has such a pathetic imagination. She can't cope with dreams, and is confined to the daily. You read in the Bible of truly wonderful dreams; like Jacob's ladder or Joseph putting his brothers in their place by boasting about their measly little sheaves of corn bowing down to his great big fat one.

I think a few dreams would be fun and a much better way of getting spiritual guidance because you could chat for hours with your friends about interpretations and Freud and sex and things. But do I dream? No, I don't. All I get are her clichés, and her interfering pettiness, and her tedious scruples.

Of course, she doesn't agree. She says the reason I don't get dreams is because I sleep so soundly, for which—in her opinion— I ought to be grateful. I find this terribly unromantic but it's true: frankly the minute I turn the light out I slump asleep and practically never wake up again until the alarm clock rings. But you might well think a half-way competent angel would be able to deal with such a minor impediment. It makes you wonder. If I were God the very least I'd do is check that all the guardian angels had *some* creative flair, and ones like mine who are so totally prosaic and mundane would be kept in heaven, well out of the way of delicate and aspiring souls.

Anyway, all this is pretty irrelevant; because as it happens this story did take place in the night. At twelve minutes past three to be precise. The very worst imaginable time to be woken up by an angel with a slightly common accent manifesting herself all of a sudden, and saying "I've just popped in to say goodbye."

"Go away," I muttered. In my own defence I must stress that I was nine-tenths asleep. Then I remembered with a horrid jerk that I had said much the same thing to my daughter one night when she was ten years old and had been woken up two hours later by my very angry oldest son reporting that she was retching and shivering and swallowing her pain in the bathroom, and telling him not to wake me or I would be cross. She had acute appendicitis; and had been wheeled into surgery still apologizing for having disturbed me.

(By the way, in fairness since I am always complaining about Angel, I should mention that she was completely marvelous that night, and came with us all the way in the ambulance and did try to comfort me, and reassure me that I could go on being a mother. Unlike usual, she didn't rub my face in guilt. I refused her consolation though—I knew all about my inadequacy and awfulness on that occasion.)

So with that unfortunate precedent looming in my consciousness I sat up and said "Sorry, Angel, I was asleep. Is it something important?"

"I just popped in to say goodbye."

"Can't that wait?" I asked peevishly.

"You are always telling me you want divine revelations in the cold small hours of the night," she said. If anyone else had used that tone to me I would have thought they were being a bit sarcastic, but Angel is too dense for such subtleties.

"I don't see your departure exactly as a spiritual revelation," I muttered. And then it hit me. Her departure. She couldn't leave me, not just like that. I hadn't been *that* nasty to her; it was just that we disagreed about quite a lot of things. Surely angels could accept and tolerate difference? Surely she wouldn't be that small-minded? What did she expect, slavish obedience or something? Not that I minded of course; if she wanted to desert her God-given duties that was up to her; it was none of my business. It was just the principle of the thing.

"Angel . . . ," I began.

"You know we always take this Friday off," she said.

She always did too. Regular as clockwork, "Fine," I said, ignoring a great surge of relief and happiness, "I don't see why you had to wake me up for that. Did you think I'd forget or something? See you Easter Day."

There was a pause. Then she said, with what sounded, like an unusual degree of difference, "I thought I'd better remind you about fasting."

"Fasting! For Good Friday!" I exclaimed. "Oh don't be so antiquated. No one does that anymore".

She didn't argue with me, there was just one of her long silences.

"I'm not", I said boldly, "into all that body-hating, masochistic, mediaeval stuff. Do you fast in heaven?"

Her silence continued. I waited hopefully. For once, I thought, I had her where I wanted her. In the wrong. After a bit I heard her sniffle; the poor thing was probably embarrassed. I felt a moment of compassion, but, thinking about all the times she had forced me to apologize, I clung to my moment of triumph.

"Well," I said, after I thought she had been silent for long enough, "do you fast in heaven?"

The silence went on a bit longer. It was almost beginning to feel awkward; then she said, quite suddenly and almost crossly for her, "Well we can't, can we? We don't eat. We don't feel hunger."

But the odd thing was that she didn't sound the least bit pleased with herself—either for her minor victory over me, or for this abundant proof of the superiority of angels.

We fell into silence again. It went on for a long time. I thought she had finished harassing me and would dematerialize herself in her own good time, so I lay down again and tried to go back to sleep. She was still there, hovering in my left cortex as only angels can. Now and again she made a funny snuffly sound, as though she had a cold; but when someone has just reminded you, and in rather a disagreeable tone, that they don't experience hunger, you can't very well offer them a handkerchief and tell them to blow their nose.

It was all very annoying. I felt more and more obstinate. She could stay or go in her own good time, but I was not going to initiate another conversation. It was three o'clock in the morning, for goodness sake, and no time for a busy woman to be having to deal with sulky angels. And in passing I would like to say that no human being, not even the adolescent male, can sulk as efficiently and thoroughly as your average angel. All I wanted was to go back to sleep.

The snuffling however did not diminish. On the contrary. Then I realized that she was crying. I mean really crying. It was a bit embarrassing actually, like the first time a grown-up man cries those terrible awkward male tears onto you; you know it's a sort of compliment, you have an inkling of how much they need to do it, and, at the same time, you just wish they wouldn't, because they are so bad at it. Angel's tears made me squirm a bit; I nearly asked her how it was that angels could cry when they couldn't eat, and then decided that would not be very kind. But I really did feel quite strongly that it was an angel's role to comfort, not to be comforted, so I let her get on with it for a bit.

In the end it got to me; that irrepressible maternal instinct—or since I'm a feminist perhaps I should say human instinct—that simply prevents you from letting a person, or I suppose an angel for that matter, cry. I wasn't best pleased about it.

"Oh for heaven's sake, Angel," I said, when I could bear it no longer, "whatever's the matter now?"

But she didn't reply. She just went on crying. It was really getting on my nerves. I said "All right then, if it means that much to you I will fast today."

You might think that this generosity of spirit would cheer anyone up, but it didn't work with her.

"Please." I could hear myself begging. When I think of all the times that she has felt free to interrupt me and demand that I talk to her about whatever idiotic banality she chooses. And now she was refusing me the same privilege. It wasn't fair. That sounded a bit childish, so I changed my mind. It was outrageous!

"You're behaving like a teenager," I said; I tried to say it firmly rather than angrily. Three teenage children in one household is quite enough, without having to put up with a teenaged spiritual force that skulked about somewhere slightly above my top vertebra. Once my daughter locked herself in the bathroom and howled for three hours, and when she finally came out she demanded cinnamon toast and refused point blank ever to say what the matter was. I was not going through that again, especially not with a blasted angel about whom I could not even have the dubious satisfaction of murmuring "boy-friend-trouble" with the world-weariness of middle age.

"Angel," I said, "don't be such a baby." But when babies cry you can comfort them. You can kiss them and cuddle them; you can wrap them warm and safe against you, petting their pink, flushed faces. You can find their favourite teddy bear, its face already worn bald with the receiving of love and the giving of furry comfort. You cannot do any of these things, or anything like them, with an angel. Grey matter may be soft and warm, but cuddly it is not. I reached through my mind and spirit for tenderness and comfort and found my hands empty. It was very frustrating.

The crying went on and on. I had tried emotional bribery and I had tried emotional blackmail. There was nothing left except love. And, given the difficulties of our relationship, and the degree to which I felt irritated by her, it was not an easy thing to offer.

"Angel," I said, as carefully as I knew how. "I love you. When you came to say goodbye I had forgotten about the Friday bank holi-day or whatever you call it in heaven, and I thought you were leaving me permanently. I was sad. I didn't even know I was sad, but I was. I was sad because I love you. And because I need you. But hon-estly I would rather you left me if that made you happier than have you stay like this."

I felt a complete idiot when I said this. There are many things you find yourself doing as you get older which your optimistic young self would never have known how to dream of, but very high on that list for me comes sitting up in bed at four in the morning, in a flannel nightie, trying to tell *anyone*, let alone a weeping and unresponsive citizen of heaven, that you love her.

But it worked. Not magically or instantaneously or anything, but the solid flow of desolate tears turned back into the infuriating ade-noidal snuffles, and then into the hiccups of a sob-exhausted toddler.

Finally she said "It's worse than you know."

"What is?" I asked, relieved that we were getting somewhere, but weary with the strain.

"I'm jealous."

"Jealous!" I exclaimed startled. "Jealous?" I inquired in an attempt at non-judgemental open-minded interest.

There was a bit more snuffling, and then finally she said "I'm jealous of *you*."

"Me?" I said tentatively, though really I meant "What on earth are you talking about?"

"Yes you. I'm jealous of you because you can get hungry. Because you can get hurt, I mean physically hurt, because you can have pain, and suffering, and agony."

"But that's not nice. I mean, those things aren't nice. They're horrid. Why does that make you jealous?"

"Because you can be with Him today and we can't. We just can't. We tried and tried and we couldn't understand. After the Last Supper he went away from us. We thought we could rescue him and he wouldn't let us. Then we thought at least we could comfort him, and we couldn't. That peasant woman could; she may be the Queen of Heaven now, but then she was just a middle-aged woman from the sticks, but she could comfort him, and her half-daft fisherman friend and that red-headed whore from Magdala; they could comfort him because they could understand. And we, the first-born of the creation, the spinners of the seven spheres, the messengers of the Holy Spirit, the powers and dominions, cherubim and seraphim, angels and archangels; we could do nothing. He didn't need us. We could not go where he had gone. We could not understand. That's why we all take the day off; not for a holiday but because we know we're useless."

"They scourged him and we could not feel it. They crowned him with thorns and it didn't hurt us. They banged those nails through his hands and we wept for his humiliation, but we could not go where he had gone when he went into the pain-place, whatever that is. He gave you the glory, the privilege of going where he went, into the body in all its beauty and holiness, into the pain and the pleasure of the flesh. He loves you more than he loves us. And you take that privilege, that gift, that joy so lightly that you don't even care enough to fast once a year. *Of course I'm jealous.*"

She began to cry again. So did I, as a matter of fact. We wept together and we could not comfort each other.

"We don't call it Good Friday," she gulped after a while, "we call it Bad Friday."

"Angel," I said, "I really will fast today. I'll fast for me and I'll fast for you." This time the generosity of spirit was slightly more authentic.

"Thank you," she said.

It was nearly dawn, grey light was coming through the curtains. She got ready to depart. I began to think about how impressed my children would be when they saw I wasn't eating, not even the hot cross buns. It might even reconvert my middle son who was trying out existentialism at that moment. I might even become a great ascetic saint pretty soon, known for the rigours of my Sue and for my charity to lesser mortals.

Angel put a stop to that; she paused in her soft descent through my cranial cavity, and murmured "Watch it, sister; we haven't even started on hair shirts and flagellation yet, and they're tough." But she was grinning a shy, happy, little grin.

"Peace be with you," she said as usual, "and see you on Sunday."

Review Questions

1. Why did Angel visit Sara at 3:12 a.m.?

2. What did Angel remind Sara to do during the next day?

3. What did Angel say she was crying so inconsolably about?

4. Why do angels take Good Friday off?

5. What does Sara say she will do for Angel throughout the day on Friday?

In-depth Questions

1. Sara describes Angel as being rather annoying. However, Angel always seems to be challenging Sara to be holier. Do you ever feel a struggle within yourself between your conscience and other inclinations? When your conscience rules your actions, why do you think it wins? When other inclinations rule your actions, why do you think they come out on top?

2. When Sara's daughter was rushed to the hospital with appendicitis, Sara received great comfort from Angel. Describe a time that was difficult for you and you felt like you received heavenly assistance or comfort.

3. Sara speaks with Angel as familiarly as she speaks to a family member. When you pray, would you describe your prayer as more formal or more familiar? Describe the manner in which you address God.

4. Read Hebrews 4:14–16. Describe the parallels you see between this Scripture passage and the description of Jesus's humanity in "Bad Friday." Why are these parallels important? What does it tell us about Jesus?

From *The Diary of a Country Priest*

GEORGES BERNANOS

Introduction

Although the French novelist Georges Bernanos (1888–1948) wrote a handful of notable novels and a movie script, he is best remembered for his 1937 spiritual and literary masterpiece, *The Diary of a Country Priest*.

Bernanos seemed to be in a fight of one kind or another throughout much of his life. He was a poor student in most subject areas except for writing, and frequently clashed with his teachers. As a young man, he became involved in the Action Française, a militant royalist movement that sought to restore France's past glory by reinstating the monarchy. It appealed to certain French Catholics by claiming to defend the Church from those who wanted the separation of church and state. Bernanos edited a royalist weekly newspaper, but later became disillusioned with Action Française and left the movement.

The next fight Bernanos found himself in was World War I. After this conflict he married Jeanne Talbert d'Arc (a direct descendant of Joan of Arc's brother), with whom he had six children. He spent ten years working for an insurance company before publishing his first novel, *The Star of Satan*, in 1926. The novel, about an ordinary priest's struggle with the good and evil within himself, was enough of a success that Bernanos decided to fully commit himself to his writing. As a young man, he briefly considered becoming a priest; instead, he made priests central characters in many of his novels, including *The Diary of a Country Priest*.

In that novel, a young priest records his daily life among the members of a parish in rural France. Bernanos loosely modeled the priest on Thérèse of Lisieux; his diary entries echo her "Little Way," a spiritual discipline of humility and love practiced in simple, everyday acts. (See "From *The Story of a Soul*," pages 152–159.) The priest reaches out to his parishioners with genuine compassion, but they respond to his efforts with indifference and even hostility. Over the course of the novel, he is increasingly plagued by self-doubt and a persistent stomach ailment. He comes to regard himself as a failure, and yet Bernanos makes clear to the reader that the priest is not. His humility may prevent him from realizing it, but the priest is actually a saint who sacrifices himself for the sake of his flock. As he dies of stomach cancer, his ultimate triumph is revealed in his last words.

The last battle fought by Bernanos was against sin. Late in his life, he stopped writing fiction in order to write essays that envisioned a world-wide spiritual renewal led by French Catholics. That renewal failed to materialize in the way he had hoped. But like his country priest, Bernanos's efforts to promote greater holiness in the world were not a failure, for his work continues to move and inspire many around the world to greater holiness and more devout service.

GREAT CATHOLIC LITERATURE
From *The Diary of a Country Priest*

And I know now that youth is a gift of God, and like all His gifts, carries no regret. They alone shall be young, really young, whom He has chosen never to survive their youth. I belong to such a race of men. I used to wonder: what shall I be doing at fifty, at sixty? And of course I couldn't find an answer, I couldn't even make one up. There was no old man in me.

This awareness is sweet. For the first time in years — perhaps for the first time ever — I seem to stand before my youth and look upon it without mistrust; I have rediscovered a forgotten face. And my youth looks back at me, forgives me. Disheartened by the sheer clumsiness in me which always kept me back, I demanded of my youth what youth alone can't give, and I said it was a stupid thing and was ashamed of being young. But now, both weary with our silly quarrels, we can rest awhile, silent by the road, and breathe in the deep peace of evening where we shall enter together.

It greatly comforts me also, to think that nobody has been guilty of real harshness towards me — not to say the great word: injustice. I certainly respect those victims of iniquity who are able to find in that knowledge some basis of strength and hope. Somehow I should always hate to think myself — though unwittingly — the cause, or merely the pretext of another's sin.

Even from the Cross, when Our Lord in His agony found the perfection of His saintly Humanity — even then He did not own Himself a victim of injustice: *They know not what they do.* Words that have meaning for the youngest child, words some would like to call childish, but the spirits of evil must have been muttering them ever since without understanding, and with ever-growing terror. Instead of the thunderbolts they awaited, it is as though a Hand of innocence closed over the chasm of their dwelling.

And so I find great joy in thinking that much of the blame, which sometimes hurts me, arose from a common ignorance of my true destiny. A sensible man like the Dean of Blangermont was obviously over inclined to anticipate what I should be later, and he was unconsciously reproaching me now for mistakes that were to come.

I have loved without guile (I think that is the only way I can love). Such guilelessness was a danger in the end, both for myself and for others. I know it. I always struggled against this natural impulse, and so ineffectually that I may believe it was invincible. The thought that this conflict is over—there is no more reason for it— had already occurred to me this morning, but I was still dazed by Dr. Laville's revelation. It seeped into me only very slowly, like tiny drops from a stream at first. But now there are rising waters freshening to my spirit, overflowing. Quiet and peace.

Of course, during the last weeks or months that God may spare to me, while I can still look after a parish, I shall do my best, as always, to be careful. But I shall give less thought to the future, I shall work in the present. I feel such work is within my power. For I only succeed in small things, and when I am tried by anxiety, I am bound to say it is the small joys that release me.

This day of realization will have been like others: with nightfall fear had gone, but the coming dawn brings no glory. I do not turn my back on death, neither do I confront it bravely as M. Olivier surely would. I have tried to open my eyes to death in all the simplicity of surrender, yet with no secret wish to soften or disarm it. Were the comparison less foolish, I would say that I look upon death as I did on Sulpice Mitonnet or Mlle Chantal. . . . Alas, one would need also to become as a little child. . . .

Before I realized my fate, I often feared I should not know how to die when the time came, as there is no doubt I am too impressionable. I remember a saying of dear old Dr. Delbende, which I believe was recorded in this diary, about monks and priests not always being the best at dying. . . . But I have no more qualms about that now. I can understand how a man, sure of himself and his courage, might wish to make of his death a perfect end. As that isn't in my line, my death shall be what it can be, and nothing more. Were it not a very daring thing to say, I would like to add that to a true lover, the halting confession of his beloved is more dear than the most beautiful poem. And when you come to think of it, such a comparison should offend no one, for human agony is beyond all an act of love.

God might possibly wish my death as some form of example to others. But I would rather have their pity. Why shouldn't I? I have loved men greatly, and I feel this world of living creatures has been so pleasant. I cannot go without tears. Nothing is farther removed from me than stoic indifference, so how can I hope for the death of a stoic? Plutarch's heroes both terrify and bore me. If I were to go to heaven wearing such a mask, I think even my guardian angel would laugh at me.

Why worry, why look ahead? If I feel afraid I shall say: I am afraid, and not be ashamed of it. As soon as Our Lord appears before me, may His eyes set me at rest. . . .

I have said my rosary at the window, opened wide over a court-yard like a dark well. But above me, the east corner of the building seems to be showing lighter. I have rolled myself up in the blanket, and even drawn it a little over my head. I am not cold. My usual pain isn't troubling me, but I feel sick.

If only I could I'd get out of this house! I would love to walk again through empty streets the way I went this morning. My visit to Dr. Laville, and the time I spent in Mme Duplouy's café are now but a confused memory, and when I try to concentrate and recall precise details of those hours, I become aware of a strange insurmountable weariness. What was hurt in me then is no longer, must have died. Some part of me cannot feel any more and will not feel — until the end.

I certainly regret my show of weakness in the presence of Dr. Laville. But I should be ashamed of feeling no real remorse, consider-ing the impression of us priests I must have given to that determined, resolute gentleman! Well, it's all over now. The strange mistrust I had of myself, of my own being, has flown, I believe for ever. That con-flict is done. I cannot understand it any more. I am reconciled to myself, to the poor, poor shell of me.

How easy it is to hate oneself! True grace is to forget. Yet if pride could die in us, the supreme grace would be to love oneself in all simplicity — as one would love any one of those who themselves have suffered and loved in Christ.

Letter from Monsieur Louis Dufréty to Monsieur le Curé de Torcy:
Lille, February 19—.

MONSIEUR LE CURÉ,

I am sending you at once the information you were so kind as to request. I am writing a really detailed account of what occurred for the Lille Youth Herald, *a very modest periodical of ours to which I contribute at odd times. But owing to my present state of health I have been unable as yet to complete the article. I shall take pleasure in sending you a copy as soon as it comes out.*

My friend's visit was a great satisfaction to me. Our affection for each other sprang from the best years of our youth, and was such that time does not efface. His first intention, I believe, was just to spend the evening here with me, chatting over old times. At about seven o'clock he was not feeling too well. I decided he had better stay the night. My home, simple though it is, seemed to attract him, and I had no difficulty in persuading him to stay. But at the same time I felt it would be tactful myself to put up with a friend, whose flat was on the same landing.

Towards four o'clock in the morning, being restless and unable to sleep, I went quietly to his room and discovered my poor friend lying unconscious on the floor.

We carried him to bed. And though we used all possible care, I fear this moving him was fatal. He vomited blood in great quantities. The lady who shares my life had made a thorough study of medicine, and was able to inform me regarding his condition and do all that was required. Her diagnosis was a very grave one. But the haemorrhage had subsided. While I was awaiting the doctor, our friend regained consciousness. Yet he did not speak. Great beads of perspiration were rolling over his brow and cheeks. His eyes, which I could scarcely see under his heavy half-closed lids, told of great anguish. I felt his pulse and it was rapidly growing weak. We sent a boy to go and fetch our parish priest. The dying man motioned to me to give him his rosary. I found it in one of his pockets; and from that moment he held it pressed to his breast. Then some strength returned to him, and in a voice one could hardly hear he asked me for absolution. His face became more at peace, he smiled even. Although I realized I had no right to accede over hastily to this request, it was quite impossible in the name of humanity and friendship, to refuse him. May I add that I was able to discharge this duty in a spirit which need leave you with no possible misgivings.

The priest was still on his way, and finally I was bound to voice my deep regret that such delay threatened to deprive my comrade of the final consolations of Our Church. He did not seem to hear me. But a few moments later he put his hand over mine, and his eyes entreated me to draw closer to him. He then uttered these words almost in my ear. And I am quite sure that I have recorded them accurately, for his voice, though halting, was strangely distinct.

"Does it matter? Grace is everywhere. . . ."

I think he died just then.

Review Questions

1. As a young man, what was the country priest's attidude toward youth?

2. What does he resolve to do about the future?

3. The country priest says he is now looking at death in what way?

4. What does he say would happen if pride were to die within us?

5. What were the last words of the country priest to his friend?

In-depth Questions

1. "For I only succeed in small things, and when I am tried by anxiety, I am bound to say it is the small joys that release me." As the country priest approaches death, he seems at peace with the fact that his impact on the world will be limited. He now wants to find his happiness in small things. What are the small things that bring you joy? Do you think these are God's gifts? Please explain.

2. ". . . for human agony is beyond all an act of love." Do you think this statement is true? Please explain.

3. "If I feel afraid I shall say: I am afraid, and not be ashamed of it." At the end of his life, it seems that the priest has nothing more to hide and nothing of which to be ashamed. Do you think it is hard for a high school student to come to a similar point? How can a relationship with God affect such an attitude?

4. Many people see parallels between *The Diary of a Country Priest* and Saint Thérèse of Lisieux's "Little Way" (pages 152–159). What parallels do you see? What do you think these parallels can tell us about following and imitating Jesus?

"The Old Sailor"

BRUCE MARSHALL

Introduction

Bruce Marshall was a prolific Scottish novelist who penned historical novels, wartime thrillers, and religious comedies. Born in 1899 near Edinburgh, he converted to Catholicism in 1917. He served with the Royal Irish Fusiliers in World War I, during which he lost a leg. After the war, he completed his education, becoming an accountant and incorporating that experience into a suspense novel, *The Bank Audit*. He moved to France, where he lived for most of his life, although he remained fiercely proud of his Scottish heritage.

His first great success came in 1931 with the publication of *Father Malachy's Miracle*. That book and many of his later Catholic novels — *The World, the Flesh, and Father Smith* (1945), *A Thread of Scarlet* (1959), *Father Hilary's Holiday* (1965), *Month of the Falling Leaves* (1963) — feature several religious themes: the tension between temptation and responsibility among the clergy and vowed religious; the power of grace to transform lives; and the intrinsic value of society's poor, forgotten, and scorned. *The World, the Flesh, and Father Smith*, from which "The Old Sailor" is taken, reflects many of these themes. Father Smith asserts that although the Church (at least in Scotland) is made up of the poor and derelict, it is stronger for this fact, because material poverty makes the Church spiritually rich. Marshall often criticized those in the clergy who were too intent on criticizing those who were alcoholics or sexually promiscuous. In his view, the rich and powerful might be guilty of the greater sin, at least to the extent that they teach the young that wealth and power are the ultimate good in life. After all, these quiet sins corrupt the innocent, and ultimately spread themselves throughout society. On the other hand, Marshall also has Father Smith observe that a man who visits the brothel is actually on a misguided search for God.

GREAT CATHOLIC LITERATURE
"The Old Sailor"

"Father, there's an old sailor dying at Mistress Flanigan's and the auld besom's sent a laddie for to tell ye to come at once."

With difficulty Father Smith repressed a snort of impatience. He was hungry and he was tired and he had been long enough a priest to bear a grudge against sinners for always choosing to die at awkward moments—in the middle of the night or when a poached egg had just been served. He remembered, however, the shock with which he had once heard Father Bonnyboat say on an Easter Sunday, "I'm sick to death of giving holy communion," and reminded himself that death was no less death to the sinner who was dying because others had died before him and that he was Christ's priest who had been marked and anointed and ordained to save human souls.

As he had no permanent church, Father Smith had to reserve the Blessed Sacrament in Montrose Street, where he had rented two rooms for a presbytery. Tearing out of his cassock, he hurried away down on his bicycle. The streets were still slippy and slimy from the rain and his back tyre skidded twice and once his front wheel got caught in the tram line. Even when she heard that someone was dying, his landlady wanted him to have his lunch first, saying that the roast beef would spoil if it were kept in the oven much longer, but the priest told her sharply that the fate of a human soul was much more important than any amount of roast beef, and rushed into the chapel, where with blundering fingers he plucked a Host out of the ciborium and hung it in a silver pyx round his neck and under

CIBORIUM AND PYX

A ciborium (suh-BORE-ee-uhm) looks similar to a chalice and is used to hold the Blessed Sacrament in a tabernacle. The Blessed Sacrament is reserved in the tabernacle so that people can come and pray before the Real Presence of Jesus and so that the sick can receive the Blessed Sacrament outside of Mass. When the Blessed Sacrament is brought to the sick, it is carried in a small, round metal container called a pyx (PICKS).

his coat. He also took the holy oils with him as well, to anoint the sailor's eyes, ears, nose, mouth, hands, and feet and cleanse him from his sins of sense.

Because it was raining again when he came out, he took the tram because there was a direct line to John Knox Street and he didn't want to run the risk of a fall when he was carrying the Blessed

Sacrament. The tram was empty because the Presbyterians and the Episcopalians had been out of church for a long time now and it was still a bit early for the brilliantined young men and their girls. The conductor took the priest's fare sullenly and then stood at the back whistling through his teeth and reading *Photo-Bits.* The tram zoomed and lurched away down the street with Father Smith making acts of adoration to the Blessed Sacrament opposite a stained-glass advertisement for Odol.

The priest knew that Mrs. Flanigan's lodging-house in Knox Street was not all that it should be, but he had no hesitations about taking the Blessed Sacrament there, because real sinners always knew how to respect our Lord and because our Lord Himself had been in even lower dives when He had lived on earth. Mrs. Flanigan was at the door to receive him, in a fine state of sweat and nerves and holding a monster lighted candle in her hand, because she knew that the priest would be carrying the Host.

"Praise be to Jasus, you've come, Father," she said. "It was only this morning that I found out that he was a Catholic and I sent for your riverence as soon as the doctor told me he was dying. Faith and he's lying cursing and swearing fit to burst himself, he is and all, but I've no doubt that yon'll be pleased enough to see you when you tell him who you are."

The priest nodded and followed Mrs. Flanigan along the passage smelling of brussels sprouts and linoleum. From an open door three pretty girls in dressing gowns poked tousled heads and two of them curtsied and crossed themselves because, although they were bad girls, they didn't hate God at all and knew that it was Jesus of Nazareth Who had walked on the Sea of Galilee Who was passing by. "Faith, ye trollops, and let the holy praist bay, will ye now," Mrs. Flanigan shouted at them as she pulled the door shut, because she wanted Father Smith to imagine that it was a hotel she ran.

In the bedroom where the sailor lay dying, Mrs. Flanigan had already placed a crucifix, two lighted candles, and a glass of water on the bed-table, because she always kept these things handy, since she didn't want to run any risks when the Lord called upon her to kick the bucket herself. The sailor himself was a very ill sailor and he lay on a high bed in a pair of widely striped pyjamas. Lying there with his eyes closed, his face looked not unlike the face of His Holiness Pope Pius X, but Father Smith suspected that the thoughts which went on behind it were slightly different. When he had laid the pyx and the chrism on the linen cloth, the priest motioned to Mrs. Flanigan to leave him alone with the dying man. When she had gone, he sat down beside the bed and took the old sailor's hand in his. The old sailor's hand was very hot and Father Smith felt very sorry for him being so ill and dying, but he knew that there was no time to be lost.

"My child, I've come to hear your confession," he said.

The old sailor opened a pair of very blue eyes. They appeared to take some time to interpret the priest's presence, but when they succeeded, they grew dark and angry.

"Leave me alone, won't you," the old sailor said, half-raising himself from his bed and falling back again.

Father Smith smiled wearily. Fifteen years ago when he had been a young priest carrying the Blessed Sacrament to deathbeds, protests like this had both shocked and frightened him, because it had been hard for a young priest of twenty-five with strong black hair to reconcile hoary sinners with God. But the strong black hair was peppered with grey now and he had knocked about with his Lord in all corners of the vineyard and had learned a thing or two about motives of pride and human respect.

"My son, you are dying and nobody is going to think you a fine fellow any longer for denying our Blessed Lord," he said. "The time for acquiring merit is short. I am God's priest and I am here to hear your confession."

As he had expected, his words had an almost immediate effect. The hostile glare vanished from the old sailor's eyes and he turned his head away from the priest and said:

"It's true, Father. I've been all sorts of a dirty swine, but it's too late now."

"It's never too late as long as you're alive," Father Smith said. "That's just where God's mercy comes in." But did it? Mightn't it have been a bit more merciful on God's part to have set a time limit on repentance, say forty-five? There would have been no inducement for sinners to keep putting things off to the last moment then and it would have been a lot easier for priests. Father Smith smiled briefly at his own impertinence and rather imagined that God was smiling too, and then he got back to the dreary business of getting a not very original sinner to acknowledge his sloth, his stupidity, and his cowardice.

It was obvious at once that the sailor had not been practising his religion for years, because he said right away that he didn't remember when he had last been to Mass or Holy Communion, although he had never gone to sleep without saying a Hail Mary, because out East a fellow never knew when he wouldn't wake up with his throat slit. Then he started off to tell the priest about all the women he had known in Buenos Aires and Hong Kong and said that he had liked the women in Hong Kong best, but Father Smith said that he thought they had better go through the Commandments from the beginning and see how many he had broken because after all it was a bigger mortal sin to have forgotten to love God all one's life than to have known tawdry Jezebels in foreign ports. The sailor said that that was quite easy and that there was no need to go through the Commandments at all, because he had broken the whole lot of them right down to coveting his neighbour's ass, and that Father Smith was quite wrong, as the women weren't tawdry at all, especially the ones in China, who had had gold on their fingernails and worn black satin slippers with high red heels, and that now that he came to think of it he wasn't sorry for having known all these women at all, since they had all been so beautiful and that he would like to know them again if he got the chance. Father Smith said that that was very wrong of the sailor and that our Lord and our Lady and Saint Joseph and the saints were very much more beautiful than any number of Chinese harlots with high heels: but the sailor said that he wasn't so sure, and that he still wasn't sorry for having known all these women, because their dresses had made such lovely sounds when they walked, and in South America it had been much the same thing and the governor general had seemed to think so too, because he had always been at old Señora Alvarez's every Saturday night. The priest said that was no way for a man to talk to God when he was dying and that the old sailor had better hurry up and be sorry for his sins if he didn't want to go to hell and lose Almighty God for ever and ever; but the old sailor said that while he was sorry for having missed the Sacraments so often and for not having loved God more, he wasn't sorry for having known all those women, because they had all been so beautiful and some of them very kind as well. In despair Father Smith asked the old sailor if he was sorry for not being sorry for having known all these women and the old sailor said that yes he was sorry for not being sorry and hoped that God would understand. Whereupon Father Smith said that he thought that perhaps God would understand, and he absolved the old sailor from his sins, pouring the merits of Christ's Passion over the old sailor's forgetfulness of God and those long-ago dresses that had made such lovely sounds.

It was easy enough to anoint the old sailor, because he lay quite still and seemed to like it when Father Smith took the holy oil of chrism and healed his limbs and his senses from walking away from and touching away from and hearing and seeing and smelling away from Jesus for so long; but it wasn't so easy for the old sailor to swallow the Blessed Sacrament, because his mouth was dry and parched and Father Smith had to help him by making him drink some water afterwards. Then the old sailor seemed to sink, into unconsciousness, although Father Smith knew that he was still alive because the stripes on his pyjamas kept going up and down. Kneeling beside the bed, the priest began to recite the prayers for the dying: "Go, Christian soul, from this world, in the Name of God the Father Almighty, Who created thee; in the Name of Jesus Christ, the Son of the Living God, Who suffered for thee; in the Name of the Holy Ghost, Who was breathed into thee; in the name of the glorious and holy virgin Mother of God Mary; in the name of blessed Joseph, the illustrious spouse of the same Virgin; in the name of angels and archangels; in the name of thrones and dominions; in the name of principalities and powers; in the name of virtues, cherubim and seraphim; in the name of patriarch and prophets; in the name of holy apostles and evangelists; in the name of holy martyrs and confessors; in the name of holy monks and hermits; in the name of holy virgins and of all God's saints."

Father Smith was still praying away when the door opened and Mrs. Flanigan and two of the girls entered and knelt with him round the bed, crossing themselves mightily. "Into Thy hands, O Lord, I commend my spirit," Father Smith began, but the stripes on the old sailor's pyjamas were going too quickly up and down for him to be able to answer, so Mrs. Flanigan and the two girls had to answer for him: "Lord Jesus, receive my soul."

Although the old sailor was too ill to be able to pray, Mrs. Flanigan said that she thought that it would be a good idea if he were to hold a crucifix in his hand, so that his eyes might get accustomed to the image of his Saviour before meeting Him face to face in the next world, and Father Smith said that he quite agreed. So they took the crucifix from the bed-table and pressed it into the old sailor's hands. At first he didn't seem to want to hold it, but at last he gripped it firmly and his eyes shone brightly and eagerly, and Father Smith told Mrs. Flanigan that he was sure that the old sailor was going to make a good death after all, and that he hoped that it would be a lesson to them all to forsake their sins, because Almighty God didn't always grant such wonderful last-minute graces.

The stripes on the old sailor's pyjamas began to go up and down more quickly and Father Smith shot out invocations at such a rate that Mrs. Flanigan and the two young ladies were unable to keep pace with him: "Saint Joseph, pray for me. Saint Joseph, with thy Blessed Virgin Spouse, open to me the breast of divine mercy. Jesus, Mary, Joseph, I give you my heart and my soul. Jesus, Mary, Joseph, be present with me in my last agony. Jesus, Mary, Joseph, let me sleep and rest in peace with you." Then the old sailor's pyjamas were very still, and his face seemed to shrink away and away as though it were trying to become a baby's face again. Father Smith prayed to the saints of God and to the angels of the Lord, that they might come and run thither and carry the old sailor's soul into the sight of the Most High, because he knew that the old sailor was dead.

Review Questions

1. What did Father Smith tell his landlady when she urged him to eat his lunch before going to the dying man?

2. Why did Father Smith not have any reservations about bringing the Blessed Sacrament into even the most sinful places?

3. When the old sailor grew angry at Father Smith's presence, what did Father Smith say to him?

4. After the old sailor refused to express sorrow for being with so many women, for what did he finally express sorrow?

5. What did the old sailor do when Mrs. Flanigan placed a crucifix in his hands?

In-depth Questions

1. The story says that Father Smith made "acts of adoration to the Blessed Sacrament" as he took the tram to Mrs. Flanigan's. Why do you think he was making such gestures on a public train?

2. When the old sailor realized that a priest was with him, he grew very angry. Why do you think people can be so resistant to committing their lives to the Lord?

3. Father Smith thought God should set an age limit on repentance. Do you agree? Why do you think it would be important to repent of one's sins prior to death?

4. It seems that the old sailor did indeed see the face of God as he died. What do you think this story says about God's mercy? Do you think this mercy can be abused? Please explain.

"The Beginnings of a Sin"

BERNARD MACLAVERTY

Introduction

Bernard MacLaverty was born in Belfast, Northern Ireland, in 1942. When he was twelve years old, his father died of lung cancer, leaving him brokenhearted. His father continues to haunt his dreams as an adult, and father-son relationships are central to much of his fiction. We see this in "The Beginnings of a Sin," where the boy's deceased father permeates the pages.

After graduating from Catholic high school, MacLaverty took work as a medical laboratory assistant. Around the same time, his interest in writing was sparked by his reading of *The Brothers Karamazov,* by Fyodor Dostoevsky. He became part of a circle of writers in Belfast in the mid-1960s, quickly becoming known for his insight into the social and political tensions that marked Northern Ireland at the time.

Northern Ireland's ethnic strife between the dominant Protestant majority and the oppressed Catholic minority was just beginning when he enrolled in Queen's University in 1970. "Troubles," as this strife has been called, erupted into a decades-long violent struggle marked by terrorist bombings, assassinations, and random killings. In order to raise his family of four children away from the violence, MacLaverty took a teaching position in Scotland, but he did not turn his back on Northern Ireland or the Troubles. In fact, the Troubles were the subject of his 1983 breakout novel, *Cal.* The book, which was later made into a critically acclaimed movie, is about a young member of the Irish Republican Army (one of the Northern Irish terrorist organizations) who falls in love with the widow of a man he has just killed. At one point in his career, MacLaverty's work was so closely identified with the Troubles that critics joked that he would not know what to write if peace ever came to Ireland. Such violence between groups with Christian names, Protestant and Catholic, can be a cause of strain on one's faith, and such a strain is found in the current story.

"The Beginnings of a Sin" was published in 1982, but it is set at an earlier time, when the Mass was in Latin. The story confronts the reader, as it confronts the boy in the story, with a painful reality: human imperfection. The Church is a unique institution; in the Nicene Creed, Catholics lift their voices in faith that God indeed works in the Church as the sacrament of salvation. Nonetheless, it is made up of humans, who are always imperfect. Coming face-to-face with the sinfulness of individual representatives of the Church is always painful, but it can contribute to a mature relationship with God and the Church, and to a deeper understanding of oneself.

GREAT CATHOLIC LITERATURE
"The Beginnings of a Sin"

I believe he's late again thought Colum. He took a clean white surplice from his bag and slipped it over his head, steadying his glasses as he did so. It was five to eight. He sat on the bench and changed his shoes for a black pair of gutties. Father Lynch said that all his altarboys must move as quietly as shadows. When he was late he was usually in his worst mood. Sometimes he did not turn up at all and Miss Grant, the housekeeper, would come over and announce from the back of the church that Father Lynch was ill and that there would be no Mass that day.

At two minutes to eight Colum heard his footstep at the vestry door. Father Lynch came in and nodded to the boy. Colum had never seen anyone with such a sleep-crumpled face in the mornings. It reminded him of a bloodhound, there was such a floppiness about his deeply wrinkled skin. His whole face sagged and sloped into lines of sadness. His black hair was parted low to the side and combed flat with Brylcreem. Colum thought his neat hair looked out of place on top of the disorder of his features.

"Is everything ready?" Father Lynch asked him.

"Yes, Father."

Colum watched him as he prepared to say Mass. He began by putting on the amice, like a handkerchief with strings, at the back of his neck. Next, a white alb like a shroud, reaching to the floor. The polished toecaps of his everyday shoes peeped out from underneath. He put the cincture about his waist and knotted it quickly. He kissed the embroidered cross on his emerald stole and hung it round his neck. Lastly he put on the chasuble, very carefully inserting his head through the neck-hole. Colum couldn't make up his mind whether he did not want to stain the vestments with hair-oil or wreck his hair. The chasuble was emerald green with yellow lines. Colum liked the feasts of the martyrs best, with their bright blood colour. Father Lynch turned to him.

"What are you staring at?"

"Nothing, Father."

"You look like a wee owl."

"Sorry."

"Let's get this show on the road," Father Lynch said, his face still like a sad bloodhound. "We're late already."

None of the other altar-boys liked Father Lynch. When they did something wrong, he never scolded them with words but instead would nip them on the upper arm. They said he was too quiet and you could never trust anybody like that. Colum found that he was not so quiet if you asked him questions. He seemed to like Colum better than the others, at least Colum thought so. One day he had asked him why a priest wore so much to say Mass and Father Lynch had spoken to him for about ten minutes, keeping him late for school.

"Normally when people wear beautiful things it is to make their personality stand out. With a priest it is the opposite. He wears so much to hide himself. And the higher up the Church you go, the more you have to wear. Think of the poor Pope with all that trumpery on him."

After Mass Father Lynch asked him how the ballot tickets were going.

"Great. I've sold—"

"Don't tell me. Keep it as a surprise."

In the darkness Colum stood at the door waiting. He had rolled up a white ballot ticket and was smoking it, watching his breath cloud the icy air. He pulled his socks up as high as he could to try and keep his legs warm. There was a funny smell from the house, like sour food. The woman came back out with her purse. She was still chewing something.

"What's it in aid of?"

"St. Kieran's Church Building Fund."

"How much are they?"

"Threepence each."

The woman hesitated, poking about in her purse with her index finger. He told her that the big prize was a Christmas hamper. There was a second prize of whiskey and sherry. She took four tickets, finishing his last book.

"Father Lynch'll not be wanting to win it outright, then."

He was writing her name on the stubs with his fountain pen.

"Pardon?"

"You're a neat wee writer," she said. He tore the tickets down the perforations and gave them to her. She handed him a shilling, which he dropped into his jacket pocket. It was swinging heavy with coins.

"There's the snow coming on now," said the woman, waiting to close the front door. He ran the whole way home holding on to the outside of his pocket. In the house he dried his hair and wiped the speckles of melted snow from his glasses. Two of his older brothers, Rory and Dermot, were sitting on the sofa doing homework balanced on their knees and when he told them it was snowing they ran out to see if he was lying.

He took down his tin and spilled it and the money from his pocket onto the table. He added it all together and counted the number of books of stubs. For each book sold the seller was allowed to keep sixpence for himself. Over the past weeks Colum had sold forty-two books around the doors. He took a pound note and a shilling and slipped them into his pocket. He had never had so much money in his life and there was still a full week to sell tickets before the ballot was drawn.

His mother stood at the range making soda farls on a griddle. When they were cooked they filled the house with their smell and made a dry scuffling noise as she handled them. He heard the front door close and Michael shout "Hello." At eighteen he was the eldest and the only wage earner in the house.

"Come on, Colum," said his mother. "Clear that table. The hungry working man is in."

After tea they always said the Family Rosary. Colum would half kneel, half crouch at the armchair with his face almost touching the seat. The cushion smelt of cloth and human. He tried to say the Rosary as best he could, thinking of the Sacred Mysteries, while his mouth said the words. He was disturbed one night to see Michael kneeling at the sofa saying the prayers with the Sunday paper between his elbows. Colum counted off the Hail Mary's, feeding his shiny lilac rosary beads between his finger and thumb. They were really more suitable for a woman but they had come all the way from Lourdes. Where the loop of the beads joined was a little silver heart with a bubble of Lourdes water in it — like the spirit level in his brother's tool kit.

When it came to his turn to give out the prayer Colum always waited until the response was finished — not like his brothers who charged on, overlapping the prayer and the response, slurring their words to get it finished as quickly as possible. They became annoyed with him and afterwards, in whispers, accused him of being "a creeping Jesus."

At the end of each Rosary their mother said a special prayer "for the Happy Repose of the Soul of Daddy." Although he had been dead two years, it still brought a lump to Colum's throat. It wouldn't have been so bad if she had said father or something but the word

Daddy made him want to cry. Sometimes he had to go on kneeling when the others had risen to their feet in case they should see his eyes.

It was Colum's turn to do the dishes. They had their turns written up on a piece of paper so that there would be no argument. He poured some hot water into the basin from the kettle on the range. It had gone slightly brown from heating. He didn't like the look of it as much as the cold water from the pump. In the white enamel bucket under the scullery bench it looked pure and cool and still. Where the enamel had chipped off, the bucket was blue-black. If you put your hand in the water the fingers seemed to go flat.

He dipped a cup into the basin, rinsed it out and set it on the table. Father Lynch had funny fingers. He had tiny tufts of black hair on the back of each of them. They made Colum feel strange as he poured water from a cruet onto them. The priest would join his trembling index fingers and thumbs and hold them over the glass bowl, then he would take the linen cloth ironed into its folds and wipe them dry. He would put it back in its creases and lay it on Colum's arm. He had some whispered prayers to say when he was doing that. Colum always wondered why Father Lynch was so nervous saying his morning Mass. He had served for others and they didn't tremble like that. Perhaps it was because he was holier than them, that they weren't as much in awe of the Blessed Sacrament as he was. What a frightening thing it must be, to hold Christ's actual flesh — to have the responsibility to change the bread and wine into the body and blood of Jesus.

He dried the dishes and set them in neat piles before putting them back on the shelf. Above the bench Michael had fixed a small mirror for shaving. Colum had to stand on tiptoe to see himself. He was the only one of the family who had to wear glasses. He took after his father. For a long time he had to wear National Health round ones with the springy legs that hooked behind his ears, but after months of pleading and crying his mother had given in and bought him a good pair with real frames.

He went to the back door and threw out a basinful of water with a slap onto the icy ground. It steamed in the light from the scullery window. It was a still night and he could hear the children's voices yelling from the next street.

The kitchen was warm when he came back in again. Radio Luxembourg was on the wireless. Colum took all his money in his pocket and put the stubs in a brown paper bag.

"I'm away, Mammy," he said,

She was having a cigarette, sitting with her feet up on a stool.

"Don't be late," was all she said.

He walked a lamppost, ran a lamppost through the town until he reached the hill which led to the Parochial House. It was a large building made of the same red brick as the church. He could see lights on in the house so he climbed the hill. It was still bitterly cold and he was aware of his jaw shivering. He kept both hands in his pockets, holding the brown bag in the crook of his arm. He knocked at the door of the house. It was the priest's housekeeper who opened it a fraction. When she saw Colum she opened it wide.

"Hello, Miss Grant. Is Father Lynch in?"

"He is busy, Colum. What was it you wanted?"

"Ballot tickets, Miss. And to give in money."

She looked over her shoulder down the hallway, then turned and put out her hand for the money.

"It's all loose, Miss," said Colum, digging into his pocket to let her hear it.

"Oh, you'd best come in then—for a moment."

Miss Grant brought him down the carpeted hallway to her quarters—she had a flat of her own at the back of the house. She closed the door and smiled a jumpy kind of smile—a smile that stopped in the middle. Colum emptied the bag of stubs on the table.

"There's forty-two books . . ." he said.

"Goodness, someone has been busy."

". . . and here is five pounds, five shillings." He set two pound notes and a ten shilling note on the table and handfulled the rest of the coins out of his pocket. They rang and clattered on the white-wood surface. She began to check it, scraping the coins towards her quickly and building them into piles.

"All present and correct," she said.

Colum looked at the sideboard. There was a bottle of orange juice and a big box of biscuits which he knew was for the ticket sellers. She saw him looking.

"All right, all right," she said.

She poured a glass of juice and allowed him to choose two biscuits. His fingers hovered over the selection.

"Oh come on, Colum, don't take all night."

He took a chocolate one and a wafer and sat down. He had never seen Miss Grant so snappy before. Usually she was easygoing. She was very fat, with a chest like stuffed pillows under her apron. He had heard the grown-ups in the town say that if anybody had earned heaven it was her. They spoke of her goodness and kindness. "There's one saint in that Parochial House," they would say. For a long time Colum thought they were talking about Father Lynch.

In the silence he heard his teeth crunching the biscuit. Miss Grant did not sit down but stood by the table waiting for him to finish. He swallowed and said,

"Could I have ten more books, please?"

"Yes, dear." She put her hands in her apron pocket and looked all around her, then left the room.

Colum had never been in this part of the house before. He had always gone into Father Lynch's room or waited in the hallway. Although it was a modern house, it was full of old things. A picture of the Assumption of Our Lady in a frame of gold leaves hung by the front door. The furniture in Father Lynch's room was black and heavy. The dining room chairs had twisted legs like barley sugar sticks. Everything had a rich feel to it, especially the thick patterned carpet. Miss Grant's quarters were not carpeted but had some rugs laid on the red tiled floor. It was the kind of floor they had at home, except that the corners of their tiles were chipped off and they had become uneven enough to trip people.

"Vera!" he heard a voice shout. It was Father Lynch.

Vera's voice answered from somewhere. Colum looked up and Father Lynch was standing in the doorway with his arm propped against the jamb.

"Hello, Father."

"Well, if it isn't the owl," said Father Lynch.

He wasn't dressed like a priest but was wearing an ordinary man's collarless shirt, open at the neck.

"What brings you up here, Colum?"

He moved from the door and reached out to put his hand on a chair back. Two strands of his oiled hair had come loose and fallen over his forehead. He sat down very slowly on the chair.

"Ballot tickets, Father. I've sold all you gave me."

Father Lynch gave a loud whoop and slapped the table loudly with the flat of his hand. His eyes looked very heavy and he was blinking a lot.

"That's the way to do it. Lord, how the money rolls in."

He was slurring his words as if he was saying the Rosary. Miss Grant came into the room holding a wad of white ballot tickets.

"Here you are now, Colum. You'd best be off."

Colum finished his juice and stood up.

"Is that the strongest you can find for the boy to drink, Vera?" He laughed loudly. Colum had never heard him laugh before. He slapped the table again.

"Father—if you'll excuse us, I'll just show Colum out now."

"No. No. He came to see me—didn't you?"

Colum nodded.

"He's the only one that would. Let him stay for a bit."

"His mother will worry about him."

"No she won't," said Colum.

"Of course she won't," said Father Lynch. He ignored Miss Grant. "How many books did you sell?"

"Forty-two, Father."

The priest raised his eyes to heaven and blew out his cheeks. Colum smelt a smell like altar wine.

"Holy Saint Christopher. Forty-two?"

"Yes."

Miss Grant moved behind Colum and began to guide him with pressure away from the table.

"That calls for a celebration." Father Lynch stood up unsteadily. "Forty-two!"

He reached out to give Colum a friendly cuff on the back of the head but he missed and instead his hand struck the side of the boy's face, scattering his glasses on the tiled floor.

"Aw Jesus," said the priest. "I'm sorry." Father Lynch hunkered down to pick them up but lurched forward onto his knees. One lens was starred with white and the arc of the frame was broken. He hoisted himself to his feet and held the glasses close to his sagging face, looking at them.

"Jesus, I'm so sorry," he said again. He bent down, looking for the missing piece of frame, and the weight of his head seemed to topple him. He cracked his skull with a sickening thump off the sharp edge of a radiator. One of his legs was still up in the air trying to right his balance. He put his hand to the top of his head and Colum saw that the hand was slippery with blood. Red blood was smeared from his Brylcreemed hair onto the radiator panel as the priest slid lower. His eyes were open but not seeing.

"Are you all right, Father?" Miss Grant's voice was shaking. She produced a white handkerchief from her apron pocket. The priest shouted, his voice suppressed and hissing and angry. He cursed his housekeeper and the polish on her floor. Then he raised his eyes to her without moving his head and said in an ordinary voice,

"What a mess for the boy."

Miss Grant took the glasses which he was still clutching and put them in Colum's hand. Father Lynch began to cry with his mouth half open. Miss Grant turned the boy away and pushed him towards the door. Both she and Colum had to step over the priest to get out. She led him by the elbow down the hallway.

"That's the boy. Here's your ballot tickets."

She opened the front door.

"Say a wee prayer for him, Colum. He's in bad need of it"

"All right, but—"

"I'd better go back to him now."

The door closed with a slam. Colum put his glasses on but could only see through his left eye. His knees were like water and his stomach was full of wind. He tried to get some of it up but he couldn't. He started to run. He ran all the way home. He sat panting on the cold doorstep and only went in when he got his breath back. His mother was alone.

"What happened to you? You're as white as a sheet," she said, looking up at him. She was knitting a grey sock on three needles shaped into a triangle. Colum produced his glasses from his pocket. Within the safety of the house he began to cry.

"I bust them."

"How, might I ask?" His mother's voice was angry.

"I was running and they just fell off. I slipped on the ice."

"Good God, Colum, do you know how much those things cost? You'll have to get a new pair for school. Where do you think the money is going to come from? Who do you think I am, Carnegie? Eh?"

Her knitting needles were flashing and clacking. Colum continued to cry, tears rather than noise.

"Sheer carelessness. I've a good mind to give you a thumping."

Colum, keeping out of range of her hand, sat at the table and put the glasses on. He could only half see. He put his hand in his pocket and took out his pound note.

"Here," he said, offering it to his mother. She took it and put it beneath the jug on the shelf.

"That'll not be enough," she said, then after a while, "Will you stop that sobbing? It's not the end of the world."

The next morning Colum was surprised to see Father Lynch in the vestry before him. He was robed and reading his breviary, pacing the strip of carpet in the centre of the room. They said nothing to each other.

At the Consecration Colum looked up and saw the black congealed wound on the thinning crown of Father Lynch's head, as he lifted the tail of the chasuble. He saw him elevate the white disc or the host and heard him mutter the words,

"Hoc est enim corpus meum."

Colum jangled the cluster of bells with angry twists of his wrist. A moment later when the priest raised the chalice full of wine he rang the bell again, louder if possible.

In the vestry afterwards he changed as quickly as he could and was about to dash out when Father Lynch called him. He had taken off his chasuble and was folding it away.

"Colum."

"What?"

"Sit down a moment."

He removed the cincture and put it like a coiled snake in the drawer. The boy remained standing. The priest sat down in his alb and beckoned him over.

"I'm sorry about your glasses."

Colum stayed at the door and Father Lynch went over to him, Colum thought his face no longer sad, simply ugly.

"Your lace is loosed." He was about to genuflect to tie it for him but Colum crouched and tied it himself. Their heads almost collided.

"It's hard for me to explain," said Father Lynch, "but . . . to a boy of your age sin is a very simple thing. It's not."

Colum smelt the priest's breath sour and sick.

"Yes, Father."

"That's because you have never committed a sin. You don't know about it."

He removed his alb and hung it in the wardrobe.

"Trying to find the beginnings of a sin is like . . ." He looked at the boy's face and stopped. "Sin is a deliberate turning away from God. That is an extremely difficult thing to do. To close Him out from your love . . ."

"I'll be late for school, Father."

"I suppose you need new glasses?"

"Yes."

Father Lynch put his hand in his pocket and gave him some folded pound notes.

"Did you mention it to your mother?"

"What?"

"How they were broken?"

"No."

"Are you sure? To anyone?"

Colum nodded that he hadn't. He was turning to get out the door. The priest raised his voice, trying to keep him there.

"I knew your father well, Colum," he shouted. "You remind me of him a lot."

The altar-boy ran, slamming the door after him. He heard an empty wooden coat-hanger rattle on the hardboard panel of the door and it rattled in his mind until he reached the bottom of the hill. There he stopped running. He unfolded the wad of pound notes still in his hand and counted one — two — three — four of them with growing disbelief.

Review Questions

1. What was Colum selling, and for what purpose?

2. What did Colum's mother say at the end of the Rosary that some-times made him cry?

3. Why did Colum go the Parochial House on the night his glasses were broken?

4. How were Colum's glasses broken?

5. How did he tell his mother that his glasses had been broken?

In-depth Questions

1. When talking about all of the garments that a priest wears when he celebrates the Eucharist, Father Lynch says, "Normally when people wear beautiful things it is to make their personality stand out. With a priest it is the opposite. He wears so much to hide himself." What makes this section of the story so significant? (To learn more, research the Catholic teaching called *ex opera operato*.)

2. When Colum returned to his house, he put his glasses on and "he could only half see." Do you think that this was meant as a symbol of Colum's faith? Did Colum lose some of his faith when his glasses were broken? Explain your answer.

3. Father Lynch said: "Sin is a deliberate turning away from God. That is an extremely difficult thing to do." Do you think this shows a confidence in God's mercy or an abuse of God's mercy? Please explain your answer.

4. The last line of the story, "with growing disbelief," seems to indicate that Colum became disillusioned by this experience and began to lose his faith. How do you think you would respond if you saw the sinful side of someone you admired?

PART THREE
GREAT CATHOLIC
SPIRITUAL WRITINGS

OUR LADY GUADALUPE

ST. ANTHONY OF THE DESERT

SAINT THÉRÈSE OF LISIEUX

GREAT CATHOLIC SPIRITUAL WRITINGS: READING 1

Selections from *The Sayings of the Desert Fathers*

THE DESERT FATHERS AND MOTHERS

Introduction

Being a Christian was quite dangerous in the first few centuries after Christ had risen from the dead. It could mean the loss of one's family, social rejection, and, during the Roman Empire's periodic persecutions, possibly even death. All of that changed when the emperor Constantine legalized Christianity in AD 313. Within a few decades, Christianity was not only tolerated by the Roman Empire, but had become its most favored religion. It became socially acceptable, and even advantageous, to be a Christian. These and other factors led large numbers of people into the Church.

However, not everyone thought this was a good thing. Some thought Christians were better off when they had to risk death and make sacrifices in order to practice the faith. In fact, some Christians regretted that they no longer had the opportunity to die for their faith.

Thousands of these men and women sought to "die" in another way: by fleeing civilization to live alone in the desert. There, they hoped to grow closer to God through prayer, study, simple work, and asceticism.

ASCETICISM
Asceticism is self-denial for the sake of spiritual growth.

By denying themselves such basic comforts as food, water, sleep, and human contact, they hoped to overcome all worldly and demonic temptations so they could concentrate completely on God. Some of their ascetic practices seem extreme by modern standards, but the people of the time considered these solitary monks of the desert to be examples of holiness, and often sought their advice.

The thousands of holy men and women who fled to the desert during the fourth century followed the example of John the Baptist and other biblical figures who encountered God in the wilderness. But Jewish and Christian faith also emphasize the importance of seeking holiness through community and relationships with others. Over time, the men and women of the desert began to form communities so that they could support one another in the quest for holiness; these were the first Christian monasteries.

Within a few centuries, life in communal monasteries largely replaced the solitary lifestyle of the desert hermit. But the wisdom of the desert fathers and mothers was preserved in stories and sayings that were passed along orally. Sometime in the sixth century, an unknown editor collected many of those stories and sayings in the *Apophthegmata Patrum*, or *The Sayings of the Desert Fathers*.

Besides providing the foundation for Christian monasticism, the desert fathers and mothers greatly influenced the development of Christian spirituality; their wisdom has inspired countless saints over the centuries. The seeds they sowed through their prayer and sacrifice have borne great fruit in the Church; in that sense, they fulfilled Isaiah's prophecy that the desert "shall blossom abundantly" (35:2).

GREAT CATHOLIC SPIRITUAL WRITINGS
From *The Sayings of the Desert Fathers*

ANTHONY THE GREAT

On How to Be Saved

The brethren came to the Abba Anthony and said to him, "Speak a word; how are we to be saved?" The old man said to them, "You have heard the Scriptures. That should teach you how." But they said, "We want to hear from you too, Father." Then the old man said to them, "The Gospel says, 'if anyone strikes you on one cheek, turn to him the other also.'" (Matt. 5.39) They said, "We cannot do that." The old man said, "If you cannot offer the other cheek, at least allow one cheek to be struck." "We cannot do that either," they said. So he said, "If you are not able to do that, do not return evil for evil," and they said, "We cannot do that either." Then the old man said to his disciple, "Prepare a little brew of corn for these invalids. If you cannot do this, or that, what can I do for you? What you need is prayers."

On Renouncing the World

A brother renounced the world and gave his goods to the poor, but he kept back a little for his personal expenses. He went to see Abba Anthony. When he told him this, the old man said to him, "If you want to be a monk, go into the village, buy some meat, cover your naked body with it and come here like that." The brother did so, and the dogs and birds tore at his flesh. When he came back the old man asked him whether he had followed his advice. He showed him his wounded body, and Saint Anthony said, "Those who renounce the world but want to keep something for themselves are torn in this way by the demons who make war on them."

On the Weakness of Today's People
He also said, "God does not allow the same warfare and temptations to this generation as he did formerly, for men are weaker now and cannot bear so much."

On Attacks on Rational People
Abbot Anthony said, "A time is coming when men will go mad, and when they see someone who is not mad, they will attack him saying, 'You are mad, you are not like us.'"

On Helping Those Who Are Down
A brother in a monastery was falsely accused of fornication and he arose and went to Abba Anthony. The brethren also came from the monastery to correct him and bring him back. They set about proving that he had done this thing, but he defended himself and denied that he had done anything of the kind. Now Abba Paphnutius, who is called Cephalos, happened to be there, and he told them this parable: "I have seen a man on the bank of the river buried up to his knees in mud and some men came to give him a hand to help him out, but they pushed him further in up to his neck." Then Abba Anthony said this about Abba Paphnutius: "Here is a real man, who can care for souls and save them." All those present were pierced to the heart by the words of the old man and they asked forgiveness of the brother. So, admonished by the Fathers, they took the brother back to the monastery.

On Loving God
Abba Anthony said, "I no longer fear God, but I love Him. For love casts out fear." (John IV, 18).

On Fearing God
He also said, "Always have the fear of God before your eyes. Remember him who gives death and life. Hate the world and all that is in it. Hate all peace that comes from the flesh. Renounce this life, so that you may be alive to God. Remember what you have promised God, for it will be required of you on the day of judgement. Suffer hunger, thirst, nakedness, be watchful and sorrowful; weep, and groan in your heart; test yourselves, to see if you are worthy of God; despise the flesh, so that you may preserve your souls."

On Being Watchful of One's Actions

Abba David said, "Abba Arsenius told us the following, as though it referred to someone else, but in fact it referred to himself. An old man was sitting in his cell and a voice came to him which said, 'Come, and I will show you the works of men.' He got up and followed. The voice led him to a certain place and showed him an Ethiopian cutting wood and making a great pile. He struggled to carry it but in vain. But instead of taking some off, he cut more wood which he added to the pile. He did this for a long time. Going on a little further, the old man was shown a man standing on the shore of a lake drawing up water and pouring it into a broken receptacle, so that the water ran back into the lake. Then the voice said to the old man, 'Come, and I will show you something else.' He saw a temple and two men on horseback, opposite one another, carrying a piece of wood crosswise. They wanted to go in through the door but could not because they held their piece of wood crosswise. Neither of them would draw back before the other, so as to carry the wood straight; so they remained outside the door. The voice said to the old man, 'These men carry the yoke of righteousness with pride, and do not humble themselves so as to correct themselves and walk in the humble way of Christ. So they remain outside the Kingdom of God. The man cutting the wood is he who lives in many sins and instead of repenting he adds more faults to his sins. He who draws the water is he who does good deeds, but mixing bad ones with them, he and, as far as I could, I have never let anyone go to sleep with a grievance against me.'"

ABBA AGATHON

On Rejecting Heresy

It was said concerning Abba Agathon that some monks came to find him having heard tell of his great discernment. Wanting to see if he would lose his temper they said to him, "Aren't you that Agathon who is said to be a fornicator and a proud man." "Yes, it is very true," he answered. They resumed, "Aren't you that Agathon who is always talking nonsense." "I am." Again they said, "Aren't you Agathon the heretic?" But at that he replied "I am not a heretic." So

HERETIC

A heretic is a baptized person who rejects a formally defined doctrine of the Catholic Church.

they asked him, "Tell us why you accepted everything we cast at you, but repudiated this last insult." He replied "The first accusations I take to myself, for that is good for my soul. But heresy is separation from God. Now I have no wish to be separated from God." At this saying they were astonished at his discernment and returned, edified.

On Caring Only About What God Thinks
It was said of Abba Agathon that he spent a long time building a cell with his disciples. At last when it was finished, they came to live there. Seeing something during the first week which seemed to him harmful, he said to his disciples, "Get up, let us leave this place." But they were dismayed and replied, "If you had already decided to move, why have we taken so much trouble building the cell? People will be scandalized at us, and will say, 'Look at them, moving again, what unstable people!'" He saw they were held back by timidity and so he said to them, "If some are scandalized, others, on the contrary, will be much edified and will say, 'How blessed are they who go away for God's sake, having no other care.' However, let him who wants to come, come; as for me, I am going." Then they prostrated themselves to the ground and besought him to allow them to go with him.

On Bearing Good Fruit
Someone asked Abba Agathon, "Which is better, bodily asceticism or interior vigilance?" The old man replied, "Man is like a tree, bodily asceticism is the foliage, interior vigilance the fruit. According to that which is written, 'Every tree that bringeth not forth good fruit shall be cut down and cast into the fire.' (Matt. 3, 10) It is clear that all our care should be directed towards the fruit, that is to say, guard of the spirit; but it needs the protection and the embellishment of the foliage, which is bodily asceticism."

On the Greatness of Prayer
The brethren also asked him "Amongst all good works, which is the virtue which requires the greatest effort?" He answered, "Forgive me, but I think there is no labour greater than that of prayer to God. For every time a man wants to pray, his enemies, the demons, want to prevent him, for they know that it is only by turning him from prayer that they can hinder his journey. Whatever good work a man undertakes, if he perseveres in it, he will attain rest. But prayer is warfare to the last breath."

On Perfect Charity
Abba Agathon said, "If I could meet a leper, give him my body and take his, I should be very happy." That indeed is perfect charity.

On Seeking God through Trials

Amma Syncletica said, "In the beginning there are a great many battles and a good deal of suffering for those who are advancing towards God and afterwards, ineffable joy. It is like those who wish to light a fire; at first they are choked by the smoke and cry, and by this means obtain what they seek (as it is said: 'Our God is a consuming fire' [Heb. 12.24]): so we also must kindle the divine fire in ourselves through tears and hard work."

On Swerving from Salvation

She also said, "My children, we all want to be saved, but because of our habit of negligence, we swerve away from salvation."

Review Questions

1. What does Abba Anthony say one must do to be saved?

2. Why did Abba Anthony instruct a brother to cover his naked body with raw meat?

3. Why was Abba Agathon able to bear any insult except being called a heretic?

4. What virtue does Abba Agathon say requires the greatest effort?

In-depth Questions

1. Abba Anthony says the people are weaker now than they used to be. Do you think that is true for your generation? Is your generation weaker, or are today's temptations stronger? Please explain.

2. Abba Anthony speaks of both loving God and fearing God. How would you describe the fear of God to someone else?

3. Abba Agathon describes his desire to please God rather than please other people. Do you think this is a difficult principle to live out? Please explain.

4. Amma Syncletica describes the difficulties that lie ahead of a person as they begin their relationship with God. Why do you think such beginnings are so difficult?

5. Read the selections from Thomas Merton on pages 58–61 and 190–196. Are you able to identify the thoughts of the desert fathers and mothers in his writings?

Selections from *The Life of Brother Juniper*

THE UNKNOWN AUTHOR OF *THE LIFE OF BROTHER JUNIPER*

Introduction

If you know something about Saint Francis of Assisi, you have a good head start on getting to know Brother Juniper. Francis was the son of a rich merchant, and he gave up everything he had—even the clothes on his back—so that he would be more free to serve God. At first the townspeople of Assisi ridiculed him, but his joy and radical commitment to the Gospel soon attracted other young men; Brother Juniper was among these early followers.

"The Life of Brother Juniper" is from a larger collection of stories about Francis and his companions, *The Little Flowers of Saint Francis*. No one knows who wrote that book, but the first version was probably written sometime in the last half of the thirteenth century. The author probably relied on popular stories that had been passed along by word of mouth.

Besides being one of Francis's first companions, Juniper was apparently one of the most foolish. That was not necessarily a bad thing—such holy foolishness was considered a virtue by Francis and his followers. They called themselves "fools for Christ" because the world considered them foolish for following the Gospel so zealously. Humility, selflessness, detachment from material goods, joy in the face of adversity, and radical love of others—especially the poor and the sinner—were marks of this holy foolishness. Even the Pope tried to persuade Francis that his order's commitment to poverty was too harsh! But Brother Juniper's foolishness was excessive even by Franciscan standards, making him a model by which other Franciscans measured their spiritual growth.

"The Life of Brother Juniper" is not a biography, which is to say that recording the historical facts and circumstances of Juniper's life is not its main purpose. Rather, it is a hagiography: a form of literature that tells the story of a saint's life in order to show what it means for a Christian to be holy. Hagiographies are written to provide an inspiring example for others to imitate. "The Life of Brother Juniper" is about a historical person. But as a hagiography, we can assume that certain elements of his history have been exaggerated or embellished in order to provide a lesson about what it means to be a "fool for Christ."

Although "The Life of Brother Juniper" aims to teach its readers something about holiness, do not be surprised if you find yourself smiling as you read it. "The Life of Brother Juniper" seems bent on making us laugh, as if to say that a generous sense of humor, tempered by a good dose of humility, will take us a long way toward Juniper's ideal of joyful holiness and a delightful relationship with Jesus.

GREAT CATHOLIC SPIRITUAL WRITINGS
"The Life of Brother Juniper"

HOW BROTHER JUNIPER CUT OFF THE FOOT OF A PIG, TO GIVE TO ONE WHO WAS SICK.

ONE of the most chosen disciples and first companions of Saint Francis was a certain Brother Juniper, a man of profound humility, of great fervour and charity, with regard to whom Saint Francis said once, speaking with some of his saintly companions: "He would be a good Friar Minor who had conquered the world and himself like Brother Juniper."

FRIAR MINOR
From the same root word as "fraternal," friar means "brother." To be a friar minor is to be a "little brother."

It came to pass once, at St. Mary of the Angels, that, inflamed with the love of God, he went to visit a sick Brother, and with great compassion asked him: "Can I do you any service?" The patient replied: "It would be a great comfort to me if you could get me a pig's foot to eat." Immediately Brother Juniper said: "Leave it to me, you shall have it at once." Away he goes and snatches a knife from the kitchen, and runs in fervour of spirit to the wood, where a number of pigs were feeding, and having thrown himself upon one of them, cuts off its foot and flees, leaving the pig thus mutilated. He returns and washes and dresses and cooks the foot, and with much diligence having well prepared it, he bears it with great charity to the invalid; who ate it with avidity, to the great consolation and joy of Brother Juniper, whilst he in high spirits, to amuse the sick man, recounted his assault on the pig.

In the meantime, the keeper of the pigs, who had seen him cutting off the foot, went and told the whole affair in detail with great indignation to his master, who when he had heard it, came to the house of the Brothers, calling them hypocrites, thieves, liars, rascals, and good-for-nothings, and saying: "Why did you cut off my pig's foot?" At the great disturbance at which he made, Saint Francis came out with all the Brothers, and humbly excusing himself and them, as ignorant of what had happened, tried to pacify him by promising to compensate him to the last farthing. But for all this the man was not pacified, but went away in a rage, still uttering menaces and threats, and repeating over and over, how maliciously they had cut off the foot of his pig. And listening to neither excuse nor promise, he departed as angry as he came, leaving all the Brothers stupified and amazed.

But, Saint Francis, full of prudence, thought it over and said in his heart: "Can Brother Juniper have done this through indiscreet zeal?" And he had Brother Juniper called to him secretly, and asked him saying: "Did you cut off the foot of a pig in the wood?" And Brother Juniper, not as one who had committed a fault, but rather as one who had performed a great act of charity, answered him joyously: "It is true sweet Father mine, that I cut off the foot of a pig, and for the reason, be pleased to listen, my Father, feelingly. I went out of charity to visit the sick Brother;" and then he told him in detail all he had done, and added: "I tell thee, thus that considering the consolation it brought our sick Brother, and the pleasure he took in it, if I had cut off the feet of a hundred pigs, as I did of that one, I am sure it would have been pleasing to God." To which St. Francis, in just anger and very great displeasure replied: "O Brother Juniper, why hast thou caused such a great scandal? Not without reason does this man complain and rail so greatly against us: and perhaps at this moment he is in the town, spreading an accusation against us of such ill-doing and with very great cause. Wherefore I command thee by holy obedience to run after him and overtake him, and throw thyself at his feet and tell him thy fault, promising to make such satisfaction to him, as that he shall have nothing to complain of against us, for certainly this has been too great an excess."

Brother Juniper was astonished at these words; and full of wonder that anyone should be angered by such an act of charity, because it seemed to him that temporal goods were nothing at all, except in as far as they were charitably shared with one's neighbour, he answered: "Doubt not, my Father, that I will soon compensate the man, and make him content. And why should I be troubled, seeing that this pig, whose foot I cut off, belonged more to God than it did to him, and that I did it for so great a charity?" And with this, he ran off and overtook the man, who had by no means recovered his equanimity, but was still angry beyond measure; and he narrated to him how and why he cut off the foot of the pig; and this with as much fervour and exultation and joy as if he had done him a great service, for which he ought to be greatly rewarded.

The man, full of anger and beside himself with fury, gave Brother Juniper many bad names, calling him a fool and a madman, a robber and the worst of brigands. But Brother Juniper cared nothing for these insulting words, and marveled within himself, for he rejoiced in being abused; and thought he could have well understood the man, because there seemed to him room rather for praise than for blame. So he told the story over again, and throwing himself on the man's neck, kissed and embraced him, and told him how he had done it solely out of charity, inviting and pressing him to do the same with the rest of the pig; and with so much affection, simplicity, and humility that the man came back to himself, and not without many tears fell on his knees; and acknowledged his own fault in speaking and acting so violently against the Brothers, and goes and catches the pig and kills it, and having cut it up and cooked it he bears it with much devotion and with many tears to St. Mary of the Angels, and gives it to the holy Brothers to eat in compensation for the abuse he had given them.

Then St. Francis, considering the simplicity and patience under adversity of the said holy Brother Juniper, said to his companions and the others who were present: "Would to God, my Brothers, that I had a whole forest of such Junipers!"

An instance of the great power which Brother Juniper had the demons.

INASMUCH as the demons could not endure the purity of Brother Juniper's innocence and the depth of his humility, the following instance took place, by which this was most clearly shown. A certain person who was possessed, suddenly threw himself out of the way he was going, and contrary to all his usual customs, fled hither and thither by devious paths for about seven miles. And when his relatives, who pursued him, with great grief, had overtaken and interrogated him, asking why he had fled with such precipitancy he replied: "The reason is this; because that idiot Juniper was passing along the way, and I cannot endure his presence or his aspect, therefore I fled into the woods." And they certified themselves of the truth that it was even so; that Brother Juniper had passed by at the same hour, as the demon had said. Wherefore St. Francis, when they brought him the possessed that he might heal them, if the evil spirit did not immediately depart at his command, used to say: "If thou depart not forthwith from this creature of God, I will fetch hither against thee Brother Juniper;" and immediately the demons, fearing the presence of Brother Juniper and unable to sustain the virtue of St. Francis, departed from them.

How Brother Juniper gave to the poor, for the love of God, all that he had in his power to give.

Such pity and compassion had Brother Juniper for the poor, that whenever he saw anyone naked, or badly clothed, he immediately took off his tunic and the hood from his head, and gave it to them: wherefore the Guardian forbade him under obedience to give away the whole of his tunic, or any part of his habit, to anyone. It came to pass that a few days after he met a poor man half-naked, who prayed

Guardian

The Guardian was the superior of the friars. Each brother was required to do as the Guardian asked, as an expression of holy obedience.

Brother Juniper for an alms, for the love of God, to whom the Brother with much compunction replied: "I have nothing could give thee, except my tunic; and I am bound under obedience by my Superior not to give that to anyone, or even a part of my habit; but if you pull it off my back, I shall not resist you."

He spoke not to the deaf; and forthwith the beggar pulled his tunic over his head, and went his way, leaving Brother Juniper naked. And when he returned home, they asked him where his tunic was; to which he replied: "A good man pulled it off my back, and went away with it." And this virtue of compassion still growing in him, he was no longer content with giving away his tunic, but gave also the mantles of the others, and the books and ornaments of the church, and all he could lay his hands on, to the poor. And for this reason the Brothers left nothing open or lying about, because Brother Juniper gave everything away for the love of God, and to His praise.

HOW BROTHER JUNIPER ONCE COOKED A FORTNIGHT'S DINNER FOR THE BROTHERS.

As Brother Juniper was once staying in a very small house belonging to the Friars, it happened that for some reason all the Brothers were obliged to go out, and only Brother Juniper remained in the house. Therefore the Guardian said: "Brother Juniper, all of us are going out, so see that, when we come home, you have cooked some small refreshment for the Brothers on their return." And Brother Juniper replied very willingly: "Leave it all to me." When all the others were gone, said Brother Juniper to himself: "What useless care and solicitude is this, that one Brother should be lost in the kitchen, and kept away from prayer? For a certainty, I am appointed to cook for this once; I will do so much at a time, that all the Brothers, and more, if more there were, shall have enough for a whole fortnight." So, full of

FORTNIGHT

A fortnight is a two-week period of time.

business, he went off to the farm and brought several large earthenware pots for cooking, and procured fresh and dried meat, fowls, eggs and herbs, also firewood in plenty, and lighting his fire, put all on to boil—fowls in their feathers, and eggs in their shells, and all the other things in the same fashion.

When the Brothers returned home, one of them, who was well aware of Brother Juniper's simplicity, went straight to the kitchen, and there found many and huge pots on raging fire; and sat himself down, looking on with astonishment, and saying nothing but watching with what solicitude Brother Juniper attended to his cooking. Because the fire was very fierce, and that he could not well get near his pots to skim them, he took a plank, and tied it tightly in front of him with cords to his body, and thus jumping from one pot to another, made a delightful spectacle. After watching him for some time, to his great amusement, the other Brother went out of the kitchen, found the rest, and said to them: "I assure you that Brother Juniper is cooking for a wedding." The Brothers took his words for a joke; but Brother Juniper presently lifted his pots from the fire, and rang the bell for the repast. And as they went in to dinner, he entered the refectory, with all his dishes, his face crimsoned with fatigue and the heat of the fire; and said to them all: "Eat well, and then let us all go to prayer, and none think of cooking any more for awhile, for I have cooked dinner enough to-day to last a fortnight." And he placed his stew, of which there was not a pig in all the Roman province famished enough to have eaten, on the table before the Brothers. But Brother Juniper praised up his cooking, to give them an appetite; and seeing that the Brothers ate nothing, he said: "Now such fowls as these are comforting food for the brain, and such a stew as this will strengthen our bodies, it is so good." And the Brothers remained lost in devout astonishment at Brother Juniper's piety and simplicity.

But the Guardian, annoyed at such stupidity, and so much waste of good food, reproved him with great severity. Then Brother Juniper, all at once threw himself on the ground on his knees before the Guardian, and acknowledged his fault against him and against all the Brothers, saying: "I am the worst of men, such a one commits such a crime, and has his eyes put out for it; but I deserve much more; another is hanged for his faults, but I am more deserving of it for my evil deeds, who am always wasting the good things of God and of the Order." And thus sorrowfully he went away, and would not appear before any of the Brothers all that day. But when he was gone, the Guardian said: "Well-beloved Brothers, I would that every day this Brother of ours spoilt as many good things as to-day if we had them, solely for our own edification; for out of his great simplicity and charity he has done it all."

HOW BROTHER JUNIPER DETACHED SOME BELLS FROM THE ALTAR, AND GAVE THEM AWAY FOR THE LOVE OF GOD.

BROTHER JUNIPER was one day at Assisi, deeply meditating before the altar of the convent; and it was near the time of the Nativity of our Lord. Now this altar was very richly decked and adorned; and the sacristan begged him to remain and watch by it, whilst he went away to get something to eat. And as he continued in devout meditation a poor woman came, and begged an alms for the love of God. Then said Brother Juniper: "Wait a little, and I will see whether I can get thee something from the ornaments of the altar." And there was on this altar a fringe of gold, richly worked, and with little silver bells of great value. And Brother Juniper said: "These bells are a superfluity;" and he took a knife, and cut off the whole of them, and gave them to the poor woman, out of compassion.

The sacristan had not eaten three or four mouthfuls before he began to bethink himself of Brother Juniper's ways, and to misdoubt greatly what might become of the ornaments of the altar, which he had left in his charge; he feared lest he should do some mischief out of the excess of his charity. And all in haste and in great suspicion, he rose from the table, and went back to the church, and looked to see if the ornaments of his altar were safe, and none missing; and there he saw the fringe cut up, and all the bells gone, at which he was greatly angered and scandalized. But Brother Juniper, seeing his perturbation said: "Do not put yourself out about these bells, for I have given them to a poor woman, who was in the greatest need of them; and here they were of no use whatever, but a piece of vain and worldly pomp." Hearing this, the sacristan, in much distress immediately ran through the church, and all over the city, seeking everywhere if perchance he might find them again: but he neither found them, nor any person who had seen anything of them. Wherefore, returning to the convent in a rage, he took up the fringe and carried it to the General who was then at Assisi, and said: "Father General, I crave justice against Brother Juniper, who has spoilt my fringe, the best there was in the sacristy; now see how he has cut it to pieces, and torn off all the silver bells, and says that he has given them away to a poor woman." The General answered: "Brother Juniper has not done this, but your own stupidity; for you ought to know, at this time of day, his way of going on; and I tell you that I marvel he has not given away the whole thing, but all the same, I will correct him severely for this affair." And calling all the Brothers together in Chapter, he summoned Brother Juniper, and in the presence of all the community, rebuked him severely on account of the said silver bells; and so wrath was he, that he raised his voice until he became quite hoarse.

Chapter

In religious communities such as the Franciscans, the Chapter is the gathering of the entire community that addresses important issues.

Brother Juniper cared little or almost nothing for his words, because he delighted in reproaches and in being well abused; but he began to think of a remedy for the hoarseness of the Father General; and having received his reproof, he went off to the city, and ordered a porridge to be made of flour and butter. And when a good part of the night was past, he returned, lighted a candle, and went with his porridge to the cell of the General, and knocked. The General opened the door, and seeing him there, with the lighted candle and the porridge in his hand, asked softly; "What is this?" Brother Juniper replied: "My Father, when you reproved me today for my faults, I noticed that your voice became hoarse—I think that it must have been through excess of fatigue; and therefore I considered how to find a remedy, and had this porridge made for you; therefore I pray you eat it, for I assure you it will soften your chest and your throat." The General answered him: "What an hour is this to come and disturb people!" And Brother Juniper said: "See, it is made on purpose for you; I pray you eat it without more ado, for it will do you a great deal of good." But the General, angry at the lateness of the hour and his importunity, commanded him to be off, saying that at such an hour he had no desire to eat, and calling him names, as a rascal and a good-for-nothing. Brother Juniper therefore, seeing that neither prayers, nor coaxing, would move him, said: "My Father, since you will not eat, and this porridge was made on purpose for you, do this much for me: hold the candle and I will eat it." Then the General, being a pious and devout man, and perceiving the simplicity and piety of Brother Juniper, and that all this was done by him out of pure devotion, said to him: "Well, see now, since thou wilt have it so, thou and I will eat it together." And together they ate the porridge with a fervent charity each for the other; and much more were they refreshed by each other's devotion, than they were by the bodily nourishment.

Review Questions

1. Why was Brother Juniper astonished that Saint Francis chastised him so severely when he cut the foot off of the pig?

2. How did Saint Francis threaten evil spirits if they did not leave a person at his command?

3. Brother Juniper was bound by obedience never to give away his tunic. How then did the half-naked beggar acquire it?

4. Why did Brother Juniper think it would be a good idea to cook two-weeks' worth of food at once?

5. What did Brother Juniper think about while the Father General rebuked him for giving away the bells and the fringe from the altar?

In-depth Questions

1. In these stories, there seems to be a pattern. Brother Juniper would make a foolish mistake with the purest of motives. People at first were angered by his mistake, but they later experienced a loving admiration for Brother Juniper. Please explain why you think this was a pattern.

2. Brother Juniper showed no attachment to material things. He would give away his own possessions and the possessions of the other

brothers. Of all your possessions, what would you be most upset about if you discovered Brother Juniper had given it away? Why?

3. Brother Juniper seemed to tolerate it well when he was chastised, even if it was not warranted. How do you respond when you have been wrongly chastised? What do you think the holy, or correct, response is when you are being chastised unjustly?

4. Brother Juniper is described as "simple" and his simplicity is seen as a holy attribute. On the other hand, the readings from Saint Thomas Aquinas on pages 14–16 and Blaise Pascal on pages 20–22 are far from simple; yet they are also viewed as holy. How can things so different from each other both be viewed as holy?

GREAT CATHOLIC SPIRITUAL WRITINGS: READING 3

Selections from *The Cloud of Unknowing*

THE UNKNOWN AUTHOR OF *THE CLOUD OF UNKNOWING*

Introduction

No one knows the name of the person who wrote *The Cloud of Unknowing*, but the author's writing reveals a few basic facts. He or she wrote in English rather than Latin, which was the scholarly language of the time. The author probably wrote in the late fourteenth century, during the same turbulent times that Julian of Norwich (see pages 162–171, *Showings*) experienced. He or she is clearly a master of the spiritual life, and fluent in theology — facts that lead many scholars to believe that the author was an English priest or a monk. Five or six other spiritual guides are attributed to the same unidentified author.

The author writes to a young spiritual apprentice, and repeatedly makes clear that *The Cloud of Unknowing* is not meant for everyone. The book "will mean nothing" to anyone but those who are called to contemplation — in other words, the most advanced seekers of God. That warning is appropriate; *The Cloud of Unknowing* is written in a conversational style with concrete imagery and a wry sense of humor, but its content is not nearly as straightforward as its prose style is.

The author is concerned with how one might begin to achieve union with God here on earth. In the previous century, Scholastic theologians such as Thomas Aquinas (see pages 14–16, "The Five Ways") took a very rational, almost scientific, approach to describing and understanding God. Without totally dismissing the value of using our minds to understand God, this author takes a different approach: the *via negativa* (literally, "the negative way"). According to this approach, all our images, words, and thoughts about God ultimately fail to describe his full reality. When people try to strictly define who and what God is, they actually cut themselves off from the possibility of being surprised by God and experiencing a fuller union with him. Instead of trying to define who God *is*, those who follow the *via negativa* attempt to strip their mind of all that God *is not*. Once their mind is cleared of these distractions, union with God becomes possible through love experienced in contemplative prayer.

The author of *The Cloud of Unknowing* profoundly influenced the Christian mystics who followed him. Modern mystics like Thomas Merton (see pages 58–61 "Things in Their Identity," and pages 190–196, "Day of a Stranger") have continued to develop the insights of the *Cloud* author. However, most modern spiritual writers would disagree with the author's distinction between the "active" and "contemplative" life. Nonetheless, *The Cloud of Unknowing* is among the greatest spiritual masterpieces in the Catholic tradition. Its message that God is most fully known not with the mind, but with the heart, is especially relevant in an age that too often values scientific knowledge above all other ways of knowing.

GREAT CATHOLIC SPIRITUAL WRITINGS
From *The Cloud of Unknowing*

MY FRIEND IN GOD: CHAPTER I

It seems to me, in my rough and ready way, that there are four states or kinds of Christian life, and they are these: Common, Special, Solitary, and Perfect. Three of them may be begun and ended in this life; the fourth, by the grace of God, may be begun here, but it goes on forever in the bliss of Heaven! And just as you will notice that I have set these four in a certain sequence (Common, Special, Solitary, Perfect) so I think that our Lord in his great mercy has called you in the same order and in the same way, leading you on to himself by your heart-felt desire.

For you are well aware that, when you were in the Common state of the Christian life, living with your friends in the world, God, through his everlasting love (which made and fashioned you when you were nothing, and then, when you were lost with Adam, bought you with the price of his precious blood) would not allow you to live the kind of life that was so far away from him. In that most gracious way of his, he kindled your desire for himself, and bound you to him by the chain of such longing, and thus led you to that more Special life, a servant among his own special servants. He did this that you might learn to be more especially his and to live more spiritually than ever you could have done in the common state of life.

And there is more: it appears that he is not content to leave you just there — such is the love of his heart which he has always had for you — but in his own delightful and gracious way he has drawn you to this third stage, the Solitary. It is in this state that you will learn to take your first loving steps to the life of Perfection, the last stage of all.

Chapter 2

Pause for a moment, you wretched weakling, and take stock of yourself. Who are you, and what have you deserved, to be called like this by our Lord? How sluggish and slothful the soul that does not respond to Love's attraction and invitation!

At this stage, wretched man, you must keep an eye on your enemy. You must not think yourself any holier or better because of the worthiness of your calling, and because you live the solitary life. Rather the opposite: you are even more wretched and cursed unless you are doing your very best to live answerably to your calling, helped as you are by grace and direction. You ought to be all the more humble and loving to your spiritual husband who is Almighty God, King of Kings and Lord of Lords and yet has so humbly come down to your level, and so graciously chosen you out of his flock to be one of his "specials," and has set you in rich pasture to be fed with the sweet food of his love, a foretaste of your inheritance in the Kingdom of Heaven.

So go on, I beg you, with all speed. Look forward, not backward. See what you still lack, not what you have already; for that is the quickest way of getting and keeping humility. Your whole life now must be one of longing, if you are to achieve perfection. And this longing must be in the depths of your will, put there by God, with your consent. But a word of warning: he is a jealous lover, and will brook no rival; he will not work in your will if he has not sole charge; he does not ask for help, he asks for you. His will is that you should look at him, and let him have his way. You must, however, guard your spiritual windows and doorways against enemy attacks. If you are willing to do this, you need only to lay hold upon God humbly in prayer, and he will soon help you. Lay hold of him then, and see how you fare. God is ready when you are, and is waiting for you.

But what am I to do, you say, and how am I to "lay hold"?

Chapter 3

Lift up your heart to God with humble love: and mean God himself, and not what you get out of him. Indeed, hate to think of anything but God himself, so that nothing occupies your mind or will but only God. Try to forget all created things that he ever made, and the purpose behind them, so that your thought and longing do not turn or reach out to them either in general or in particular. Let them go, and pay no attention to them. It is the work of the soul that pleases God most. All saints and angels rejoice over it, and hasten to help it on with all their might. All the fiends, however, are furious at what you are doing, and try to defeat it in every conceivable way. Moreover, the whole of mankind is wonderfully helped by what you are doing, in ways you do not understand. Yes, the very souls in purgatory find their pain eased by virtue of your work. And in no better way can you yourself be made clean or virtuous than by attending to this. Yet it is the easiest work of all when the soul is helped by grace and has a conscious longing. And it can be achieved very quickly. Otherwise it is hard and beyond your powers.

Do not give up then, but work away at it till you have this longing. When you first begin, you find only darkness, and as it were a cloud of unknowing. You don't know what this means except that in your will you feel a simple steadfast intention reaching out towards God. Do what you will, this darkness and this cloud remain between you and God, and stop you both from seeing him in the clear light of rational understanding, and from experiencing his loving sweetness in your affection. Reconcile yourself to wait in this darkness as long as is necessary, but still go on longing after him whom you love. For if you are to feel him or to see him in this life, it must always be in this cloud, in this darkness. And if you will work hard at what I tell you, I believe that through God's mercy you will achieve this very thing.

CHAPTER 4

So that you may make no mistake, or go wrong in this matter, let me tell you a little more about it as I see it.

This work does not need a long time for its completion. Indeed, it is the shortest work that can be imagined! It is no longer, no shorter, than one atom, which as a philosopher of astronomy will tell you is the smallest division of time. It is so small that it cannot be analyzed: it is almost beyond our grasp. Yet it is as long as the time of which it has been written, "All the time that is given to thee, it shall be asked of thee how thou hast spent it." And it is quite right that you should have to give account of it. It is neither shorter nor longer than a single impulse of your will, the chief part of your soul.

For there can be as many movements or desires of your will within the hour as there are atoms of time. If grace had restored your soul to the state of Adam's soul before the Fall, you would be in control of your every impulse. None would go astray, but all would reach out to the sovereign of all desires, the peak of all that can be willed, God himself.

For he comes down to our level, adapting his Godhead to our power to comprehend. Our soul has some affinity with him, of course, because we have been created in his image and likeness. Only he himself is completely and utterly sufficient to fulfill the will and longing of our souls. Nothing else can. The soul, when it is restored by grace, is made wholly sufficient to comprehend him fully by love. He cannot he comprehended by our intellect or any man's — or any angel's for that matter. For both we and they are created beings. But only to our intellect is he incomprehensible: not to our love.

All rational beings, angels and men, possess two faculties, the power of knowing and the power of loving. To the first, to the intellect, God who made them is forever unknowable, but to the second, to love, he is completely knowable, and that by every separate individual. So much so that one loving soul by itself, through its love, may know for itself him who is incomparably more than sufficient to fill all souls that exist. This is the everlasting miracle of love, for God always works in this fashion, and always will. Consider this, if by God's grace you are able to. To know it for oneself is endless bliss; its contrary is endless pain.

If any man were so refashioned by the grace of God that he heeded every impulse of his will, he would never be without some sense of the eternal sweetness, even in this life, nor without its full realization in the bliss of heaven. So do not be surprised if I urge you on. It is this very thing that man would be doing today if he had not sinned — as you will be hearing later. For this was man made, and all else was made to help him achieve this end. It is by this that man shall be restored. And it is because he does not heed that a man falls ever more deeply into sin, becoming ever more estranged from God. Yet on the other hand, it is by constantly heeding and attending to this very thing and nothing else that a man gets more free from sin, and nearer to God.

So be very careful how you spend time. There is nothing more precious. In the twinkling of an eye heaven may be won or lost. God shows that time is precious, for he never gives two moments of time side by side, but always in succession. To do otherwise he would have to alter the whole course of creation. Time is made for man, not man for time. And God, who orders nature, fitted time in with the nature of man — and man's natural impulses occur one at a time. Man will have no excuse before God at the Day of Judgement when he gives account of how he spent his time. He cannot say: "Thou dost give two times at once, when I have but one impulse at the same moment."

But now you are anxious, and say, "What am I to do? If what you are saying is true, how am I to give account of each moment of time? Here am I, twenty-four years old, altogether heedless of time! Were I to amend straight away, you know perfectly well from what you have already written that neither in nature nor in grace are there any moments of time over and to spare with which I could make satisfaction for my misspent past. I have only those times which are coming to work on. And what is more, I know very well that because of my appalling weakness and dull-wittedness I should only be able to heed one impulse in a hundred. What a plight I am in! Help me, now, for the love of Jesus!"

How right you are to say "for the love of Jesus." For it is in the love of Jesus that you have your help. The nature of love is such that it shares everything. Love Jesus, and everything he has is yours. Because he is God, he is maker and giver of time. Because he is Man, he has given true heed to time. Because he is both God and Man he is the best judge of the spending of time. Unite yourself to him by love and trust, and by that union you will be joined both to him and to all who like yourself are united by love to him . . . with our lady, Saint Mary, who, full of grace, perfectly heeded every passing moment; with all the angels in heaven, who have never let time pass; and with all the saints in heaven and on earth, who by their love, and by Jesus's grace, take proper account of every moment.

This is a great comfort. Really understand it, and get profit therefrom. But let me emphasize this: I cannot see that anyone can claim fellowship in this matter with Jesus or his righteous Mother, his angels or his saints, unless he is doing everything in his power, with the help of grace, to attend to each moment of time . . . so that he can be seen to be doing his part to strengthen the fellowship, however little it may be, as each of them, in his turn, is doing his.

So pay great attention to this marvelous work of grace within your soul. It is always a sudden impulse and comes without warning, springing up to God like some spark from the fire. An incredible number of such impulses arise in one brief hour in the soul who has a will to this work! In one such flash the soul may completely forget the created world outside. Yet almost as quickly it may relapse back to thoughts and memories of things done and undone—all because of our fallen nature. And as fast again it may rekindle.

This then, in brief, is how it works. It is obviously not make-believe, nor wrong thinking, nor fanciful opinion. These would not be the product of a devout and humble love, but the outcome of the pride and inventiveness of the imagination. If this work of grace is to be truly and genuinely understood, all such proud imaginings must ruthlessly be stamped out!

For whoever hears or reads about all this, and thinks that it is fundamentally an activity of the mind, and proceeds then to work it all out along these lines, is on quite the wrong track. He manufactures an experience that is neither spiritual nor physical. He is dangerously misled and in real peril. So much so, that unless God in his great goodness intervenes with a miracle of mercy and makes him stop and submit to the advice of those who really know, he will go mad, or suffer some other dreadful form of spiritual mischief and devilish deceit. Indeed, almost casually as it were, he may be lost eternally, body and soul. So for the love of God be careful, and do not attempt to achieve this experience intellectually. I tell you truly it cannot come this way. So leave it alone.

Do not think that because I call it a "darkness" or a "cloud" it is the sort of cloud you see in the sky, or the kind of darkness you know at home when the light is out. That kind of darkness or cloud you can picture in your mind's eye in the height of summer, just as in the depth of a winter's night you can picture a clear and shining light. I do not mean this at all. By "darkness" I mean "a lack of knowing" —just as anything that you do not know or may have forgotten may be said to be "dark" to you, for you cannot see it with your inward eye. For this reason it is called "a cloud," not of the sky, of course, but "of unknowing," a cloud of unknowing between you and your God.

Review Questions

1. What are the four states of Christian life?

2. If a person's soul has been restored to the condition of Adam's soul before the Fall, what would that person experience?

3. If God cannot be comprehended by our intellect, what part of our humanity can comprehend God?

4. What two powers, or faculties, do rational beings possess?

5. How are we supposed to spend our time?

In-depth Questions

1. The author urges the reader to give one's heart to God from a desire to love God rather than a desire to get something from God. Why do you think this is important? If you are a person of prayer, do you pray to love God, get something from God, or both? Please explain.

2. The author says that we can feel a darkness when we begin to seek God. Have you experienced such feelings? Do you agree with the

author that you should continue to seek God, despite this feeling? Please explain.

3. The author is convinced of the importance of time. Overall, do you think you spend your time wisely? Do you think you give God enough of your time? If you were to change the way you spend your time, what would you change?

4. There is a great difference between the way *The Cloud of Unknowing* speaks about knowing God and the way Saint Thomas Aquinas speaks about knowing God in "The Five Ways" on pages 14–16. Do you prefer one way over another? Please explain.

GREAT CATHOLIC SPIRITUAL WRITINGS: READING 4

Selections from *The Story of a Soul*

SAINT THÉRÈSE OF LISIEUX

Introduction

Thérèse Martin longed to be a priest, a missionary, and a martyr. She never was any of those things. Instead, she lived what seemed to be a quiet life. When she died in 1897 at the age of twenty-four, she was virtually unknown beyond the walls of her convent; yet her hidden life and "little way" would soon be known by millions of people. Today, she is widely considered to be one of the Church's greatest saints. The principle reason for such devotion to her lies in the huge popularity of her autobiography, *The Story of a Soul*.

In 1873, Saint Thérèse was born in the French village of Lisieux. She enjoyed a happy family, full of love and good humor; yet Thérèse experienced sadness and depression at a young age. Her mother died of breast cancer when she was only four; and when Thérèse was nine, her sister Pauline entered the convent. Pauline had become a second mother to Thérèse. This second loss made her so sad that she became physically ill for many months. Perhaps because of these losses, her family doted on her: she was her sister's "baby," her father's "little Queen" — and she often acted like one. She burst into tears over the smallest disappointment or perceived offense, and increasingly withdrew into herself.

Whatever her childhood faults were, she had a great love of God from an early age. That devotion led to what she would later call her "conversion" shortly before her fourteenth birthday. After returning from Christmas Mass, she accidentally overheard her normally affectionate father make a critical comment about her childishness. She typically would have burst into tears; instead, strengthened by the grace of the Eucharist, she cheerfully responded to the comment. This sort of response to everyday difficulties reflects the heart of her "little way."

Practically overnight, grace transformed the childish Thérèse into a strong, confident young woman. Seeking greater spiritual maturity, she entered the Carmelite convent. Thérèse had a witty sense of humor and a talent for mimicking others that she used to entertain the other nuns with stories from her childhood. It was after one of these storytelling sessions that her sister, Pauline, who was also the convent prioress, asked Thérèse to write down her childhood memories. Thérèse did so in a way that revealed her deep spiritual wisdom. The prioress who succeeded Pauline asked her to write more about her spiritual insights. These writings became *The Story of a Soul*.

Some modern readers are turned off by Saint Thérèse's writing, especially the seeming trivialness of her "little way." Yet the genius of her spirituality lies in its littleness: by becoming "little," she emptied herself of her own cares so that God could fill her with the grace to love more deeply. She realized that she did not need to become a missionary, a martyr, or a priest to do great things, because the greatness of our actions is not measured by their size or importance, but by love.

After Thérèse's death in 1897, *The Story of a Soul* was circulated to the other Carmelite convents in place of an obituary. The work spread quickly, as did the number of miracles attributed to her intercession. She was declared a saint in 1925, and in 1997 she was declared one of the thirty-three Doctors of the Church, an honor that recognizes her unique contribution to the Church's understanding of the faith. She never left Lisieux after entering the convent, but more than 100 million copies of her *The Story of a Soul* have circled the globe in fifty different languages.

GREAT CATHOLIC SPIRITUAL WRITINGS
From *The Story of a Soul*

CHAPTER 9

You, Reverend Mother, have said that I should write — for you — the end of my hymn to the mercies of the Lord. I do not want to argue, but I must smile as I pick up my pen to tell you of things you know as well as I do. Yet I obey you. I will not ask what can be the use of this manuscript. And I assure you that I should not be a bit upset if you burnt it in front of me without troubling to read it.

The nuns think that you have spoilt me in every possible way from the very moment I entered Carmel, but "man seeth those things that appear, but the Lord beholdeth the heart." I thank you for not having spared me. Jesus knew very well that His little flower needed the life-giving water of humiliation. She was not strong enough to take root without it, and she owes that priceless favour to you.

LITTLE FLOWER

Saint Thérèse of Lisieux is also known as Saint Thérèse the Little Flower. It is a constant image that she used for herself, and Little Flower has become another name by which she is known.

For several months Jesus has completely changed His method of cultivating His little flower. He found, no doubt, that she had had enough of that bitter water, so now He sees to it that she grows beneath the warmth of a genial sun. Now He gives her only smiles— something entirely owing to you, Reverend Mother. This sun never withers the Little Flower. It makes her grow wonderfully. Deep within her petals she treasures the precious drops of dew she received in days gone by. They always remind her how small and weak she is. Everyone can stoop down over her, admire her, and shower flattery on her, but it won't give her a scrap of that foolish self-satisfaction which would spoil the real happiness she has in knowing that is nothing but a poor little nonentity in God's eyes. When I say that all praise leaves me unmoved, I'm not thinking of the love and confidence you show me. I'm very moved by it, but I feel that I now need have no fear of praise and that I can accept it calmly. For I attribute to God all the goodness with which He has endowed me. It is nothing to do with me if it pleases Him to make me seem better than I am. He is free to do what He wants . . .

You know, Mother, that I have always wanted to become a saint. Unfortunately when I have compared myself with the saints, I have always found that there is the same difference between the saints and me as there is between a mountain whose summit is lost in the clouds and a humble grain of sand trodden underfoot by passers-by. Instead of being discouraged, I told myself: God would not make me wish for something impossible and so, in spite of my littleness, I can aim at being a saint. It is impossible for me to grow bigger, so I put up with myself as I am, with all my countless faults. But I will look for some means of going to heaven by a little way which is very short and very straight, a little way that is quite new. We live in an age of inventions. We need no longer climb laboriously up flights of stairs; in well-to-do houses there are lifts. And I was determined to find a lift to carry me to Jesus, for I was far too small to climb the steep stairs of perfection. So I sought in Holy Scripture some idea of what this lift I wanted would be, and I read these words from the very mouth of eternal Wisdom: "Whosoever is a little one, let him come to me." I drew nearer to God, fully realizing that I had found what I was looking for. I also wanted to know how God would deal with a "little one," so I continued my search and found this: "You shall be carried at the breasts and upon the knees; as one whom the mother caresseth, so will I comfort you." Never before had I been gladdened by such sweet and tender words. It is Your arms, Jesus, which are the lift to carry me to heaven. And so there is no need for me to grow up. In fact, just the opposite: I must stay little and become less and less. O God, You have gone beyond anything I hoped for and I will sing of Your mercies: "Thou hast taught me, O Lord, from my youth, and till now I have declared Thy wonderful works and shall do so unto old age and grey hairs."

Among the countless graces I have received this year, perhaps the greatest has been that of being able to grasp in all its fullness the meaning of charity. I had never before fathomed Our Lord's words: "The second commandment is like to the first: Thou shalt love thy neighbour as thyself." I had striven above all to love God, and in loving Him I discovered the secret of those other words: "Not everyone that saith to me: Lord, Lord! shall enter into the kingdom of heaven, but he that doeth the will of my Father." Jesus made me understand what this will was by the words He used at the Last Supper when He gave His "new commandment" and told His apostles "to love one another as He had loved them." I began to consider just how Jesus had loved His disciples. I saw it was not for their natural qualities, for I recognized they were ignorant men and often preoccupied with earthly affairs. Yet He calls them His friends and His brethren. He wants to see them near Him in the kingdom of His Father and to open this kingdom to them He wills to die on the Cross, saying: "Greater love than this no man hath, that a man lay down his life for his friends." As I meditated on these words of Jesus, I saw how imperfect was my love for the other nuns and I knew that I did not love them as Jesus loves them. But now I realize that true charity consists in putting up with all one's neighbour's faults, never being surprised by his weakness, and being inspired by the least of his virtues. Above all, I learnt that charity is not something that stays shut up in one's heart for "no man lighteth a candle and putteth it in a hidden place, nor under a bushel; but upon a candlestick, that they who come in may see the light." This candle represents that charity which must illumine and cheer not only those dearest to me but "All those who are of the household."

When God, under the old law, told His people to love their neighbours as themselves, He had not yet come down to earth. As He knew how much we love ourselves, He could not ask us to do more. But when Jesus gave His apostles a "new commandment, His own commandment," He did not ask only that we should love our neighbours as ourselves but that we should love them as He loves them and as He will love them to the end of time. O Jesus, I know You command nothing that is impossible. You know how weak and imperfect I am, and You know only too well that I could never love the other nuns as You love them if You Yourself did not love them *within me*. It is because You wish to grant me this grace that You have given a new commandment. How I cherish it, for it assures me that it is Your will *to love in me* all those whom You command me to love.

When I act and think with charity, I feel it is Jesus who works within me. The closer I am united with Him, the more I love all the other dwellers in Carmel. If I want this love to grow deeper and the devil tries to show me the faults of a sister, I hasten to think of all her virtues and of how good her intentions are. I tell myself that though I have seen her commit a sin, she may very well have won many spiritual victories of which I know nothing because of her humility. What seems a fault to me may very well be an act of virtue because of the intention behind it. I have experienced that myself. During recreation one day the portress came to ask for a sister to help her with a certain job. I wanted to take a hand in that particular bit of work and sure enough I was chosen. I at once began to fold up my sewing, but I was slow about it so that the nun next to me was able to fold hers before me, for I knew how pleased she would be to take my place. When she saw me in so little of a hurry, the portress said with a smile: "Ah! I felt sure you would not add this pearl to your crown. You are too slow." And the whole community thought this slowness was natural. I benefited tremendously from this little incident. It has made me very understanding. It still stops my having any feeling of pride when people think well of what I do, for I say to myself: Since any small good deed I do can be mistaken for a fault, the mistake of calling a fault a virtue can be made just as easily. Then I say with St. Paul: "To me it is a very small thing to be judged by you, or by man's day. But neither do I judge myself. He that judgeth me is the Lord." As it is Jesus who judges me, and as He said: "Judge not and ye shall not be judged," I want always to have charitable thoughts so that He will judge me favourably—or, rather, not judge me at all.

To return to the Gospels where Our Lord teaches me so clearly what His new commandment is. In St. Matthew I read: "You have heard that it hath been said, Thou shall love thy neighbour and hate thy enemy: but I say unto you, love your enemies and pray for them that persecute you." In Carmel, of course, one has no enemies, but one certainly has natural likes and dislikes. One feels attracted to a certain sister and one would go out of one's way to dodge meeting another. Jesus tells me that it is this very sister I must love, and I must pray for her even though her attitude makes me believe she has no love for me. "If you love them that love you, what thanks are to you? For sinners also love those that love them." It is not enough to love. We must prove that we do. We naturally like to please a friend, but that is not charity, for so do sinners.

Jesus also teaches me: "Give to everyone that asketh thee; and of him that taketh away thy goods, ask them not again." It is not so pleasant to give to everyone who asks as it is to offer something freely and spontaneously; and it is easy to give when you are asked nicely, but if we are asked tactlessly, we at once want to refuse unless perfect charity strengthens us. We find a thousand reasons for saying no, and it is not until we have made the sister aware of her bad manners that we give her what she wants *as a favour,* or do her a slight service which takes a quarter of the time needed to tell her of the obstacles preventing our doing it or of our fancied rights.

If it is hard to give to anyone who asks, it is very much harder to let what belongs to us be taken without asking for it back. I say that it is hard, but I should really say that it *seems* hard, for "the yoke of the Lord is sweet and His burden light." The moment we accept it, we feel how light it is.

I have said that Jesus does not want me to ask for the return of what belongs to me. That seems very right, as nothing really does belong to me. So I should rejoice when I have the chance of experiencing that poverty to which I am solemnly vowed. I used to believe I had no possessiveness about anything; but since I have really grasped what Jesus means, I see how far I am from being perfect. If, for example, I settle down to start painting and find the brushes in a mess, or a ruler or a penknife gone, I very nearly lose my patience and have to hold on to it with both hands to prevent my asking bad-temperedly for them. Of course I can ask for these essential tools and I do not disobey Jesus if I ask *humbly.* I behave like poor people who hold out their hands for the necessities of life. As no one owes them anything, they are never surprised at being rebuffed. What peace pours over the soul once it soars above natural feelings! There is no joy like that known by the truly poor in spirit. Our Lord's counsel is: "If any man, take away thy coat, let go thy cloak also unto him," and these poor in spirit are following this counsel when they ask, with detachment, for some necessary thing and it is refused them and an effort is made to snatch away even what they have. To give up one's coat means to renounce one's last rights and to regard oneself as the servant and the slave of others. Without one's cloak, it is much easier to walk and run, and so Jesus adds: "And whosoever will force thee one mile, go with him another two." It is not enough for me to give to all who ask me: I must go beyond what they want. I must show how grateful and honoured I am to serve them and if anything I use is taken away, I must appear glad to be rid of it.

There are times, though, when I cannot always keep strictly to the words of the Gospel. Occasions crop up when I have to refuse something. But when charity is deeply rooted in the soul, it shows outwardly. It is possible to refuse in such a gracious manner that the refusal gives as much pleasure as the gift would have done. It is true that people are less embarrassed at asking from those who always show themselves willing to oblige, but I must not avoid the sisters who ask for things easily on the pretext that I shall have to refuse. Our Lord says: "From him that would borrow of thee turn not away." Nor must I be kind just for appearances' sake or in the hope that the sister I oblige will one day do the same for me, for Our Lord also says: "If you lend to them of whom you hope to receive, what thanks are to you? For sinners also lend to sinners for to receive as much. But you do good and lend, hoping for nothing thereby, and your reward shall be great." And the reward is great indeed, even on earth. It is only the first step which counts along this path. It seems hard to lend "hoping for nothing thereby." One would prefer to give, for something given no longer belongs to one. Someone comes up to you and says very earnestly: "Sister, I need your help for a few hours. But don't worry. Reverend Mother has given me permission and I will repay the time you lend me." But I know very well that this borrowed time will never be given back and I would rather say: "I give it you!" But that would feed my self-love, for it is more generous to give than to lend and it would, as well, make the sister feel that I did not rely on her to repay me. Oh, how contrary to human nature are the divine teachings! Without the help of grace, it would be impossible not only to follow them but even to understand them.

Dear Mother, I feel that, more than ever, I have expressed myself very badly. I do not know how you can take any interest in reading all these muddled thoughts. But, after all, I am not writing a literary work, and if I have bored you by this homily on charity, you will at least see that your child has given proof of her goodwill.

I am, I confess, far from practicing what I know I should, yet the mere desire I have to do so gives me peace. If it happens that I fall and commit a fault against charity, I rise again at once. For some months I have no longer even had to struggle. I can say with our Father St. John of the Cross: "My house is entirely at peace," and I attribute this deep peace to a certain battle which I won. Ever since this victory the hosts of heaven come to my aid, for they cannot bear to see me wounded after I fought so valiantly on the occasion I am going to describe.

Formerly one of our nuns managed to irritate me whatever she did or said. The devil was mixed up in it, for it was certainly he who made me see so many disagreeable traits in her. As I did not want to give way to my natural dislike for her, I told myself that charity should not only be a matter of feeling but should show itself in deeds. So I set myself to do for this sister just what I should have done for someone I loved most dearly. Every time I met her, I prayed for her and offered God all her virtues and her merits. I was sure this would greatly delight Jesus, for every artist likes to have his works praised and the divine Artist of souls is pleased when we do not halt outside the exterior of the sanctuary where He has chosen to dwell but go inside and admire its beauty.

I did not remain content with praying a lot for this nun who caused me so much disturbance. I tried to do as many things for her as I could, and whenever I was tempted to speak unpleasantly to her, I made myself give her a pleasant smile and tried to change the subject. *The Imitation* says: "It is more profitable to leave to everyone his way of thinking than to give way to contentious discourses."

When I was violently tempted by the devil and if I could slip away without her seeing my inner struggle, I would flee like a soldier deserting the battlefield. And after all this she asked me one day with a beaming face: "Sister Thérèse, will you please tell me what attracts you so much to me? You give me such a charming smile whenever we meet." Ah! it was Jesus hidden in the depth of her soul who attracted me, Jesus who makes the bitterest things sweet!

I have just told you, Mother, of my last resolve for avoiding a defeat in the struggles of life — *desertion*. I used this rather dishonourable trick when I was a novice and it was always completely successful. I will give you a striking example which, I think, will make you smile.

You had been ill for some days with bronchitis and we were very worried. One morning I came very guiltily to the infirmary to put back the keys of the Communion grille, for I was sacristan. I was feeling delighted at having this opportunity of seeing you, but I took good care not to let it be seen. One of the sisters, full of zeal, thought I was going to waken you and tried to take the keys quietly from me. I told her, as politely as possible, that I was just as eager as she was to make no noise, and added that it was my duty to return the keys. Nowadays I realize that it would have been far better simply to have given her them, but I did not understand that then and tried to push my way into the room in spite of her.

Then what we feared happened. The noise we made woke you and all the blame fell on me! The sister I had opposed hastened to make quite a speech, the gist of which was: "It was Sister Thérèse of the Child Jesus who made the noise." I burned to defend myself, but fortunately I had a bright idea. I knew, without a shadow of a doubt, that if I began to speak up for myself I should lose my peace of soul; I knew too that I was not virtuous enough to let myself be accused without saying a word, my only hope of safety was to run away. No sooner thought than done: I fled . . . but my heart beat so violently that I could not go far and I sat down on the stairs to enjoy in peace the fruits of my victory. It was undoubtedly a queer kind of courage, but I think it is better not to fight when defeat is certain.

Alas! When I remember my days as a novice, I see how imperfect I was. I laugh now at some of the things I did. How good God is to have lifted up my soul and given it wings! All the nets of the hunters cannot frighten me, for "a net is set in vain before the eyes of them that have wings."

In the days to come it may be that my present state will seem most imperfect, but I am no longer surprised by anything and I feel no distress at seeing my complete helplessness. On the contrary, I glory in it and every day I expect to discover fresh flaws in myself. In fact, this revelation of my nothingness does me much more good, than being enlightened on matters of faith.

I remember that "charity covereth a multitude of sins" and I draw from the rich mine opened by the Lord in the Gospels. I ransack the depths of His adorable words and I cry with David: "I have run the way of Thy commandments when Thou didst enlarge my heart." Charity alone can enlarge my heart. . . . O Jesus, ever since its gentle flame has consumed my heart, I have run with delight along the way of Your "new commandment" and I want to continue until that blessed day when, with Your company of virgins, I shall follow You through infinite realms singing your *new canticle*—the canticle of LOVE.

Review Questions

1. What Scripture passage did Saint Thérèse find to describe her "lift" into heaven?

2. How did Saint Thérèse describe "true charity"?

3. When did Saint Thérèse feel that Jesus was working within her?

4. One nun in particular was irritating to Saint Thérèse. What would Saint Thérèse do every time she met her?

5. What was so attractive about the irritating nun, according to Saint Thérèse?

In-depth Questions

1. Review Saint Thérèse's definition of "true charity." Why do you think it is generally difficult to endure the faults of others?

2. Saint Thérèse was quite aware of others' faults. But she was also aware of her own faults. How can an awareness of one's own faults help our relationships with others?

3. Saint Thérèse wrote, "The closer I am united with Him, the more I love all the other dwellers in Carmel." Why do you think union with Jesus is important in order to love others?

4. Saint Thérèse said her way to holiness was by following the "little way." Can you list five little ways in your daily life that Jesus might be asking you to imitate him?

Great Catholic Spiritual Writings: Reading 5

Selections from *Showings*

Julian of Norwich

Introduction

Little is known about Julian of Norwich other than what she wrote about herself in her book, *Showings*. She was born in 1342 in Norwich, England and lived until at least 1416. This was a time of great turmoil: England and France were fighting, peasants revolted against landowners, and different factions in the Church fought for control of the papacy. But the most-feared threat to Europeans was the bubonic plague. Between 1346 and 1351, about one-third of Europeans died as a result of the bubonic plague that swept the continent. The plague had a huge impact on European society, including its attitudes toward religion.

People wondered why God would allow such widespread death and suffering. During this time, the ravages of the plague greatly tested people's faith, and many people abandoned their faith in God. But others responded to the plague by seeking God all the more. Among those who deepened their devotion to God were women called anchoresses.

These women confined themselves to a small room attached to the wall of a church. They lived in this room, called an anchorhold, in order to devote their lives completely to prayer and contemplation. Julian was one of these anchoresses, living in the anchorhold of the Church of Saint Julian in Norwich (anchoresses usually took the name of the church in which they resided). Openings in the anchorhold allowed her to participate in the Mass, receive food and other necessities, and talk with the many visitors who sought her counsel.

When she was young, Julian longed to have a vision of Christ's Passion—his suffering and death on the cross—so that she would understand it as well as if she had actually been at the foot of the cross. Her wish was fulfilled when she became seriously ill at the age of thirty. During this illness, she received sixteen divine revelations, or "showings," which contained vivid visions of Christ's suffering and death. But while her contemporaries generally interpreted Christ's Passion as necessary to appease God's anger and vengeance, Julian's vision of the

Passion revealed the power of God's love to create, sustain, and save all of creation. In a time when many people were very focused on the reality of sin and suffering, God revealed to Julian the power of His grace to overcome all evil.

GREAT CATHOLIC SPIRITUAL WRITINGS
From *Showings*

THE SECOND CHAPTER

This revelation was made to a simple, unlettered creature, living in this mortal flesh, the year of our Lord one thousand, three hundred and seventy-three, on the thirteenth day of May; and before this the creature had desired three graces by the gift of God. The first was recollection of the Passion. The second was bodily sickness. The third was to have, of God's gift, three wounds. As to the first, it seemed to me that I had some feeling for the Passion of Christ, but still I desired to have more by the grace of God. I thought that I wished that I had been at that time with Magdalen and with the others who were Christ's lovers, so that I might have seen with my own eyes the Passion which our Lord suffered for me, so that I might have suffered with him as others did who loved him. Therefore I desired a bodily sight, in which I might have more knowledge of our saviour's bodily pains, and of the compassion of our Lady and of all his true lovers who were living at that time and saw his pains, for I would have been one of them and have suffered with them. I never desired any other sight of God or revelation, until my soul would be separated from the body, for I believed that I should be saved by the mercy of God. This was my intention, because I wished afterwards, because of that revelation, to have truer recollection of Christ's Passion. As to the second grace, there came into my mind with contrition—a free gift which I did not seek—a desire of my will to have by God's gift a bodily sickness. I wished that sickness to be so severe that it might seem mortal, so that I might in it receive all the rites which Holy Church has to give me, whilst I myself should think that I was dying, and everyone who saw me would think the same; for I wanted no comfort from any human, earthly life in that sickness. I wanted to have every kind of pain, bodily and spiritual, which I should have, if I had died, every fear and temptation from devils, and every other kind of pain except the departure of the spirit. I intended this because I wanted to be purged by God's mercy, and afterwards live more to his glory because of that sickness; because I hoped that this would be to my reward when I should die, because I desired soon to be with my God and my Creator.

These two desires about the Passion and the sickness which I desired from him were with a condition, for it seemed to me that this was not the ordinary practice of prayer; therefore I said: Lord, you know what I want, if it be your will that I have it, and if it be not your will, good Lord, do not be displeased, for I want nothing which you do not want. When I was young I desired to have this sickness when I would be thirty years old.

As to the third, by the grace of God and the teaching of Holy Church I conceived a great desire to receive three wounds in my life, that is, the wound of true contrition, the wound of loving compassion and the wound of longing with my will for God. Just as I asked for the other two conditionally, so I asked urgently for this third without any condition. The two desires which I mentioned first passed from my mind, and the third remained there continually.

THE THIRD CHAPTER

And when I was thirty and a half years old, God sent me a bodily sickness in which I lay for three days and three nights, and on the third night I received all the rites of Holy Church, and did not expect to live until day. And after this I lay for two days and two nights, and on the third night I often thought that I was on the point of death, and those who were with me often thought so. And yet in this I felt a great reluctance to die, not that there was anything on earth which it pleased me to live for, or any pain of which I was afraid, for I trusted in the mercy of God. But it was because I wanted to live to love God better and longer, so that I might through the grace of that living have more knowledge and love of God in the bliss of heaven. Because it seemed to me that all the time that I had lived here was very little and short in comparison with the bliss which is everlasting, I thought: Good Lord, can my living no longer be to your glory? And I understood by my reason and the sensation of my pains that I should die; and with all the will of my heart I assented to be wholly as was God's will.

So I lasted until day, and by then my body was dead from the middle downwards, as it felt to me. Then I was helped to sit upright and supported, so that my heart might be more free to be at God's will, and so that I could think of him whilst my life would last. My curate was sent for to be present at my end; and before he came my eyes were fixed upwards, and I could not speak. He set the cross before my face, and said: I have brought the image of your saviour; look at it and take comfort from it. It seemed to me that I was well, for my eyes were set upwards towards heaven, where I trusted that I by God's mercy was going; but nevertheless I agreed to fix my eyes on the face of the crucifix if I could, and so I did, for it seemed to me that I would hold out longer with my eyes set in front of me rather than upwards. After this my sight began to fail. It grew as dark around me in the room as if it had been night, except that there was ordinary light trained upon the image of the cross, I did not know how. Everything around the cross was ugly and terrifying to me, as if it were occupied by a great crowd of devils.

After this the upper part of my body began to die, until I could scarcely feel anything. My greatest pain was my shortness of breath and the ebbing of my life. Then truly I believed that I was at the point of death. And suddenly at that moment all my pain was taken from me, and I was as sound, particularly in the upper part of my body, as ever I was before. I was astonished by this sudden change, for it seemed to me that it was by God's secret doing and not natural; and even so, in this ease which I felt, I had no more confidence that I should live, nor was the case I felt complete for me, for I thought that I would rather have been delivered of this world, because that was what my heart longed for.

Then suddenly it came into my mind that I ought to wish for the second wound as a gift and a grace from our Lord, that my body might be filled full of recollection and feeling of his blessed Passion, as I had prayed before, for I wished that his pains might be my pains, with compassion which would lead to longing for God. So it seemed to me that I might with his grace have the wounds which I had before desired; but in this I never wanted any bodily vision or any kind of revelation from God, but the compassion which I thought a loving soul could have for our Lord Jesus, who for love was willing to become a mortal man. I desired to suffer with him, living in my mortal body, as God would give me grace.

THE FOURTH CHAPTER

And at this, suddenly I saw the red blood running down from under the crown, hot and flowing freely and copiously, a living stream, just as it was at the time when the crown of thorns was pressed on his blessed head. I perceived, truly and powerfully, that it was he who just so, both God and man, himself suffered for me, who showed it to me without any intermediary.

And in the same revelation, suddenly the Trinity filled my heart full of the greatest joy, and I understood that it will be so in heaven without end to all who will come there. For the Trinity is God, God is the Trinity. The Trinity is our maker, the Trinity is our protector, the Trinity is our everlasting lover; the Trinity is our endless joy and our bliss, by our Lord Jesus Christ and in our Lord Jesus Christ. And this was revealed in the first vision and in them all, for where Jesus appears the blessed Trinity is understood, as I see it. And I said: Blessed be the Lord! This I said with a reverent intention and in a loud voice; and I was greatly astonished by this wonder and marvel, that he who is so to be revered and feared would be so familiar with a sinful creature living in this wretched flesh.

I accepted it that at that time our Lord Jesus wanted, out of his courteous love, to show me comfort before my temptations began; for it seemed to me that I might well be tempted by devils, by God's permission and with his protection, before I would die. With this sight of his blessed Passion, with the divinity which I saw in my understanding, I knew well that this was strength enough for me, yes, and for all living creatures who were to be saved, against all the devils of hell and against all their spiritual enemies.

In this he brought our Lady St. Mary to my understanding. I saw her spiritually in her bodily likeness, a simple, humble maiden, young in years, grown a little taller than a child, of the stature which she had when she conceived. Also God showed me part of the wisdom and the truth of her soul, and in this I understood the reverent contemplation with which she beheld her God, who is her Creator, marveling with great reverence that he was willing to be born of her who was a simple creature created by him. And this wisdom and truth, this knowledge of her Creator's greatness and of her own created littleness, made her say very meekly to Gabriel: Behold me here, God's handmaiden. In this sight I understood truly that she is greater, more worthy and more fulfilled, than everything else which God has created, and which is inferior to her. Above her is no created thing, except the blessed humanity of Christ, as I saw.

THE FIFTH CHAPTER

At the same time as I saw this sight of the head bleeding, our good Lord showed a spiritual sight of his familiar love. I saw that he is to us everything which is good and comforting for our help. He is our clothing, who wraps and enfolds us for love, embraces us and shelters us, surrounds us for his love, which is so tender that he may never desert us. And so in this sight I saw that he is everything which is good, as I understand.

And in this he showed me something small, no bigger than a hazelnut, lying in the palm of my hand, as it seemed to me, and it was as round as a ball. I looked at it with the eye of my understanding and thought: What can this be? I was amazed that it could last, for I thought that because of its littleness it would suddenly have fallen into nothing. And I was answered in my understanding: It lasts and always will, because God loves it; and thus everything has being through the love of God.

In this little thing I saw three properties. The first is that God made it, the second is that God loves it, the third is that God preserves it. But what did I see in it? It is that God is the Creator and the protector and the lover. For until I am substantially united to him, I can never have perfect rest or true happiness, until, that is, I am so attached to him that there can be no created thing between my God and me.

This little thing which is created seemed to me as if it could have fallen into nothing because of its littleness. We need to have knowledge of this, so that we may delight in despising as nothing everything created, so as to love and have uncreated God. For this is the reason why our hearts and souls are not in perfect ease, because here we seek rest in this thing which is so little, in which there is no rest, and we do not know our God who is almighty, all wise and all good, for he is true rest. God wishes to be known, and it pleases him that we should rest in him; for everything which is beneath him is not sufficient for us. And this is the reason why no soul is at rest until it has despised as nothing all things which are created. When it by its will has become nothing for love, to have him who is everything, then is it able to receive spiritual rest.

And also our good Lord revealed that it is very greatly pleasing to him that a simple soul should come naked, openly and familiarly. For this is the loving yearning of the soul through the touch of the Holy Spirit, from the understanding which I have in this revelation: God, of your goodness give me yourself, for you are enough for me, and I can ask for nothing which is less which can pay you full worship. And if I ask anything which is less, always I am in want; but only in you do I have everything.

And these words of the goodness of God are very dear to the soul, and very close to touching our Lord's will, for his goodness fills all his creatures and all his blessed works full, and endlessly overflows in them. For he is everlastingness, and he made us only for himself, and restored us by his precious Passion and always preserves us in his blessed love; and all this is of his goodness.

This revelation was given to my understanding to teach our souls wisely to adhere to the goodness of God; and in that same time our habits of prayer were brought to my mind, how in our ignorance of love we are accustomed to employ many intermediaries. Then I saw

Intermediaries

"Intermediaries" or "means" refers to the vast array of images and other persons, such as saints or friends, which we may use in our approach to God. Julian recommends a direct contact rather than indirect contact.

truly that it is more honour to God and more true delight if we faithfully pray to him for his goodness, and adhere to this by grace, with true understanding and steadfast belief, than if we employed all the intermediaries of which a heart may think. For if we employ all these intermediaries, this is too little and it is not complete honour to God; but his goodness is full and complete, and in it is nothing lacking.

For what I shall say came to my mind at the same time. We pray to God for his holy flesh and for his precious blood, his holy Passion, his precious death and his glorious wounds, for all the blessings of nature and the endless life that we have of all this, it is of the goodness of God. And we pray to him for the love of the sweet mother who bore him, and all the help that we have of her, it is of his goodness. And we pray for his holy Cross on which he died, and all the help and the strength that we have of that Cross, it is of his goodness. And in the same way, all the help that we have from particular saints and from all the blessed company of heaven, the precious love and the holy, endless friendship that we have from them, it is of his goodness. For the intermediaries which the goodness of God has ordained to help us are very lovely and many. Of them the chief and principal intermediary is the blessed nature which he took of the virgin, with all the intermediaries which preceded and followed, which are a part of our redemption and of our endless salvation.

Therefore it pleases him that we seek him and honour him through intermediaries, understanding and knowing that he is the goodness of everything. For the highest form of prayer is to the goodness of God, which comes down to us to our humblest needs. It gives life to our souls and makes them live and grow in grace and virtue. It is nearest in nature and promptest in grace, for it is the same grace which the soul seeks and always will, until we truly know our God, who has enclosed us all in himself.

A man walks upright, and the food in his body is shut in as if in a well-made purse. When the time of his necessity comes, the purse is opened and then shut again, in most seemly fashion. And it is God who does this, as it is shown when he says that he comes down to us in our humblest needs. For he does not despise what he has made, nor does he disdain to serve us in the simplest natural functions of our body, for love of the soul which he created in his own likeness. For as the body is clad in the cloth, and the flesh in the skin, and the bones in the flesh, and the heart in the trunk, so are we, soul and body, clad and enclosed in the goodness of God. Yes, and more closely, for all these vanish and waste away; the goodness of God is always complete, and closer to us, beyond any comparison. For truly our lover desires the soul to adhere to him with all its power, and us always to adhere to his goodness. For of all the things that the heart can think, this pleases God most and soonest profits the soul. For it is so preciously loved by him who is highest that this surpasses the knowledge of all created beings. That is to say, there is no created being who can know how much and how sweetly and how tenderly the Creator loves us. And therefore we can with his grace and his help persevere in spiritual contemplation, with endless wonder at this high, surpassing, immeasurable love which our Lord in his goodness has for us; and therefore we may with reverence ask from our lover all that we will, for our natural will is to have God, and God's good will is to have us, and we can never stop willing or loving until we possess him in the fullness of joy. And there we can will no more, for it is his will that we be occupied in knowing and loving until the time comes that we shall be filled full in heaven.

And therefore this lesson of love was revealed, with all that follows, as you will see, for the strength and foundation of everything was revealed in the first vision. For of all things, contemplating and loving the Creator makes the soul to seem less in its own sight, and fills it full with reverent fear and true meekness, and with much love for its fellow Christians.

THE SEVENTH CHAPTER

And to teach us this, as I understand, our good Lord showed our Lady St. Mary at the same time, that is to signify the exalted wisdom and truth which were hers as she contemplated her Creator. This wisdom and truth showed her in contemplation how great, how exalted, how mighty and how good was her God. The greatness and nobility of her contemplation of God filled her full of reverent fear; and with this she saw herself so small and so humble, so simple and so poor in comparison with her God that this reverent fear filled her with humility. And founded on this, she was filled with grace and with every kind of virtue, and she surpasses all creatures.

And during all the time that our Lord showed me this spiritual vision which I have now described, I saw the bodily vision of the copious bleeding of the head persist. The great drops of blood fell from beneath the crown like pellets, looking as if they came from the veins, and as they issued they were a brownish red, for the blood was very thick, and as they spread they turned bright red. And as they reached the brows they vanished; and even so the bleeding continued until I had seen and understood many things. Nevertheless, the beauty and the vivacity persisted, beautiful and vivid without diminution.

The copiousness resembles the drops of water which fall from the eaves of a house after a great shower of rain, falling so thick that no human ingenuity can count them. And in their roundness as they spread over the forehead they were like a herring's scales.

At the time three things occurred to me: The drops were round like pellets as the blood issued, they were round like a herring's scales as they spread, they were like raindrops off a house's eaves, so many that they could not be counted. This vision was living and vivid and hideous and fearful and sweet and lovely; and in all this vision which I saw, what gave me most strength was that our good Lord, who is so to be revered and feared, is so familiar and so courteous, and most of all this filled me full of delight and certainty in my soul.

And so that I might understand this, he showed me this plain example. It is the greatest honour which a majestic king or a great lord can do for a poor servant, to be familiar with him; and especially if he makes this known himself, privately and publicly, with great sincerity and happy mien, this poor creature will think: See, what greater honour and joy could this noble lord give me than to demonstrate to me, who am so little, this wonderful familiarity? Truly, this is a greater joy and delight to me than if he were to give me great gifts, and himself always to remain distant in his manner. This bodily example was shown, so exalted that this man's heart could be ravished and he could almost forget his own existence in the joy of this great familiarity.

So it is with our Lord Jesus and us, for truly it is the greatest possible joy, as I see it, that he who is highest and mightiest, noblest and most honourable, is lowest and humblest, most familiar and courteous. And verily and truly he will manifest to us all this marvelous joy when we shall see him. And our good Lord wants us to believe this and trust, rejoice and delight, strengthen and console ourselves, as we can with his grace and with his help, until the time that we see it in reality. For the greatest abundance of joy which we shall have, as I see it, is this wonderful courtesy and familiarity of our Father, who is our Creator, in our Lord Jesus Christ, who is our brother and our saviour. But no man can know this wonderful familiarity in this life, unless by a special revelation from our Lord, or from a great abundance of grace, given within by the Holy Spirit. But faith and belief together with love deserve the reward, and so it is received by grace. For our life is founded on faith with hope and love. This is revealed to whom God wills, and he plainly teaches and expounds and declares it, with many secret details which are a part of our faith and belief, which are to be known to God's glory. And when the revelation, given only for a time, has passed and is hidden, then faith preserves it by the grace of the Holy Spirit to the end of our lives. And so in the revelation there is nothing different from the faith, neither less nor more, as will be seen by our Lord's intention in this same matter, when the whole revelation is completed.

THE EIGHTH CHAPTER

And as long as I saw this vision of the copious bleeding of the head, I could not stop saying these words:

> Blessed be the Lord! In this revelation I understood six things. The first is the tokens of his blessed Passion and the plentiful shedding of his precious blood. The second is the virgin who is his beloved mother. The third is the blessed divinity, that always was and is and shall be, almighty, all wisdom and all love. The fourth is everything which he has made, for I know well that heaven and earth and all creation are great, generous and beautiful and good. But the reason why it seemed to my eyes so little was because I saw it in the presence of him who is the Creator. To any soul who sees the Creator of all things, all that is created seems very little. The fifth is that he who created it created everything for love, and by the same love is it preserved, and always will be without end, as has been said already. The sixth is that God is everything which is good, as I see, and the goodness which everything has is God.

God showed me this in the first vision, and he gave me space and time to contemplate it. And then the bodily vision ceased, and the spiritual vision persisted in my understanding. And I waited with reverent fear, rejoicing in what I saw and wishing, as much as I dared, to see more, if that were God's will, or to see the same vision for a longer time.

In all this I was greatly moved in love towards my fellow Christians, that they might all see and know the same as I saw, for I wished it to be a comfort to them, for all this vision was shown for all men.

Then I said to those who were with me: Today is my Doomsday. And I said this because I expected to die; because on the day that a man or a woman dies he receives particular judgment as he will be forever, as I understand. I said this because I wished them to love God better, and to make them mindful that this life is short, of which they could see me as an example. For in all this time I was expecting to die, and that was wonderful to me and somewhat surprising, for it seemed to me that this vision was revealed for those who would go on living.

Everything that I say about me I mean to apply to all my fellow Christians, for I am taught that this is what our Lord intends in this spiritual revelation. And therefore I pray you all for God's sake, and I counsel you for your own profit, that you disregard the wretch to whom it was shown, and that mightily, wisely and meekly you contemplate upon God, who out of his courteous love and his endless goodness was willing to show it generally, to the comfort of us all. For it is God's will that you accept it with great joy and delight, as Jesus has shown it to you.

Review Questions

1. Before the revelation began, what three graces did Julian desire by the gifts of God?

2. Julian saw a vision through which she received her revelation. What did she see?

3. During the revelation, Julian says, "the Trinity filled my heart full of the greatest joy . . ." She continues with a fourfold description of the Trinity. What are the four ways that describe the Trinity?

4. Julian uses the description "greater, more worthy and more fulfilled, than everything else which God has created, . . ." To what or whom is Julian referring?

5. Why does Julian say that "our hearts and souls are not in perfect ease"?

6. What is the human person's natural will, according to Julian? What is God's will for the human person?

In-depth Questions

1. Julian mentions her desire for three "wounds": "true contrition," "loving compassion," and "longing with my will for God." Why do you think the first two desires passed away from her, yet the longing for God remained?

2. To the modern reader, a desire to suffer seems bizarre. Why do you think many of the great spiritual writers, such as Julian of Norwich, desired to suffer?

3. Julian of Norwich said, "Always I am in want; but only in you do I have everything." If God was enough for you, how would you treat your possessions? your friends? your family?

4. Julian said, "I wished them [people] to love God better." After reading this writing from Julian of Norwich, how do you think you can love God better?

Nican Mopohua

Luis Laso de la Vega

Introduction

When the Spanish arrived in what is now Mexico in 1519, the Aztec empire was among the greatest on earth. Aztec warriors had conquered millions of people from the Atlantic to the Pacific. Aztec scientists and engineers had built Tenochtitlan (tae-notch-TEE-tlan), a city of towering temples, wide plazas, and aqueducts that teemed with hundreds of thousands of people. Merchants filled huge marketplaces with goods from across the Americas. But amid this splendor, the Aztecs sacrificed thousands of people to Huitzilopochtli (WEE-tzee-low-POTCH-tlee), one of their many gods. Their prophets had predicted that the world would end soon, and they believed that such sacrifices might stall the coming apocalypse. It didn't.

In 1521, the Spanish set fire to Tenochtitlan, leveled its temples, and enslaved its citizens. Huge numbers of the native population died of smallpox; others, seeing no hope for the future, committed suicide.

This destruction and humiliation is the historical context for the events recounted in the *Nican Mopohua* (NEE-kan mo-PO-wah), a poem that describes the Virgin Mary's appearance to an Indian named Juan Diego in 1531. According to the poem, Mary instructs Juan Diego to deliver her wish to the bishop: that a chapel be built on the site of the apparition.

Among the many remarkable elements in the *Nican Mopohua* is the extent to which it incorporates and affirms the native Indian culture. The poem is masterfully written in the native Aztec language, Nahuatl (NAH-wahtel), using images and sayings that would have been familiar to the Indians—the flowers and birdsong that accompany the apparition are Aztec symbols of heaven, for instance. Mary appears as an Indian maiden and speaks to Juan Diego, in a respectful way, using his own language. The image she paints on his mantle is rich with Aztec symbols that point to Jesus as Lord of the universe. Mary identifies herself as the mother of God, but she uses Nahuatl names for God. All such names for

God had been rejected by the Christian missionaries. The respectful attitude reflected in *Nican Mopohua* stands in stark contrast to the attitudes most Spanish had toward Indians.

Tradition holds that Antonio Valeriano, a widely respected Indian scholar and governor of Mexico City, wrote the *Nican Mopohua* based on Juan Diego's testimony sometime between 1540 and 1580. But recent research suggests that the *Nican Mopohua* was actually written in 1649 by Luis Laso de la Vega, who was the parish priest at Guadalupe, the site of the apparition. He probably wrote the poem with the help of Indians skilled in the Nahuatl language, and probably drew on the Indians' oral accounts of the apparition. In his introduction to the pamphlet containing the *Nican Mopohua*, he says he is writing about the apparition account because previous generations had failed to do so and the apparition was in danger of being forgotten.

Devotion to Our Lady of Guadalupe (as the apparition came to be called) began to spread among all Mexicans after the *Nican Mopohua* was published, and it continues to grow today. Her image is revered worldwide, and some ten million people visit Our Lady of Guadalupe's basilica in Mexico City every year. They come to see her image on the mantle and to ask for the love, compassion, help, and protection that she promised to the Indian who once wore it.

GREAT CATHOLIC SPIRITUAL WRITINGS
The Text of the *Nican Mopohua*

Translated by Francisco Schulte, OSB, STD

INTRODUCTION

Here is told, is set down in order, the story of how a little while ago the Perfect Virgin, Holy Mary, the Mother of God and our Queen, miraculously appeared on Tepeyac hill, now renowned as Guadalupe.

First she graciously allowed herself to be seen by a humble Indian, Juan Diego by name; and afterwards her Precious Image appeared in the presence of the recently appointed Bishop of Mexico, Don Fray Juan de Zumárraga.

VOCABULARY

- Tepeyac (te-pe-YAHK) – This mountain was the site on which the Aztecs worshiped one of their goddesses.

- Cuauhtitlán (kwau-tee-TLAHN) – This was known as the "place of the eagles."

- Tlaltelolco (tla-te-LOL-co) – This was an ancient ceremonial center that became a center for Spanish evangelization.

POEM

Ten years after the city of Mexico had been conquered, when the arrows and shields lay scattered on the ground, when there was peace in all the towns, the knowledge of the One who is the source of all life, the true God, was now growing green and blossoming, just as it had once sprouted.

At that time, in the year 1531, a few days into the month of December, it happened that there was a simple Indian, a man of the people, whose name was Juan Diego, said to be the owner of houses which in Cuauhtitlán, as far as ecclesiastical things are concerned, belonged to Tlaltelolco.

It was Saturday, very early in the morning, when he went in search of the knowledge of God and of His commandments.

As he drew near to the hill called Tepeyac, day was just dawning.

He heard singing on the hill above, like the song of numerous fine song birds. When their voices fell silent, it seemed like the hill itself answered them, in a most gentle and pleasing way; their songs surpassed those of the *coyoltótotl* bird and of the *tzinitzcan* bird and of other fine song birds.

Juan Diego stopped to see. He said to himself: "Am I really worthy, really deserving of what I hear? Am I only dreaming it? Am I asleep and simply imagining it?

Where I am? Where do I find myself? Am I perhaps in the place that our ancestors, our grandparents always told us about: in the land of the flowers, in the land of the corn, of our flesh, of our sustenance, in the heavenly land?"

He had his gaze fixed on the top of the hill, toward the side where the sun rises, toward the place from which the precious, heavenly song was coming.

And when the song had suddenly ceased, when it was no longer heard, then he heard that he was being called from the peak of the hill; that someone was calling him to come up, saying: "My dear Juan, my dear Juan Diego."

At once, without any delay, he felt like climbing where he was called; no foreboding troubled his heart nor did anything disturb it, rather he felt totally happy and at ease. So he began to climb the hill, he went to see where he was being called.

When he arrived at the summit of the hill, he saw a Maiden standing there, who called for him to come close to her.

And when he stood before her he greatly marveled at the way her wondrous grandeur surpassed all imagining: her clothing shone like the sun, it seemed to shimmer, and the stone, the crag upon which she was standing, seemed to send out rays of light; her brilliant aura looked like the most precious jade stone, like a jewel, and the earth itself seemed to shine out with sunbeams, like a rainbow in the mist.

And the mezquite bushes and prickly pear cacti, and the other plants that grew there, seemed like emeralds. Their foliage seemed like the finest turquoise, and their trunks, their thorns, their stalks, sparkled like gold.

In her presence he bowed low. He listened to her breath [that is, her voice], her word, which was extremely gracious, thoroughly pleasing, as though coming from someone who attracted him to herself and regarded him highly.

She said to him: "Listen, my dearest son, my dear Juan. Where are you headed?"

He answered her: "My Lady, my Queen, my dear Child, I am on my way to your beloved house in Mexico Tlaltelolco. I am going to seek the things of God that our priests give us, teach us, they who are the images of Our Lord."

Right away, after this dialog with him, she made known her precious will to him, she told him: "Know, and be assured, my dearest son, that I am the Perfect Ever Virgin, Holy Mary, the Mother of the One true God, of *Ipalnemohuani* (the One through whom all live), of *Teyocoyani* (the Creator of human beings), of *Tloque Nahuaque* (the Lord of nearness and closeness), of *Ilhuicahua Tlaltipaque* (the Lord of Heaven and of Earth). I greatly desire that my beloved sacred house should be built here, in order there to show Him to you all, to exalt Him, to present Him to the peoples, He who is all my love, He who is my compassionate gaze, He who is my help, He who is my salvation.

Because I am truly the compassionate Mother of you all, yours and of all the peoples who are one in this land, and of the other varied human families, those who love me, those who cry out to me, those who seek me, those who trust in me.

For there I will hear their weeping, their sadness, in order to put right, to make well all their different hardships, their sufferings, their sorrows.

And in order to accomplish what my compassionate gaze of mercy desires, go to the palace of the Bishop of Mexico, and you tell him how I myself send you to make known to him how greatly I desire that here he provide me with a house, that he build my sanctuary for me in the plain. You shall tell him absolutely everything: all that you have seen and have marveled at and what you have heard.

And be assured that I will be very grateful to you for this and that I will repay you for it, for I will enrich you and I will glorify you; and consequently you will greatly deserve my rewarding you for your weariness, your assistance in carrying out the mission that I send you on. Now, my dearest son, you have heard my breath, my word; go and do everything that is in your power."

And immediately in her presence he bowed low; he said to her: "My Lady, my Child, I go now to carry out your venerable breath, your venerable word; for now I take my leave of you, I, your lowly servant."

Then, without delay, he went down to carry out his mission: he went to take the causeway that goes straight into Mexico.

When he had arrived at the heart of the city, he went straight to the palace of the Bishop who had recently arrived as the Governing Priest; his name was Don Fray Juan de Zumárraga, a priest of the Order of Saint Francis.

Upon arriving Juan Diego immediately tried to see the Bishop, begging his servants, his household assistants, to tell the Bishop that he was there.

After a lengthy period of time had passed they came to call him, when the Lord Bishop ordered him to enter.

As soon as Juan Diego entered, he at once knelt down before the Bishop, he bowed low. Without delay he made known to him, he recounted to him the venerable breath, the precious word of the Queen of Heaven, her message. He also told him everything that he had marveled at, what he saw, what he heard.

And having heard all of Juan Diego's narration, his message, it seemed that the Bishop did not entirely believe him.

He answered him, he said to him: "My son, you will come another time; then I will listen to you calmly, then from the very beginning I will examine, I will consider the reason you have come, your will, your desire."

Juan Diego left; he left overwhelmed by sadness because his mission had not succeeded at once.

At once he went back. A brief time later, as the day was ending, he went back from there straight to the summit of the hill, and he had the great joy of meeting the Queen of Heaven: she was waiting for him there, exactly where he had seen her the first time.

And he had barely seen her when he bowed low in her presence, he threw himself on the ground, he said to her: "My dear Patroness, my Lady, my Queen, my dearest Daughter, my dear Child, I went where you sent me as your messenger, I went to comply with your venerable breath, your beloved word. Although it was with great difficulty, I did enter the dwelling of the Chief Priest. I saw him, in his presence I made known your breath, your word, as you charged me to do.

He received me kindly and listened to me carefully, but from the way he answered me, it would seem that he didn't understand, that he wasn't convinced.

He said to me: 'You will come another time; then I will listen to you calmly, then from the very beginning I will see why you have come, your desire, your will.'

I saw clearly from the way he answered me that he thinks that the house that you wish to be built here may only be something that I made up, or that it might not be from your lips.

Therefore I earnestly beg you, my Lady, my Queen, my dear Child, to command one of the nobles, someone who is well-regarded, well-known, respected and honored, to take your venerable breath, your precious word, that he may be believed.

For truly I am a person of little worth, I am a beast of burden, I am a lowly man; I myself need to be shown the way, to be guided, carried on someone else's shoulders. The place where you send me is hardly a place for a person like me to go, hardly a place for a person like me to linger, my dear Virgin, my dear Daughter, my Lady, my Child.

So please forgive me: I fear that I will only cloud your face, your heart with sadness; I will end up falling into your anger, I will upset you, O Lady, my Patroness."

The perfect Virgin, worthy of all honor and veneration, answered him:

"Listen, my dearest son, be assured that there is no shortage of servants, of messengers, whom I could easily send to carry out my breath, my word, to carry out my will; but it is absolutely necessary that you, personally, should go, that my will, my wish should be accomplished, should be carried out through your petition, your intercession.

And I earnestly beg you, my dearest son, and with all insistence command you, to go again tomorrow to see the Bishop.

On my behalf make him know, make him hear my wish, my will, that he construct, that he make my sanctuary that I request of him.

And, once more, tell him how it is I personally who send you, I, the Ever Virgin, Holy Mary, I, who am the Mother of God."

Juan Diego, for his part, answered her, said to her: "My Lady, my Queen, my dear Child, may I not cloud your face, your heart with sadness; with the greatest pleasure will I go to fulfill your breath, your word; in no way will I fail to carry it out, nor consider the road to be too difficult.

I will go to carry out your will, but I fear that I may not be heard; and if I am heard, perhaps I will not be believed.

Tomorrow afternoon, when the sun sets, I will come to give you the answer to your word, your breath, that the Lord Bishop gives me.

Now I respectfully take my leave of you, my dearest Daughter, my dear Maiden, my Lady, my Child; rest a little while longer."

And at once Juan Diego set off for his house to rest.

On the following day, Sunday, in the last hours of night, when everything was still dark, he left from there, left from his house, and went straight to Tlaltelolco. He went to learn the divine doctrine, to be counted among those in attendance, then to see the Lord Bishop.

Around ten in the morning he was ready: he had heard Mass, the roll call had been taken and the crowd had thinned out.

So Juan Diego then went to the palace of the Lord Bishop.

As soon as he arrived he had to struggle to see him; it was with great effort that he saw the Bishop again.

At the Bishop's feet he knelt, he wept, he grew sad while speaking to him, disclosing to him the word, the breath of the Queen of Heaven, hoping against hope that the message, the will of the Perfect Virgin would be believed: to make, to build her beloved, sacred house where she had said, in the place where she wanted it.

The Lord Bishop asked him a great many things, carefully examined him, in order to ascertain where he had seen her, what she looked like. He told the Lord Bishop absolutely everything.

And although Juan Diego declared absolutely everything to the Bishop, and despite the fact that everything he saw and marveled at clearly indicated that the Lady was the Perfect Virgin, the Beloved, Glorious Mother of Our Lord and Savior Jesus Christ, nonetheless, her request was not immediately carried out.

The Bishop said that not only by Juan Diego's word, by his petition could what he asked be done, could what he asked be carried out, but that some other sign was utterly necessary in order to be able to be believed that the Queen of Heaven in person sent him.

As soon as Juan Diego heard this, he said to the Bishop: "Ruling Lord, consider which will be the sign you will ask, since I will set out at once to ask it of the Queen of Heaven who sent me."

When the Bishop saw that Juan Diego confirmed everything, that he did not hesitate or have doubts about anything, then he dispatched him.

As soon as he had gone, the Bishop quickly ordered some of his trusted household servants to follow him, carefully observing where he went, whom he saw, with whom he spoke.

And so it was done. And Juan Diego went straight away, taking the causeway.

Those who followed him lost sight of him where the ravine comes out near Tepeyac, at the wooden bridge. And though they looked everywhere, nowhere did they see him.

And so they turned back. Not only because there were greatly irritated by this, but also because their attempt had been frustrated, it angered them.

So they went to report to the Lord Bishop, putting into his head the idea that he should not believe Juan Diego; they told him that Juan Diego did nothing but tell him lies, that he did nothing but make up what he came to tell him, or that he only dreamed or imagined what he told him, what he asked of him.

And so they made up their minds that if Juan Diego came back again, returned again, they would seize him then and there and would punish him severely, to make sure that he would never come back again to tell lies or to stir up the people.

Meanwhile, Juan Diego was with the Most Holy Virgin, telling her the reply that he brought from the Lord Bishop.

When the Lady had listened to the reply, she told him:

"Very well, my dear son, you will return here tomorrow in order to take to the Bishop the sign that he has asked of you; with it he will believe you and regarding this matter he will no longer doubt, nor will he be suspicious of you.

And be assured, my dear son, that I will repay you for your care and for all the work and fatigue that you have expended for me.

So, go now; for tomorrow I await you here."

But on the following day, Monday, when Juan Diego should have taken some sign to the Bishop to be believed, he did not return.

Because when he had arrived at his house, an illness had settled upon his uncle, Juan Bernardino by name, who was by then in critical condition.

Still he went to call the doctor for him, still he did everything he could for him, but there was no time, his uncle was already on his death bed.

And when night fell, his uncle begged him that, when it was daybreak, while it was still dark out, he should set out, he should go to Tlaltelolco to call a priest to come and hear his confession, to prepare him for death, because he was sure that it was now the time, now the place for him to die, because he would not be getting out of bed, he would not be cured.

So Tuesday, while it was still very much night time, Juan Diego left there, from his house, to call the priest at Tlaltelolco.

When he was nearing the hill of Tepeyac at the end of the mountain range, at its foot where the road goes out, toward the place where the sun sets, where he had gone before, he said to himself: "If I keep to the road, won't the Lady see me? And won't she surely, as she did before, detain me so that I may take the sign to the Chief Priest as she commanded me?

First let our affliction leave us; first let me speedily call the Religious priest; my uncle is waiting for him anxiously."

At once he skirted the hill, climbed the middle part, and crossing over from there, went toward the eastern side in order to arrive rapidly at Mexico, so that the Queen of Heaven might not delay him.

He thought that by going around the way he did, she would not be able to see him, she who sees all places perfectly.

He saw how she came down from the top of the hill, and that from there she had been observing him, from there she had been watching him all along.

She came to meet him on one side of the hill, she came to intercept him; she said to him: "What's going on, my dearest son? Where are you going, where are you headed?"

And he was perhaps a little sorry, perhaps he was ashamed; or perhaps he was frightened, perhaps he grew fearful?

In her presence he bowed low, he greeted her, he said to her: "My dear Maiden, my dearest Daughter, my Child, I pray that you are in good spirits. How did you awaken this morning? Are you feeling well, my Lady, my Child?

I fear that I will cloud your face, your heart with sadness: I want you to know, my dear Child, that a servant of yours, an uncle of mine, is on his death bed.

An awful disease has settled itself upon him, and soon he will surely die from it.

Now I will go with haste to your beloved house in Mexico to call one of the loved ones of Our Lord, one of our priests, so that he may go to hear my uncle's confession and prepare him for death; because truly for this we were born: we came into this world to prepare for the undertaking of our death.

But, if I go to carry out this mission, as soon as I am finished I will return here to bring to the Bishop your breath, your word, my Lady, my dear Maiden.

I beg you to forgive me, to have a little patience with me still, because I am not deceiving you in this, my dearest Daughter, my Child; tomorrow without fail I will come with all haste."

As soon as she heard Juan Diego's explanation, the Compassionate, Perfect Virgin answered him: "Listen, know this in your heart of hearts, my dearest son: the thing that frightened you, that distressed you, is nothing; do not let your face, your heart be troubled; do not fear this illness or any other illness, nor any hurtful, distressing thing whatsoever.

Am I not here, I, who am your mother? Are you not beneath my shade and in my shelter? Am I not the source of your joy? Are you not in the folds of my mantle, in the embrace of my arms? Do you need anything else?

Let nothing else distress you, trouble you; do not let the illness of your uncle weigh down upon you with sorrow, because he will not die from it for now. Be assured that he is already well."

(And at that very moment she healed his uncle, as it later came to be known.)

And Juan Diego, when he heard the beloved word, the beloved breath of the Queen of Heaven, was greatly consoled by it, his heart experienced a genuine peace from it.

He implored her to send him immediately to see the Lord Bishop, to take something to him by way of a sign, a proof, so that the Bishop might believe.

The Heavenly Queen at once directed him to climb to the crest of the hill, to the place where he had seen her before.

She said to him: "Climb up, my dearest son, to the top of the hill, to where you saw me and where I gave you instructions.

There you will see various flowers: cut them, gather them up, put them all together; then come down here; bring them here, to me."

And Juan Diego at once climbed the hill.

When he reached the top, he greatly marveled at how many varied, beautiful and precious flowers bloomed there, how they had opened their petals, when it was still not the season for them: because precisely in that season the ice was at its worst.

The flowers were giving off a most delicate fragrance and were covered by drops of the night dew, like precious pearls.

Without delay he began to cut them, gathered them all together, put them in the hollow of his *tilma*.

The top of that hill was definitely not a place where any flowers grow; only rocky ground, thistles and thorns abound there; only prickly pear cacti and mezquite bushes, and perhaps some other small plants grew there; for it was then the month of December, when the ice devours everything, destroys everything.

At once he went down, went to carry to the Heavenly Child the different flowers that he had gone to cut.

And when she saw them, with her venerable hands she took them; then she promptly arranged them, all together, in the hollow of his *ayate*, and said to him: "My dear son, these varied flowers are the proof, the sign that you will take to the Bishop; on my behalf you will say to him that he must see in them my wish, and that by this sign he must carry out my wish, my will.

And you, you who are my messenger, in you I place absolutely all my trust; and I firmly instruct you that only in the presence of the Bishop shall you spread open your *ayate,* shall you show him what you bear.

To him you will recount everything precisely, you will tell him that I directed you to climb to the top of the hill to cut the flowers, and each thing that you saw and marveled at, so that you may convince the Lord Bishop, so that he may immediately do what is within his power to build, to raise the sanctuary that I have requested."

And as soon as the Heavenly Queen gave him his commission, he set out on the causeway, he went straight to Mexico; and this time he went in high spirits.

This time his heart was free from worry, because his mission would turn out well, because he would accomplish it perfectly.

He went along taking great care of what was in the folds of his garments, lest anything should fall out; he went along taking great pleasure in the fragrance of the various precious flowers.

When he arrived at the palace of the Bishop, the doorman and the other servants of the Lord Bishop came out to meet him, and he begged them to tell the Bishop how he wished to see him, but no one wanted to do so. They didn't want to pay any attention to him, perhaps because it was still very dark out, or perhaps because they already knew him, that he did nothing but bother them, pester them, plus their companions had already told them about him, the ones who lost sight of him when they followed after him.

During a very long period of time he was kept waiting for a reply.

And when they saw that he had been there for such a long time, standing crestfallen, doing nothing, waiting to see if he would be called, and noticed how he seemed to be carrying something in the fold of his *tilma,* they swiftly approached him to see what he carried and to humor themselves.

When Juan Diego saw that it was impossible to hide from them what he carried, and that they would probably bully him, that they would likely throw him out or would perhaps rough him up, then he showed them just the littlest bit that they were flowers.

And when they saw that they were all fine, varied flowers, and knowing that it was not the season for them, they marveled at them greatly: how fresh they were, how wide open their petals were, how fragrant they were, how beautiful they looked; and they coveted them, yearned to get hold of some of them, to run off with some of them.

Three times they dared to grab the flowers, but they failed to do so, because each time they tried to take them they could no longer see flowers, but rather what seemed like something painted, or embroidered, or sewn on the *tilma*.

With that they immediately went to tell the Lord Bishop what they had seen, how the lowly Indian who had come other times wished to see him now, and that he had already been waiting a long time for a reply, because he wanted to see him.

And the Lord Bishop, as soon as he heard this, realized that it must be the proof sent to convince him, to accomplish what that poor man had been requesting.

At once he issued the order that Juan Diego should come in to see him.

And having entered, he bowed low in the Bishop's presence, as he had already done before.

Once more he told the Bishop what he had seen, what he had marveled at, and his message.

He said to him: "My Lord Bishop, I have already done, I have already accomplished what you charged me to do; thus I went to tell the Lady, my Mistress, the Heavenly Child, Holy Mary, the Beloved Mother of God, that you asked for a sign in order to be able to believe me, in order to construct her beloved house, in the place where she asked you to build it.

I also told her that I had given you my word to come to bring you some sign, some proof of her will, as you charged me.

She gladly heard your breath, your word, and received with pleasure your petition for the sign, for the proof, so that her beloved will might be done, might come true.

And today, while it was still night, she ordered me to come and see you again; and I asked her for the proof to be believed, as she had said that she would give me one, and immediately she satisfied my request.

She sent me to the top of the hill where I had seen her previously, that I might cut there various, precious flowers.

And after I went to cut them, I brought them down; and with her holy hands she took them, again in the hollow of my *ayate* she placed them, so that I might bring them to you, so that I might give them to you personally.

Even though I knew perfectly well that the top of the hill is not a place for flowers to grow, because there is only an abundance of rocky ground, thistles, thorny shrubs, prickly pear cacti and mezquite bushes there, even so I did not doubt, even so I did not hesitate.

When I arrived at the summit of the hill I saw to my astonishment that it was now paradise.

There were all the different varieties of precious flowers, all perfect, the finest that there are, full of dew, dazzling, so I at once began to cut them.

She told me that I should give them to you on her behalf, which I now do, so that in them you may recognize the sign that you asked of her to accomplish her beloved will, and so that the truth of my word, of my message may be clearly demonstrated.

Here you have them, do me the favor of receiving them.

And with that, standing up, he spread open his white *tilma,* in whose folds he carried the flowers.

Thus as all the varied, precious flowers fell to the ground, at that very instant the Beloved Image of the Perfect Virgin, Holy Mary, Mother of God, became a sign, appeared suddenly in the same form and figure as it now is, where it is now kept in her dearly beloved house, in her dear, sacred house at Tepeyac, which is called Guadalupe.

As soon as the Lord Bishop saw it, and all those who were there, they knelt down, they greatly marveled at it.

They stood up to see it, they grew sad, they were moved, their hearts and their thoughts lifted on high.

The Lord Bishop with weeping, with sadness, begged her, asked her to pardon him for not having immediately carried out her holy will, her venerable breath, her beloved word.

When he stood up, from the neck of Juan Diego where it had been knotted, he untied his *tilma,* his garment, upon which the Heavenly Queen appeared, upon which she became a sign, and at once he bore it away; he went to place it in his chapel.

And Juan Diego passed the whole day in the house of the Bishop, who still kept him there.

On the following day the Bishop said to him: "Come, let us go so that you may point out where the Queen of Heaven wants her sanctuary to be built."

At once people were invited to build it, to construct it.

And Juan Diego, once he had pointed out where the Lady of Heaven had ordered her beloved, sacred house to be built, at once asked permission: he wanted to go to his house in order to see his uncle Juan Bernardino, who had been on his death bed when he left him to call a priest at Tlaltelolco to hear his uncle's confession and to prepare him for death, the one whom the Queen of Heaven had told him was already healed.

But they did not let Juan Diego go alone, rather they escorted him to his house.

Upon arriving they saw that his uncle was already healthy, that nothing pained him any longer.

Juan Bernardino, for his part, greatly marveled at the way in which his nephew was escorted and highly honored; he asked his nephew why this was happening, the reason they honored him so highly.

So Juan Diego told him how, when he left him to go to call a priest to hear his confession, to prepare him for death, there at Tepeyac the Lady of Heaven had appeared to him; and she sent him to Mexico to see the Lord Bishop, that he might build her a house there at Tepeyac.

And she told Juan Diego not to be upset, that his uncle was already at ease, and with that he was greatly consoled.

His uncle told Juan Diego that it was true, that at that exact moment she had healed him, and he saw her in the same form in which she had appeared to his nephew.

Juan Bernardino told Juan Diego how the Lady had sent him, too, to Mexico, to see the Bishop; and also that, when he went to see the Bishop, he should make known to him absolutely everything, he should tell him what he had seen and the miraculous way in which she had healed him; and that her Beloved Image should be called just so, should be named just so: the Perfect Virgin, Holy Mary of Guadalupe.

Without delay they brought Juan Bernardino into the presence of the Lord Bishop, they brought him to speak with him, to present his testimony.

And together with his nephew Juan Diego, the Bishop lodged them in his house for some days, while the beloved, sacred house of the young Queen was being built over at Tepeyac, where she had deigned to let herself be seen by Juan Diego.

The Lord Bishop transferred the Precious Image of the Beloved Heavenly Child to the Principal Church.

He thought it best to remove her Beloved Image from his palace, from his chapel where it had been, so that all might see it and marvel at it.

And absolutely all the inhabitants of the city, without exception, were profoundly moved when they came to see and marvel at her Precious Image.

They came to recognize its divine nature.

They came to present their prayers to her.

Many of them marveled at the miraculous way it had appeared, since absolutely no one on earth painted her Beloved Image.

Review Questions

1. Where was Juan Diego going before dawn on that early December morning?

2. Why did the lady want a sacred house to be built at Tepeyac?

3. How did the bishop respond after Juan Diego told him of the Lady from Heaven's desire to have a sacred house built at Tepeyac?

4. What did the bishop need in order to proceed with the Ever-Virgin's wishes?

5. After the third meeting of Juan Diego with the Virgin, what did he find on the top of the hill that deeply surprised him?

6. When Juan Diego met with the bishop for the third time, Juan Diego opened his mantle and its contents fell to the ground. What else happened at that moment?

In-depth Questions

1. The *Nican Mopohua* contains accounts of many miracles. But without considering the miracles, what would you say is the important message in the *Nican Mopohua*?

2. The appearance of Mary, the Mother of God, to Saint Juan Diego is one of many such appearances in the Church's history. Many of these appearances have been to people in society's underclass. Reading Luke 1:46–55 and the *Nican Mopohua*, why do you think Mary chooses the poor?

3. Mary declares that she "will hear their [all the nations'] laments and remedy and cure all their miseries, misfortunes, and sorrows." As a nation, what do you think we need a remedy or a cure for? As a global community, what do you think we need a remedy or a cure for?

4. Read Revelation 12:1–6. Describe the parallels you see between the woman described in this Bible passage and the Lady from Heaven in the *Nican Mopohua*. Do you think the parallels are important? Why or why not?

GREAT CATHOLIC SPIRITUAL WRITINGS: READING 7

"Day of a Stranger"

THOMAS MERTON

Introduction

Merton wrote "Day of a Stranger" in the summer of 1965, about three years before his death and shortly after he moved into his cottage in the woods on the grounds of the Trappist monastery at Gethsemane. It was a time of great turbulence and change: the United States and the Soviet Union had recently stepped to the brink of nuclear war, the Vietnam War raged, and people were marching for civil rights in the South. Also, the Church was being transformed by the Second Vatican Council. Merton was attuned to all of these events, and discussed them in his correspondence with some of the greatest figures of the time, including Dorothy Day; Aldous Huxley; Martin Luther King Jr.; ecologist Rachel Carson; Zen master D. T. Suzuki; and Popes John XXIII and Paul VI. In fact, "Day of a Stranger" came out of his correspondence; Merton wrote it in response to a question from someone in Latin America about how he spent his day.

Toward the end of his life, Merton became deeply interested in the wisdom of eastern spirituality and "Day of a Stranger" makes reference to some of the Zen Buddhists he was studying. Merton believed that the interreligious dialogue promoted by Vatican II could build peace in the world, and in fact he died while attending an international conference of Christian monks in Bangkok, Thailand, in 1968.

Merton is widely considered one of the spiritual giants of the twentieth century because he wrote wisely about the spiritual needs of the modern world. In his life and in his words, he showed that contemplation, prayer, and silence are not obstacles to a life that is actively engaged with the world; rather, such practices nourish and strengthen the active life, making it more deeply meaningful and holy.

For more information on Thomas Merton, refer to pages 57–58.

"Day of a Stranger"

The hills are blue and hot. There is a brown, dusty field in the bottom of the valley. I hear a machine, a bird, a clock. The clouds are high and enormous. Through them the inevitable jet plane passes: this time probably full of passengers from Miami to Chicago. What passengers? This I have no need to decide. They are out of my world, up there, busy sitting in their small, isolated, arbitrary lounge that does not even seem to be moving — the lounge that somehow unaccountably picked them up off the earth in Florida to suspend them for a while with timeless cocktails and then let them down in Illinois. The suspension of modern life in contemplation that *gets you somewhere!*

There are also other worlds above me. Other jets will pass over, with other contemplations and other modalities of intentness.

I have seen the SAC plane, with the bomb in it, fly low over me and I have looked up out of the woods directly at the closed bay of the metal bird with a scientific egg in its breast! A womb easily and mechanically opened! I do not consider this technological mother to be the friend of anything I believe in. However, like everyone else, I live in the shadow of the apocalyptic cherub. I am surveyed by it, impersonally. Its number recognizes my number. Are these numbers preparing at some moment to coincide in the benevolent mind of a computer? This does not concern me, for I live in the woods as a reminder that I am free not to be a number.

There is, in fact, a choice.

In an age where there is much talk about "being yourself" I reserve to myself the right to forget about being myself, since in any case there is very little chance of my being anybody else. Rather it seems to me that when one is too intent on "being himself" he runs the risk of impersonating a shadow.

Yet I cannot pride myself on special freedom, simply because I am living in the woods. I am accused of living in the woods like Thoreau instead of living in the desert like St. John the Baptist. All I can answer is that I am not living "like anybody." Or "unlike anybody." We all live somehow or other, and that's that. It is a compelling necessity for me to be free to embrace the necessity of my own nature.

I exist under trees. I walk in the woods out of necessity. I am both a prisoner and an escaped prisoner. I cannot tell you why, born in France, my journey ended here in Kentucky. I have considered going further, but it is not practical. It makes no difference. Do I have a "day"? Do I spend my "day" in a "place"? I know there are trees here. I know there are birds here. I know the birds in fact very well, for there are precise pairs of birds (two each of fifteen or twenty species) living in the immediate area of my cabin. I share this particular place with them: we form an ecological balance. This harmony gives the idea of "place" a new configuration.

As to the crows, they form part of a different pattern. They are vociferous and self-justifying, like humans. They are not two, they are many. They fight each other and the other birds, in a constant state of war.

PASSIONATE READER

Merton describes the many writers that he likes to read. Among those he lists are Zen masters, literary giants, the pillars of Christian thought, humble poets, artists, and sacred Scripture. His reading list demonstrates Merton's belief that a broad mind is able to live in peace.

There is a mental ecology, too, a living balance of spirits in this corner of the woods. There is room here for many other songs besides those of birds. Of Vallejo, for instance. Or Rilke, or René Char, Montale, Zukofsky, Ungaretti, Edwin Muir, Quasimodo or some Greeks. Or the dry, disconcerting voice of Nicanor Parra, the poet of the sneeze. Here also is Chuang Tzu whose climate is perhaps most the climate of this silent corner of woods. A climate in which there is no need for explanation. Here is the reassuring companionship of many silent Tzu's and Fu's; Kung Tzu, Lao Tzu, Meng Tzu, Tu Fu. And Hui Neng. And Chao-Chu. And the drawings of Sengai. And a big graceful scroll from Suzuki. Here also is a Syrian hermit called Philoxenus. An Algerian cenobite called Camus. Here is heard the clanging prose of Tertullian, with the dry catarrh of Sartre. Here the voluble dissonances of Auden, with the golden sounds of John of Salisbury. Here is the deep vegetation of that more ancient forest in which the angry birds, Isaias and Jeremias, sing. Here should be, and are, feminine voices from Angela of Foligno to Flannery O'Connor, Theresa of Avila, Juliana of Norwich, and, more personally and warmly still, Raissa Maritain. It is good to choose the voices that will be heard in these woods, but they also choose themselves, and send themselves here to be present in this silence. In any case, there is no lack of voices.

The hermit life is cool. It is a life of low definition in which there is little to decide, in which there are few transactions or none, in which there are no packages to be delivered. In which I do not bundle up packages and deliver them to myself. It is not intense. There is no give and take of questions and answers, problems and solutions.

Problems begin down the hill. Over there under the water tower are the solutions. Here there are woods, foxes. Here there is no need for dark glasses. "Here" does not even warm itself up with references to "there." It is just a "here" for which there is no "there." The hermit life is that cool.

The monastic life as a whole is a hot medium. Hot with words like "must," "ought" and "should." Communities are devoted to high definition projects: "making it all clear!" The clearer it gets the clearer it has to be made. It branches out. You have to keep clearing the branches. The more branches you cut back the more branches grow. For one you cut you get three more. On the end of each branch is a big bushy question mark. People are running all around with packages of meaning. Each is very anxious to know whether all the others have received the latest messages. Has someone else received a message that he has not received? Will they be willing to pass it on to him? Will he understand it when it is passed on? Will he have to argue about it? Will he be expected to clear his throat and stand up and say "Well the way I look at it St. Benedict said . . . ?" Saint Benedict saw that the best thing to do with the monastic life was to cool it but today everybody is heating it up. Maybe to cool it you have to be a hermit. But then they will keep thinking that *you* have got a special message. When they find out you haven't . . . Well, that's their worry, not mine.

This is not a hermitage—it is a house. ("Who was that hermitage I seen you with last night? . . .") What I wear is pants. What I do is live. How I pray is breathe. Who said Zen? Wash out your mouth if you said Zen. If you see a meditation going by, shoot it. Who said "Love?" Love is in the movies. The spiritual life is something that people worry about when they are so busy with something else they think they ought to be spiritual. Spiritual life is guilt. Up here in the woods is seen the New Testament: that is to say, the wind comes through the trees and you breathe it. Is it supposed to be clear? I am not inviting anybody to try it. Or suggesting that one day the message will come saying NOW. That is none of my business.

I am out of bed at two-fifteen in the morning, when the night is darkest and most silent. Perhaps this is due to some ailment or other. I find myself in the primordial lostness of night, solitude, forest, peace, a mind awake in the dark, looking for a light, not totally reconciled to being out of bed. A light appears, and in the light an ikon. There is now in the large darkness a small room of radiance with psalms in it. The psalms grow up silently by themselves without effort like plants in this light which is favorable to them. The plants hold themselves up on stems which have a single consistency, that of mercy, or rather great mercy. *Magna misericordia*. In the formlessness of night and silence a word then pronounces itself: Mercy. It is surrounded by other words of lesser consequence: "destroy iniquity" "wash me" "purify" "I know my iniquity." *Peccavi.* Concepts without interest in the world of business, war, politics, culture, etc. Concepts also often without interest to ecclesiastics.

Other words: Blood. Guile. Anger. The way that is not good. The way of blood, guile, anger, war.

Out there the hills in the dark lie southward. The way over the hills is blood, guile, dark, anger, death: Selma, Birmingham, Mississippi. Nearer than these, the atomic city, from which each day a freight car of fissionable material is brought to be laid carefully beside the gold in the underground vault which is at the heart of this nation.

"Their mouth is the opening of the grave; their tongues are set in motion by lies; their heart is void."

Blood, lies, fire, hate, the opening of the grave, void. Mercy, great mercy.

The birds begin to wake. It will soon be dawn. In an hour or two the towns will wake, and men will enjoy everywhere the great luminous smiles of production and business.

—Why live in the woods?
—Well, you have to live somewhere.
—Do you get lonely?
—Yes, sometimes.
—Are you mad at people?
—No.
—Are you mad at the monastery?
—No.
—What do you think about the future of monasticism?
—Nothing. I don't think about it.
—Is it true that your bad back is due to Yoga?
—No.
—Is it true that you are practicing Zen in secret?
—Pardon me, I don't speak English.

All monks, as is well known, are unmarried, and hermits more unmarried than the rest of them. Not that I have anything against women. I see no reason why a man can't love God and a woman at the same time. If God was going to regard women with a jealous eye, why did he go and make them in the first place? There is a lot of talk about a married clergy. Interesting. So far there has not been a great deal said about married hermits. Well, anyway, I have the place full of icons of the Holy Virgin.

One might say I had decided to marry the silence of the forest. The sweet dark warmth of the whole world will have to be my wife. Out of the heart of that dark warmth comes the secret that is heard only in silence, but it is the root of all the secrets that are whispered by all the lovers in their beds all over the world. So perhaps I have an obligation to preserve the stillness, the silence, the poverty, the virginal point of pure nothingness which is at the center of all other loves. I attempt to cultivate this plant without comment in the middle of the night and water it with psalms and prophecies in silence. It becomes the most rare of all the trees in the garden, at once the primordial paradise tree, the *axis mundi*, the cosmic axle, and the Cross. *Nulla silva talem profert.* There is only one such tree. It cannot be multiplied. It is not interesting.

It is necessary for me to see the first point of light which begins to be dawn. It is necessary to be present alone at the resurrection of Day, in the blank silence when the sun appears. In this completely neutral instant I receive from the Eastern woods, the tall oaks, the one word "DAY," which is never the same. It is never spoken in any known language.

Sermon to the birds: "Esteemed friends, birds of noble lineage, I have no message to you except this: be what you are: be *birds.* Thus you will be your own sermon to yourselves!"

Reply: "Even this is one sermon too many!"

Rituals. Washing out the coffee pot in the rain bucket. Approaching the outhouse with circumspection on account of the king snake who likes to curl up on one of the beams inside. Addressing the possible king snake in the outhouse and informing him that he should not be there. Asking the formal ritual question that is asked at this time every morning: "Are you in there, you bastard?"

More rituals. Spray bedroom (cockroaches and mosquitoes). Close all the windows on south side (heat). Leave windows open on north and east sides (cool). Leave windows open on west side until maybe June when it gets very hot on all sides. Pull down shades. Get water bottle. Rosary. Watch. Library book to be returned.

It is time to visit the human race.

I start out under the pines. The valley is already hot. Machines out there in the bottoms, perhaps planting corn. Fragrance of the woods. Cool west wind under the oaks. Here is the place on the path where I killed a copperhead. There is the place where I saw the fox run daintily and carefully for cover carrying a rabbit in his mouth. And there is the cement cross that, for no reason, the novices rescued from the corner of a destroyed wall and put up in the woods: people imagine someone is buried there. It is just a cross. Why should there not be a cement cross by itself in the middle of the woods?

A squirrel is kidding around somewhere overhead in midair. Tree to tree. The coquetry of flight.

I come out into the open over the hot hollow and the old sheep barn. Over there is the monastery, bugging with windows, humming with action.

The long yellow side of the monastery faces the sun on a sharp rise with fruit trees and beehives. This is without question one of the least interesting buildings on the face of the earth. However, in spite of the most earnest efforts to deprive it of all character and keep it ugly, it is surpassed in this respect by the vast majority of other monasteries. It is so completely plain that it ends, in spite of itself, by being at least simple. A lamentable failure of religious architecture— to come so close to non-entity and yet not fully succeed! I climb sweating into the novitiate, and put down my water bottle on the cement floor. The bell is ringing. I have duties, obligations, since here I am a monk. When I have accomplished these, I return to the woods where I am nobody. In the choir are the young monks, patient, serene, with very clear eyes, then, reflective, gentle, confused. Today perhaps I tell them of Eliot's *Little Gidding*, analyzing the first movement of the poem ("Midwinter spring is its own season"). They will listen with attention thinking that some other person is talking to them about some other poem.

Chanting the *alleluia* in the second mode: strength and solidity of the Latin, seriousness of the second mode, built on the *Re* as though on a sacrament, a presence. One keeps returning to the *re* as to an inevitable center. *Sol-Re, Fa-Re, Sol-Re, Do-Re*. Many other notes in between, but suddenly one hears only the one note. *Consonantia*: all notes, in their perfect distinctness, are yet blended in one. (Through a curious oversight Gregorian chant has continued to be sung in this monastery. But not for long.)

In the refectory is read a message of the Pope, denouncing war, denouncing the bombing of civilians, reprisals on civilians, killing of hostages, torturing of prisoners (all in Vietnam). Do the people of this country realize who the Pope is talking about? They have by now become so solidly convinced that the Pope never denounces anybody but Communists that they have long since ceased to listen. The monks seem to know. The voice of the reader trembles.

In the heat of noon I return with the water bottle freshly filled, through the cornfield, past the barn under the oaks, up the hill, under the pines, to the hot cabin. Larks rise out of the long grass singing. A bumblebee hums under the wide shady eaves.

I sit in the cool back room, where words cease to resound, where all meanings are absorbed in the *consonantia* of heat, fragrant pine, quiet wind, bird song and one central tonic note that is unheard and unuttered. This is no longer a time of obligations. In the silence of the afternoon all is present and all is inscrutable in one central tonic note to which every other sound ascends or descends, to which every other meaning aspires, in order to find its true fulfillment. To ask when the note will sound is to lose the afternoon: it has already sounded, and all things now hum with the resonance of its sounding.

I sweep. I spread a blanket out in the sun. I cut grass behind the cabin. I write in the heat of the afternoon. Soon I will bring the blanket in again and make the bed. The sun is over-clouded. The day declines. Perhaps there will be rain. A bell rings in the monastery. A devout Cistercian tractor growls in the valley. Soon I will cut bread, eat supper, say psalms, sit in the back room as the sun sets, as the birds sing outside the window, as night descends on the valley. I become surrounded once again by all the silent Tzu's and Fu's (men without office and without obligation). The birds draw closer to their nests. I sit on the cool straw mat on the floor, considering the bed in which I will presently sleep alone under the icon of the Nativity.

Meanwhile the metal cherub of the apocalypse passes over me in the clouds, treasuring its egg and its message.

Review Questions

1. What does Merton describe as the apocalyptic cherub?

2. Why does Merton say that the life of a hermit is cool?

3. How has Merton seen the New Testament in the woods?

4. What does Merton say will have to be his wife?

In-depth Questions

1. Merton describes the people he reads as "voices in the woods." Who are some of the writers or artists that speak God's voice to you?

2. Would you describe Merton's life as cool? Please explain.

3. Merton describes his rituals. What are some of your rituals? Do you have rituals for honoring or thanking God?

4. Merton describes his life as filled with long times of silence. Do you have silent times in your day? If so, why are these times important? If not, what do you do to fill the silence?

PART FOUR
GREAT CATHOLIC
WRITINGS ON
SOCIAL ACTION

MOTHER TERESA

SISTER THEA BOWMAN

ARCHBISHOP
OSCAR ROMERO

Great Catholic Writings on Social Action: Reading 1

"A Hunger for God"

Mother Teresa

Introduction

On August 16, 1948, Mother Teresa left the convent school where she had been a teacher and principal for more than fifteen years. She loved teaching, but she felt called to start something new — a mission to serve the poorest of India's poor, those forgotten by everyone but God. As she left the convent that day, she had little more than the simple white sari she wore. She had no companions to help her, no possessions to speak of, and no detailed plan for accomplishing her new mission. Yet over the next forty-nine years of her life, her mission reached millions of people in more than 130 countries around the world, she won the Nobel Peace Prize, and she addressed the United Nations. How did this little nun, who started with virtually nothing, manage to accomplish so much? Simply put, she took seriously Jesus's words, "just as you did it to one of the least of these [poor] . . . you did it to me" (Matthew 25:40). She believed she would find and serve Jesus in "the least" of India's poor people — and she did.

Mother Teresa was born as Agnes Gonxha Bojaxhiu in Skopje, Macedonia, on August 27, 1910, the youngest of three children. Inspired by stories of the Jesuit missionaries to India, at age eighteen Agnes joined the Sisters of Our Lady of Loreto, a group of Irish nuns with missions in India. She chose the name Teresa after Thérèse of Lisieux, the patron saint of missions, and was assigned to teach geography and history at Saint Mary's High School in Calcutta.

The major turning point of her life occurred during a train ride to a retreat in 1946. She vividly experienced Jesus's distress at the abandonment of the poor and his call for her to help them. Two years later, she received permission to leave her religious order to begin her new mission: the Missionaries of Charity.

Soon after their founding in 1950, the Missionaries of Charity became known for their work with the dying poor. They picked up the homeless who were close to death and carried them to The Home for the Dying, where they were bathed and given basic medical care. More importantly, they treated these homeless with dignity, respect, and love. Over the years, Mother Teresa founded homes for drug addicts, prostitutes, battered women, and orphans, as well as some of the first hospices for those dying of AIDS. In spite of all that, Mother Teresa insisted that the Missionaries of Charity were not social activists, but were contemplatives in the world. They did their work out of love for Jesus, and they drew their strength from personal prayer, fellowship with each other, and the Eucharist.

This chapter contains Mother Teresa's 1982 commencement address to those graduating from Harvard University. Graduates from Harvard have been among America's most influential leaders for the past few centuries. Countless names recognized throughout the world have walked through Harvard's halls, including presidents, chemists, poets, comedians, lawyers, and software engineers. Addressing this body of graduates is a privilege that few have. Mother Teresa made the most of this opportunity as she urged these soon-to-be powerful people to recognize their own poverty and to be mindful of the poorest of the poor. Mother Teresa died in 1997.

GREAT CATHOLIC WRITINGS ON SOCIAL ACTION
"A Hunger for God"

How wonderful it is. We all long, we all want, even the unbeliever, to love God in some way or another. But where is God? How do we love God, whom we have not seen? To make it easy for us, to help us to love, he makes himself the hungry one, the naked one, the homeless one. You will, I'm sure, ask me: "Where is the hunger in our country?" Yes, there is hunger. Maybe not the hunger for a piece of bread, but there is a terrible hunger for love. There is a terrible hunger for the Word of God. I will never forget when we went to Mexico and visited very poor families. They had scarcely anything in their homes, and yet nobody asked for anything. They only asked us, "Teach us the Word of God; Give us the Word of God." Here too, in the whole world, there is a terrible hunger for God, especially among the young. We must find Jesus and satisfy that hunger. Nakedness is not only for a piece of cloth. Nakedness is the loss of human dignity, the loss of respect, the loss of that purity which was so beautiful, the loss of that virginity which is the most beautiful thing that a young man and young woman can give each other because of their love. The loss of that presence, of what is beautiful, of what is great—that is nakedness. And homelessness is not only the lack of a home made of bricks, but the feeling of being rejected, being unwanted, having no one to call your own. I will never forget one day I was walking the streets of London and I saw a man sitting there looking so sad, so lonely. So I went right up to him. I took his hand and I shook it. He looked up at me and said, "Oooh, after such a long time I feel the warmth of a human hand." That little action was so small, and yet it brought a radiating smile on a face which had forgotten to smile, a man who had forgotten the warmth of a human hand. This is what we have to find in this country and in all other countries around the world.

And where do we begin? At home. And how do we begin to love? By prayer. Prayer always gives us a clean heart, and a clean heart can see God. And if we see God in each other, we will naturally love one another. We must help each other to pray.

And where do our sisters get the strength to take care of lepers and the people dying in the streets of Calcutta, New York, London and around the world? From their union with Christ, the Bread of Life, who feeds us and gives us life. Make time to be alone with Jesus, and you will find the strength, joy, and love that your heart hungers for.

Love, to be true, must hurt. Some time back in Calcutta, we had difficulty getting sugar, and a little four-year-old boy heard; "Mother Teresa has no sugar." He went home and told his parents, "I will not eat sugar for three days. I will give my sugar to Mother Teresa." After three days the parents brought this little one to our house. They had never been to see me before and they had never given anything. But this little one, with a little bottle of sugar in his hand, brought his family to our house. That little one loved with great love. Not because he gave so much. For God, it is not how much we give but how much love we put in the giving. That love begins at home right here.

Just a few days before I left Calcutta, a young man and a young woman came to our house with a big amount of money. I asked them, "Where did you get this money?", because I knew that they gave their money to feed the poor. (In Calcutta we feed about seven thousand people each day.) They gave me the most strange answer, "Before our wedding we decided not to buy wedding clothes, not to have a wedding feast, but to give you the money to feed the poor." Then I asked them one more question, "But why, why did you do that?" That is a scandal in India, not to have a wedding feast and special clothes. And they gave me this most beautiful answer, "Out of love for each other, we wanted to give each other something special and that special something was that big sacrifice, the wonderful something." How beautiful to love each other with a pure heart. On your wedding day, resolve to give each other something beautiful. The most beautiful thing is to give a virgin heart, a virgin body, a virgin soul. That's the greatest gift that the young man can give the young woman, and the young woman can give the young man. The joy of loving gives us joy in sacrifice. And if a mistake has been made, it has been made. There is healing in God's love which renews us. One must have the courage to accept and love one's child and not to destroy the most beautiful creation of God that is life. Let us pray for each other that we may love God as he loves us. It is our turn to give that lifelong, faithful tenderness and personal friendship to him in each other.

So let us thank God. I have no gold and silver to give to the American people, but I give my sisters. I hope that together with them, you will go in haste, like Mary, to find the poor. And if you find them, if you come to know them, you will love them; and if you love them, you will do something for them. You may have the poor right in your own family. We get many young people who come to our place in Calcutta to share the joy of loving, and it's beautiful to see how devotedly they serve the poorest of the poor, with so much love, with so much care. But many families need to see in their own family the suffering, the pain, and the loneliness. I will never forget when I went to thank a family in Venezuela for a plot of land they had given us to build a children's home. When I went to see the family, I saw one of their children—I've never seen anyone so disabled, so completely handicapped—and he had the most beautiful, black, shining eyes, radiating full of joy. I asked the mother, "What is the name of your child?" And the mother answered, "We call him Professor of Love, because he keeps teaching us how to love." Such a wonderful spirit of joy in that family, because they had someone who taught them how to love.

So let us thank God for the beautiful things God has given to your children, and with your help with your prayers, they have been able to stand on their feet, and you are sending them, like Jesus sent his apostles; "Go and preach the good news." Today let us pray that they will go out and preach the good news, not just say words but by their example, by the love they give to each other, especially to the unwanted, the unloved, the uncared for. You have many poor people here. Find them, love them, put your love for them in living action for in loving them, you are loving God himself.

As the new graduates go out, I thought that the prayer of Cardinal Newman is most fitting for them, so that in going into the world, they go with Jesus, they work for Jesus, and they serve him in the distressing guise of the poor:

> Dear Jesus, help us spread your fragrance everywhere we go. Flood our souls with your spirit and life. Penetrate and possess our whole being so utterly that all our lives may only be a radiance of yours. Shine through us and be so in us that every soul we meet may feel your presence in us. Let them look up and see no longer us, but only Jesus. Stay with us and then we shall begin to shine as you shine. To shine so as to be a light to others, the light will be all from you, dear Jesus. None of it will be ours; it will be you shining on others. Let us thus praise you in the way you love best, by shining on those around us. Let us preach you without preaching; not by words, but by our example. By the catching force, the sympathetic influence of what we do, the evident fullness of the love our hearts bear for you.

This is exactly what the parents have worked for, that their sons and daughters will become the carriers of God's love. Today God loves the world through each of us, for we know in the Scripture it is written that God loved the world so much that he gave his Son, Jesus (John 3:16), who became like us in all things except sin. And he came to give us good news. He came to the poor, you and me, the poor, to give that good news that God loves us, that we are somebody special to him, that he has created us for greater things: to love and be loved. And we read in Isaiah where God speaks, "I have called you by your name. You are mine. You are precious in my sight. You are honored and I love you." And to prove that, he says: "Even, even if a mother could forget her child, I will not forget you. I have curled you in the palm of my hand."

It is good to remember this, especially in these days when there is so much fear, so much pain, so much suffering, so much distress. It is good to remember that he will not forget you, that he loves you, loves me, and that Jesus has come to give us that good news. When we look at the cross, we will understand how he loved us by his actions. And he wants us to love one another as he has loved each one of us. And when he came into the light of Mary, she accepted him as the handmaid of the Lord, and she did not speak, but what did she do? Immediately in haste, she went to her cousin's home, to do what? Just to serve. To do the small works of a handmaid. And something very strange happened: the unborn child in the womb of Elizabeth, six months old, leaped with joy. That child recognized the presence of Christ. He was the first human being to welcome Jesus, to rejoice that God's son has come.

And today it is unbelievable that we are afraid of having to feed one more child, afraid to educate one more child. A nation, people, or family that allows the death of a child, they are the poorest of the poor, because they are afraid—even of their own child.

You and I have been taught to love, to love one another, to be kind to each other, not with words but in real life. To prove that love in action as Christ has proved it. That's why we read in the gospel that Jesus made himself the Bread of Life, to satisfy our hunger for love. For he says, "whatever you do to the least of my brethren, you do to me."

My prayer for you is that you may grow in love for each other. That you grow in the likeness of Christ, in the holiness of Christ. Holiness is not the luxury of the few; it is a simple duty for you and me. And where does it begin? Right at home. God bless you.

Review Questions

1. Where is God and how do we see him?

2. How does Mother Teresa define "nakedness"?

3. Where do we begin to love and how do we begin to love?

4. What did the family from Venezuela call their severely handicapped child and why did they give him such a name?

5. Mother Teresa quotes a prayer from the nineteenth-century archbishop, Cardinal Newman. Referring to that prayer, how are we to preach the message of Jesus Christ?

In-depth Questions

1. "Love, to be true, must hurt." Looking at this quote, how do you think you have experienced "true" love? Name, in very practical terms, ways that you can truly love the following:
   • A family member
   • A friend
   • The Lord

2. Mother Teresa told the story of a couple who did not buy new clothes and did not host a party for their wedding. In India, this is scandalous. Rather, they gave the money to Mother Teresa's sisters. What do

you think would be a comparable gesture here in the United States? Could you make such a sacrifice? Please explain your answer.

3. "But many families need to see in their own family the suffering, the pain, and the loneliness." All humans experience suffering, pain, and loneliness. How do you think you can serve the "poor" in your own family?

4. Mother Teresa sees the United States as a country that has material wealth but is spiritually poor. Why do you think this is her observation? Do you think she is right? Please explain your thoughts.

From *A Consistent Ethic of Life: An American-Catholic Dialogue*

JOSEPH CARDINAL BERNARDIN

Introduction

At the beginning of the 1980s, the United States and the Soviet Union possessed nearly 54,000 nuclear weapons between them—more than one million times the power of the first atomic bomb. Despite this over-whelming destructive force, each side kept building more.

This nuclear arms race prompted the U.S. Catholic bishops to draft a pastoral letter on the issue. Doing so would be no easy task, though, since the bishops had widely differing views on the issue. To lead that effort, the bishops chose a man well-known for his ability to build bridges between people: Joseph Louis Bernardin, the Archbishop of Chicago.

Bernardin had learned to reach out to people from a very early age. Born in 1928 to Italian immigrants, he was the only Catholic boy on his block in Columbia, South Carolina. He coped by attending the Bible school sponsored by his local Baptist church—especially on the days they served ice cream. By the time he reached college he had planned to become a doctor, but after one year a call to the priesthood changed his mind. In 1952 he was ordained to the priesthood.

A sharp intelligence and amiable nature contributed to his quick rise through the Catholic hierarchy. He was made a bishop in 1966 (the youngest in the country at the time), was named Archbishop of Cincinnati in 1972, was elected president of the U.S. bishops' conference in 1974, and was named a cardinal in 1983.

Bernardin's leadership role in drafting the bishops' letter on nuclear arms and his appearance on the cover of *Time* magazine made him one of the most influential and best-known of the U.S. bishops. The resulting pastoral letter, *The Challenge of Peace*, was controversial for its criticism of the nuclear arms race and its insistence that any first use of nuclear weapons would be immoral. But it achieved the bishops' goal of starting a national conversation about the morality of nuclear weapons.

Shortly after *The Challenge of Peace* was issued in 1983, Bernardin was named chair of the U.S. bishops' Committee for Pro-Life Activities. At the time, the bishops were becoming increasingly vocal on a wide range of life-related issues besides nuclear arms. The U.S. Supreme Court had legalized capital punishment and abortion in the early 1970s, and a deepening economic recession, along with the work of Latin American theologians, drew attention to the issue of systematic poverty. It was against this background that Bernardin made this now-famous speech at Fordham University on the consistent life ethic. The speech drew national media attention for Bernardin's assertion that human life must be consistently respected in every circumstance.

Bernardin did more than talk about respect for human dignity. As the archbishop of Chicago, he became famous for his compassion and willingness to listen to others. President Clinton awarded him the Presidential Medal of Freedom, the nation's highest honor, for his unrelenting work on behalf of justice and peace. Perhaps his greatest act, though, was the way he died. He had always been afraid of a long, painful death from cancer, and in 1995 his worst fears were realized when he was diagnosed with pancreatic cancer. Rather than hide his condition, he openly shared his feelings with the public and started ministering to other cancer patients. He spent his final weeks writing a memoir about the last three years of his life called *The Gift of Peace*, and it became an instant bestseller. Bernardin died on November 14, 1996, at the age of sixty-eight.

GREAT CATHOLIC WRITINGS ON SOCIAL ACTION
From *A Consistent Ethic of Life: An American-Catholic Dialogue*

The Challenge of Peace provides a starting point for developing a consistent ethic of life but it does not provide a fully articulated framework. The central idea in the letter is the sacredness of human life and the responsibility we have, personally and socially, to protect and preserve the sanctity of life.

Precisely because life is sacred, the taking of even one human life is a momentous event. Indeed, the sense that every human life has transcendent value has led a whole stream of the Christian tradition to argue that life may never be taken. That position is held by an increasing number of Catholics and is reflected in the pastoral letter, but it has not been the dominant view in Catholic teaching and it is not the principal moral position found in the pastoral letter. What is found in the letter is the traditional Catholic teaching that there should always be a *presumption* against taking human life, but in a limited world marked by the effects of sin there are some narrowly defined *exceptions* where life can be taken. This is the moral logic which produced the "Just-War" ethic in Catholic theology.

While this style of moral reasoning retains its validity as a method of resolving extreme cases of conflict when fundamental rights are at stake, there has been a perceptible shift of emphasis in the teaching and pastoral practice of the Church in the last 30 years. To summarize the shift succinctly, the presumption against taking human life has been strengthened and the exceptions made ever more restrictive. Two examples, one at the level of principle, the other at the level of pastoral practice, illustrate the shift.

First, in a path-breaking article in 1959 in *Theological Studies*, John Courtney Murray, SJ, demonstrated that Pope Pius XII had reduced the traditional threefold justification for going to war (defense, recovery of property and punishment) to the single reason of defending the innocent and protecting those values required for decent human existence. Second, in the case of capital punishment, there has been a shift at the level of pastoral practice. While not denying the classical position, found in the writing of Thomas Aquinas and other authors, that the state has the right to employ capital punishment, the action of Catholic bishops and Popes Paul VI and John Paul II has been directed against the exercise of that right by the state. The argument has been that more humane methods of defending the society exist and should be used. Such humanitarian concern lies behind the policy position of the National Conference of Catholic Bishops against capital punishment, the opposition expressed by individual bishops in their home states against reinstating the death penalty, and the extraordinary interventions of Pope John Paul II and the Florida bishops seeking to prevent the execution in Florida last week.

Execution in Florida

On Wednesday, November 30, 1983, at 9:59 a.m. the State of Florida executed Robert A. Sullivan. For the bishops of Florida, this case clearly represented the flaws in capital punishment in both theory and practice. Sullivan was poor. He was young and, as a Massachusetts native, he found himself far from home and accused of murder. Moreover, he received a poor defense in court despite his insistence that he was innocent. Although unsuccessful, the bishops' plea for his amnesty was joined by Pope John Paul II. This demonstrated how the Church was aggressively moving toward a consistent ethic of life.

Rather than extend the specific analysis of this shift of emphasis at the levels of both principle and practice in Catholic thought, I wish to probe the rationale behind the shift and indicate what it teaches us about the need for a consistent ethic of life. Fundamental to the shift is a more acute perception of the multiple ways in which life is threatened today. Obviously questions like war, aggression and capital punishment have been with us for centuries and are not new to us. What is new, is the *context* in which these ancient questions arise, and the way in which a new context shapes the *content* of our ethic of life. Let me comment on the relationship of the context of our culture and the content of our ethic in terms of: 1) the *need* for a consistent ethic of life; 2) the *attitude* necessary to sustain it; and 3) the *principles* needed to shape it.

The dominant cultural fact, present in both modern warfare and modern medicine, which induces a sharper awareness of the fragility of human life, is our technology. To live as we do in an age of careening development of technology is to face a qualitatively new range of moral problems. War has been a perennial threat to human life, but today the threat is qualitatively different due to nuclear weapons. We now threaten life on a scale previously unimaginable. As the pastoral letter put it, the dangers of nuclear war teach us to read the Book of Genesis with new eyes. From the inception of life to its decline, a rapidly expanding technology opens new opportunities for care but also poses new potential to threaten the sanctity of life.

The technological challenge is a pervasive concern of Pope John Paul II, expressed in his first encyclical, *Redemptor Hominis,* and continuing through his address to the Pontifical Academy of Science last month when he called scientists to direct their work toward the promotion of life, not the creation of instruments of death. The essential question in the technological challenge is this: In an age when we *can* do almost anything, how do we decide what we *ought* to do? The even more demanding question is: In a time when we can do anything technologically, how do we decide morally what *we never should do?*

Asking these questions along the spectrum of life from womb to tomb creates the need for a consistent ethic of life. For the spectrum of life cuts across the issues of genetics, abortion, capital punishment, modern warfare and the care of the terminally ill. These are all distinct problems, enormously complicated, and deserving individual treatment. No single answer and no simple responses will solve them. My purpose, however, is to highlight the way in which we face new technological challenges in each one of these areas; this combination of challenges is what cries out for a consistent ethic of life.

Such an ethic will have to be finely honed and carefully structured on the basis of values, principles, rules and applications to specific cases. It is not my task today, nor within my competence as a bishop, to spell out all the details of such an ethic. It is to that task that philosophers and poets, theologians and technicians, scientists and strategists, political leaders and plain citizens are called. I would, however, highlight a basic issue: the need for an attitude or atmosphere in society which is the pre-condition for sustaining a consistent ethic of life. The development of such an atmosphere has been the primary concern of the "Respect Life" program of the American bishops. We intend our opposition to abortion and our opposition to nuclear war to be seen as specific applications of this broader attitude. We have also opposed the death penalty because we do not think its use cultivates an attitude of respect for life in society. The purpose of proposing a consistent ethic of life is to argue that success on any one of the issues threatening life requires a concern for the broader attitude in society about respect for human life.

Attitude is the place to root an ethic of life, but ultimately ethics is about principles to guide the actions of individuals and institutions. It is therefore necessary to illustrate, at least by way of example, my proposition that an inner relationship does exist among several issues not only at the level of general attitude but at the more specific level of moral principles. Two examples will serve to indicate the point.

The first is contained in *The Challenge of Peace* in the connection drawn between Catholic teaching on war and Catholic teaching on abortion. Both, of course, must be seen in light of an attitude of respect for life. The more explicit connection is based on the principle which prohibits the directly intended taking of innocent human life. The principle is at the heart of Catholic teaching on abortion; it is because the fetus is judged to be both human and not an aggressor that Catholic teaching concludes that direct attack on fetal life is always wrong. This is also why we insist that legal protection be given to the unborn.

The same principle yields the most stringent, binding and radical conclusion of the pastoral letter: that directly intended attacks on civilian centers are always wrong. The bishops seek to highlight the power of this conclusion by specifying its implications in two ways: first, such attacks would be wrong even if our cities had been hit first; second, anyone asked to execute such attacks should refuse orders. These two extensions of the principle cut directly into the policy debate on nuclear strategy and the personal decisions of citizens. James Reston referred to them as "an astonishing challenge to the power of the state."

The use of this principle exemplifies the meaning of a consistent ethic of life. The principle which structures both cases, war and abortion, needs to be upheld in both places. It cannot be successfully sustained on one count and simultaneously eroded in a similar situation. When one carries this principle into the public debate today, however, one meets significant opposition from very different places on the political and ideological spectrum. Some see clearly the application of the principle to abortion but contend the bishops overstepped their bounds when they applied it to choices about national security. Others understand the power of the principle in the strategic debate, but find its application on abortion a violation of the realm of private choice. I contend the viability of the principle depends upon the consistency of its application.

The issue of consistency is tested in a different way when we examine the relationship between the "right to life" and "quality of life" issues. I must confess that I think the relationship of these categories is inadequately understood in the Catholic community itself. My point is that the Catholic position on abortion demands of us and of society that we seek to influence an heroic social ethic.

If one contends, as we do, that the right of every fetus to be born should be protected by civil law and supported by civil consensus, then our moral, political and economic responsibilities do not stop at the moment of birth. Those who defend the right to life of the weakest among us must be equally visible in support of the quality of life of the powerless among us: the old and the young, the hungry and the homeless, the undocumented immigrant and the unemployed worker. Such a quality of life posture translates into specific political and economic positions on tax policy, employment generation, welfare policy, nutrition and feeding programs, and health care. Consistency means we cannot have it both ways. We cannot urge a compassionate society and vigorous public policy to protect the rights of the unborn and then argue that compassion and significant public programs on behalf of the needy undermine the moral fiber of the society or are beyond the proper scope of governmental responsibility.

Right to life and quality of life complement each other in domestic social policy. They are also complementary in foreign policy. *The Challenge of Peace* joined the question of how we prevent nuclear war to the question of how we build peace in an interdependent world. Today those who are admirably concerned with reversing the nuclear arms race must also be those who stand for a positive U.S. policy of building the peace. It is this linkage which has led the U.S. bishops not only to oppose the drive of the nuclear arms race, but to stand against the dynamic of a Central American policy which relies predominantly on the threat and the use of force, which is increasingly distancing itself from a concern for human rights in El Salvador and which fails to grasp the opportunity of a diplomatic solution to the Central American conflict.

The relationship of the spectrum of life issues is far more intricate than I can even sketch here. I have made the case in the broad strokes of a lecturer; the detailed balancing, distinguishing and connecting of different aspects of a consistent ethic of life is precisely what this address calls the university community to investigate. Even as I leave this challenge before you, let me add to it some reflections on the task of communicating a consistent ethic of life in a pluralistic society.

Review Questions

1. How does Bernardin summarize the shift in the Church's teaching and pastoral practice regarding the taking of human life?

2. Why have Pope Paul IV, Pope John Paul II, and the bishops argued against capital punishment?

3. How has warfare technology made a qualitative difference in the threat to human life?

4. What is the purpose of proposing a consistent ethic of life?

5. What is at the heart of the Catholic teaching on abortion?

6. When a nation considers not only the right to life, but the quality of life, what specific political issues are involved?

In-depth Questions

1. When Bernardin gave this speech, the issue of nuclear war was a major concern for Americans and was in need of a response from the Church. Now that you have read his speech, what current issues do you think need to be viewed from the perspective of the consistent ethic of life? How should the consistent ethic of life be applied in one of the situations you have named?

2. Bernardin says that some people thought the bishops should not address issues of national security. Why do you think they thought it was vital to address such issues?

3. Bernardin used the term "heroic social ethic." What do you think this term means? How do you think laypeople in the Church can be heroic for the cause of life?

4. This speech addresses the largest issues facing humanity today: abortion, war, capital punishment, euthanasia, and medical technology. These are important global issues that demand a consistent ethic of life. How do you think the consistent ethic of life can impact and challenge your attitudes and daily actions?

Great Catholic Writings on Social Action: Reading 3

"The Key to Union"

Chiara Lubich

Introduction

Taking refuge on a wooded Italian hillside, Chiara Lubich watched as bombs ripped through her neighborhood on the night of May 13, 1944. Hours earlier, she and her family had packed whatever they could into backpacks, determined to flee their town for someplace safer. So it was not the ruined house she wept for as she lay awake in the woods that night, watching the stars' transit across the dark sky. No, she wept for the relentless darkness that had swept Italy, shattering so many dreams. World War II had forced twenty-four-year-old Chiara to quit her studies in philosophy; one of her friends had lost her fiancé in the fighting; another friend's home was destroyed by a bomb. Even before the war started, the rise of Fascism in Italy had cost her socialist father his job, forcing her parents to raise four children in extreme poverty. Now she wondered whether any of her friends had survived the latest bombing raid.

Then, around four in the morning, a Latin phrase came to her almost as if someone had suggested it—*omnia vincit amor*—love conquers all. For some time, she and her friends had been searching for some ideal that no bomb could destroy, and this was it: the indestructible love of God. The next morning she tearfully parted ways with her family. As they hiked into the mountains, she went down into the ruined city of Trent to search for her friends. When she saw the extent of the city's destruction, she began crying again. Then a woman grabbed her, screaming with grief over the death of her four children. Chiara realized, as she consoled the woman, that she had to set aside her own grief in order to ease the grief of others.

Chiara found that all her friends were safe, although many of their homes had been destroyed. They began gathering in a small apartment that had been spared; the warm sense of family they found there led them to nickname the place the *focolare*, the Italian name for the family hearth (or fireplace).

During the frequent air raids, they fled to the bomb shelter carrying only a Bible. As the bombs fell, Chiara and her friends studied the Scriptures for guidance. They read: "Just as you did it to one of the least of these . . . you did it to me" (Matthew 25:40), and so they set out into the ruined town to help those in need and to invite the hungry to their dinner table. They read: "Ask, and it will be given you" (Luke 11:9), and indeed, their little apartment soon overflowed with food, clothing, and medicine for those in need. Another time they read by candlelight Jesus's prayer to the Father that his followers "may all be one" (John 17:11) as the Father and the Son are one in each other. Those words seemed especially poignant in the midst of the century's second worldwide war; the young friends felt they were born to live them out by building unity wherever they could. And they read: "This is my commandment, that you love one another as I have loved you. No one has greater love than this, to lay down one's life for one's friends" (John 15:12–13). So they gathered in a circle and committed themselves to mutual love modeled after the love of Christ, each saying to the other: "I am ready to die for you." Joy and happiness seemed to overflow in their little community, just as the Gospel said. Chiara felt she was living a miracle.

After the war, the friends went their separate ways. But rather than dying, the spirit of the Focolare traveled with them. Small Focolare communities began to spring up all over Italy, and then all over Europe. Chiara sought and received the blessing of the Church for what was becoming known as the Focolare Movement.

Some sixty years after Chiara and her friends committed themselves to imitating Christ's love for the sake of world unity, the Focolare Movement has grown to 87,000 committed members and two million associates in more than 180 nations. And although Focolare remains a Catholic movement, its commitment to unity has led it into dialogue with other Christians and other religions.

Focolare has been widely recognized for its positive contributions to society; besides receiving the enthusiastic support of Pope John Paul II, Chiara has received more than a dozen honorary doctoral degrees and countless awards, including the European Prize for Human Rights. But perhaps Chiara's greatest reward is seeing the words she heard in her darkest hour — *love conquers all* — be realized on a scale she could never have imagined.

"The Key to Union"

JUST AS ALL OF CHRISTIANITY is a mystery of love and suffering, so too the truly vital elements in our movement are love and suffering.

And just as in Christianity love generally overcomes suffering and life is victor over death, so it is, also, in the Movement.

When we started out on this new life we sometimes wondered what the most beautiful thing in the world might be: whether the stars, or flowers, or children, or men of genius, or sunsets. . . . And we arrived at the conclusion that the most beautiful thing is love, the maternal, fraternal and conjugal forms of love that God has placed in the human heart.

Jesus himself raised fraternal love to a supernatural level, making of all Christians a single brotherhood. The love of a mother seemed to us even more beautiful, since, purified by sorrow; it is more lasting and more sacred to the human heart. Yet conjugal love appeared to excel over almost every other kind of love, for it makes it possible for two creatures to abandon all other natural bonds of affection in order to found a new family.

Love is certainly a wonderful thing. "But — we wondered — what must God be like who created it? And shall we, who have left all things for his sake, be able to experience, in this life, something of the love that is God?" We often read the writings of the saints, whom we got to know one by one. They were the real experts in the love of God. They were authentic Christians who, precisely because they were such, had experienced this love while still on earth.

St. Clare of Assisi, after praying at great length before the crucifix in the church of St. Damian's, on rejoining her companions would speak to them of the things of heaven, her face all radiant with a light that she had derived from the contemplation of the divine, suffering figure on the cross.

St. Bonaventure, in his *Stimulus of Divine Love,* teaches that to reach the heart of Christ, the furnace of God's love, we must first pass through his wounds.

The soul of St. Catherine of Siena seemed wholly concentrated on two concepts: fire and blood. She felt herself to be almost identified with the very Fire of Christ's love. She once said to her companions: "I am the fire, you are the sparks," and she used other highly expressive terms that pointed out to us the necessity of passing through suffering in order to "burn" with this love. In one of her letters she writes: "Clothe yourselves in the Blood, bathe in the Blood, immerse yourselves in the Blood, drown yourselves in the Blood, inebriate yourselves in the Blood."

Every saint is different from all the others, possessing a strongly marked personality of his own. But each one has ultimately found this Love by walking along the solemn way of the Passion of Christ.

One day we heard a priest, speaking on the suffering of Christ, say that perhaps the moment when Jesus suffered most was on Calvary when he cried out: "My God, my God, why have you forsaken me?"

Commenting on these words when we got home we decided, in our desire to live well the one life we had, to choose *Jesus forsaken* — as we called him in his suffering — as our Model.

And from that moment on, he, his face, his mysterious cry, seemed to color every moment of suffering in our lives.

We too, like everybody else, at times experienced spiritual states of affliction that might be described as darkness, aridity, a sense of failure, loneliness, the heaviness of our own human nature, of our sins.

ARIDITY

Many of the great spiritual writers throughout the Christian centuries have spoken of sometimes experiencing a feeling of dryness during prayer. Coming from the word *arid*, they use the word *aridity* to describe this dryness. It is a feeling that God is not close to them or even that God has abandoned them. Many of these great writers describe this time as a real test of their faith. Yet, when they have persisted in prayer, they have told of experiences of great union with God when the aridity was over.

But was not Jesus, at the ninth hour, immersed in a blackness so thick, that it infinitely surpassed any feelings of darkness that we might ever have?

And was not this aridity so great that his divine soul seemed temporarily deprived of the loving presence of the Father?

He, the victorious one, never appeared such a great failure as at that moment. But it was then that he, the Son of God, indivisibly one with him, reunited all the children to their Father by paying the price of this most terrible desolation. He, the completely innocent one, took upon his shoulders the weight of all our sins, drawing down upon himself and absorbing, like a divine lightning conductor, the full force of God's justice.

While at first we had sluggishly dragged ourselves through moments of suffering, waiting for something unexpected to turn up that would help to make the difficulty pass, now, in similar circumstances, seeing our little sorrows in the shadow of his, we stood firm, withdrawing into the depths of our souls so as to offer this suffering to Jesus, happy to add our little droplet to the sea of his pain. And then we would continue to live moment by moment, wholeheartedly performing his will, as for example, by loving the neighbor that circumstances brought our way.

During this, our spiritual darkness, the sense of failure, aridity, all these disappeared, and we began to understand how dynamically divine is the Christian life, which knows nothing of emptiness, or the cross, or suffering, except as things that pass, and which enables us to experience the fullness of life, meaning resurrection and light and hope, even in the midst of tribulations.

Later we were to learn that there are certain forms of aridity that affect one profoundly and produce real nights of the soul, true foretastes of purgatory that may last for months or even years.

At such times, for instance, the person can no longer see, so to speak, its Spouse before it. By a special privilege of his love, Christ wishes to purify and prepare the soul to serve him in his work by identifying it with his own suffering, not even leaving it, as someone has well said, the strength to offer, but only to suffer.

All this, however, did not apply to us, since we were then just beginners in this life.

For all of us, then, Jesus forsaken was the key that invariably opened the way to union with God.

He was also the means whereby we remedied any small imperfections in the unity that had been established among us through "a constant mutual charity."

"Where charity and love are, there is God." Where love and charity are wanting, therefore, God is not present. And there were times when his consoling presence, which gave meaning to the new life we had set out upon, casting a new light on even the smallest acts performed out of love for him, clarifying for us the things that happened in the present and making us see the future as bright and beckoning . . . there were times when all this vanished. This fullness of joy that results when unity is achieved among men was lost as a consequence of the pride or egoism of one or another, of an attachment to one's own ideas or belongings, or because of a failure in charity.

Our souls would then experience confusion. They reeled about in the dark, and any progress made up till then seemed unavailing. It was as if the sun of our luminous unity had set.

Then, only the memory of Jesus in his profound abandonment, of the darkness in which his soul had been engulfed, gave us hope that all was not lost. On the contrary, our present state, being one of suffering, could actually be pleasing to God if offered to him out of love. And we strove to do this, courageously bringing about unity again by asking pardon and taking the initiative, even when it was the other who had something against us. The Gospel warned us that not even our offering at the altar was pleasing to God in a climate void of reciprocal charity.

So the sun would shine once more in our little community, the presence of Jesus among those who are united in his name.

Through love for Jesus forsaken, light and peace reigned not only in our souls, but also in the souls of all those who, being lonely, disorientated, orphaned, disillusioned, failures in life, downcast, desperate, helpless or caught up in a meaningless existence, reminded us, in one way or another, of him whom we had chosen. Such persons were sought out by the members of the Movement, who tried to share with them the troubles that filled their hearts. And then, at the right moment, they would speak to them of Jesus, of his infinite love, of his favor for the categories of people mentioned in the beatitudes, of the privilege that was theirs in being able to help him carry his cross, for their own good and that of humanity. They also explained how one must offer Him personal sorrows, always recognizing in them, the countenance of Christ.

Had not Theresa of Lisieux, when she first discovered the sickness from which she eventually died, exclaimed: "Here is the Spouse"?

In this way we gradually learned, we and all our friends, that suffering is always sacred. We were not merely to put up with it, but to actually embrace it.

So our solitude was filled with God, and with the presence of the many others who by then belonged to the Movement. In Christ forsaken, souls found an orientation for their lives. In contact with people who were all trying to do God's will, orphans, for example, found not only brothers and sisters, but fathers and mothers. The disillusioned and the weary, those who have been defeated by life, found an answer to their problems. The *why* of each one found an answer in his great *why*.

With the Incarnation, Jesus was right down at our own level; but on the cross he was crushed, and in his abandonment he seemed to be altogether annihilated. Acting as a divine, inclined plane, he made it possible for *any* man on earth, *whatever* his moral and spiritual state, to ascend to God's divine Majesty, on condition that he turn to Christ and following the example of Christ, transform the whole of his oppressive burden of sorrow into the pure gold of love.

Thus, in the course of time, many people, by means of our Movement too, have understood or experienced the truth of the words of Jesus: "Those who are well have no need of a physician, but those who are sick."

And every morning we, so as to be true Christians, repeated to ourselves on rising: "Because you are forsaken . . ." as if to say: "You, Lord, crucified, are the reason for my life, under whatever form you appear. I will not shirk this encounter with you. No, I will consider it the most precious moment of the day."

Around us were also atheists, those far from God, desecrated tabernacles, yet members of the Mystical Body, or at any rate orientated towards it.

In these brothers, also, we recognized his image.

It was this love for Jesus forsaken in them, and the testimony of unity among ourselves, that worked, with the grace of God, the most varied conversions.

There are works in the Church that do not bear visible fruit, because the supernatural good they do is mysteriously destined to reach that part of the Mystical Body which God knows to be most in need. Other organizations are dedicated to the performance of works of mercy, raising up schools, orphanages, hospitals, etc.

The function of the Movement consists, through God's grace, in bringing about the conversion of individuals, a full change of heart and mind, and in helping to lead back to God the whole of the society in which it is immersed.

The love of Jesus forsaken was also our means for the diffusion of this ideal in the world.

There is no case in which the seed of grain, cast into the earth, does not need to die and decay in order to bear much fruit. This fact was borne out every time the Movement made some advance, no matter where.

The trials were of various kinds, little or great "agonies" to which it was never easy to get accustomed.

But did not Jesus crucified, burdened under the weight of our sins, show himself to be the divine seed of grain that withers and dies to give us the life of the sons of God?

It was in his name, for love of him, that we accepted these trials, thus contributing to the conversion of the world to God.

Whenever this young tree, then, had taken root, here and there in new regions and nations, other trials would come along that reminded us of the "prunings" spoken of in the Gospel.

These sometimes led to changes in one part or another of the Focolare Movement, which were often accompanied by much suffering. But if this suffering was accepted out of love, it always procured a greater good. And for that matter, was not Jesus, in his abandonment, "pruned" by heaven itself, so as to give to men, separated from God, the possibility of regrafting themselves in him?

Furthermore, looking beyond the confines of the Movement, which was then burgeoning, we sought to see and to love him also in the great sufferings of the Church.

We saw him particularly in those sections of the Mystical Body that are impoverished by secularism, or by materialism and atheism, and are often ill-treated and martyred, undergoing subtle and atrocious forms of persecution. This part of the Church, which seemed to resound with Jesus's cry, "My God, my God, why have you forsaken me," captured our interest. It awakened in us a vocation: to bring God where he is in want.

Divisions within the faith appeared to us as a gaping wound in the Mystical Body. It is well known that among Christians not of the Roman Catholic confession, there has existed for some time a widespread ecumenical movement that aspires to unity. It seemed that the Lord wished to make use of the Movement, too, on a vast scale, to help break down age-long prejudices, and to stimulate mutual knowledge and esteem as a necessary first step toward future unity.

There are also portions of the Mystical Body wasting away for lack of spiritual nourishment. In a place like Latin America, there are very few to care for the spiritual needs of a population that is overwhelmingly Christian. These people are our brothers, who have inherited the same faith, yet they find themselves in circumstances that make it almost impossible for them to maintain this faith. They, too, reminded us of Jesus forsaken.

Throughout the world, from missionary lands to the still pagan areas where Christ is unknown, mankind seemed to be waiting for one thing: the Gospel, which alone enables men to find their true selves, because it reveals to them the Creator, in whom all things have meaning and value.

All these peoples, whether pagan or not, seemed to send out a cry of abandonment to which we had to respond, if we were to react in these circumstances as Christ himself would, he who must live in us today, in the twentieth century, with all its special needs and problems.

Putting its trust in God, the Movement wished to help meet these urgent needs of humanity, and there was no better way of doing this than to try to relive, step by step, the words that Jesus uttered when, for the sake of humanity, he was among men; to believe and to practice, with utter conviction, the things he taught, and to make our own the prayer which is both his program and his final testament: "Father, that they may all be one."

For this reason the Movement has always tried to keep in contact with all those in the world who know and live this spirit.

With the help of God's grace we would like to have for each person the same love that Jesus had for his disciples ("And having loved his own . . . he loved them to the end.") so that all of us together may form, in Christ who has called us, an ever denser network throughout the world. In this way each one may be helped to persevere and, trustingly, courageously, to overcome his trials with the aid of all the others, while at the same time giving a witness to the Gospel and the Church before as many people as possible, since Jesus prayed for all men, with none excluded.

This is our ideal: Jesus crucified and forsaken, in us and outside of us, in the whole world that is waiting to be consoled and comforted.

From our limited experience we have learned that there is no true Christian life except in those who have fully embraced the cross, for ours is one of the innumerable possible actualizations of the words of Jesus: "If any man would come after me, let him deny himself and take up his cross and follow me."

But by way of comfort to those who embark for the first time upon this divine adventure, we can say that, in a small way, we too, like our giant brothers the saints, have experienced the truth that in casting oneself into the arms of the cross, one finds not only suffering, but love, the love that is the life of God himself within us.

Review Questions

1. What did Chiara Lubich and the other members of the Focolare Movement conclude was the most beautiful thing in the world?

2. What title did they give to Jesus as the model of the proper way to suffer?

3. What kinds of people did members of the Focolare Movement seek out in an attempt to help share their troubles?

4. How does Chiara Lubich describe the function of the Focolare Movement?

5. What does Chiara Lubich describe as "a gaping wound in the Mystical Body"?

In-depth Questions

1. Chiara Lubich says every saint is unique and different from every other saint. Yet each saint has found love in Jesus Christ. Considering your uniqueness and considering Christ's love for you, what would you be remembered for if you were to become a saint?

2. One of the greatest mysteries in the history of humanity is the presence of suffering. Yet Chiara Lubich describes suffering as sacred. Can you describe a time that you saw God bring good out of suffering?

3. Chiara Lubich describes seeing God's image in atheists and those far from God. Why, do you think, does she see such people as members of Christ's body?

4. Describe the meaning of this quotation: "The Gospel . . . enables men to find their true selves, because it reveals to them the Creator, in whom all things have meaning and value."

Great Catholic Writings on Social Action: Reading 4

Selections from "The Political Dimension of the Faith from the Standpoint of the Option for the Poor"

Archbishop Oscar Romero

Introduction

Archbishop Oscar Romero celebrated Mass on the evening of March 24, 1980 with several dozen worshipers in a small, hot hospital chapel. Romero proclaimed the Gospel: "Truly, truly, I say to you, unless a grain of wheat falls into the earth and dies, it remains alone; but if it dies, it bears much fruit" (John 12:24), and preached on the need to give one's body to bring justice and peace for others. As he raised the chalice at that Mass, a single rifle shot rang out from the back of the chapel. In his dying breath, he whispered words of forgiveness for the assassins. As news of his death spread in El Salvador, some celebrated while millions wept. What had Romero done in his three short years as archbishop to win the hearts of so many, and the lethal hatred of those in power?

Oscar Arnulfo Romero y Galdames was born in 1917, entered the seminary at the age of thirteen, and was ordained to the priesthood in 1942. He was somewhat shy, and was unenthusiastic about the reforms of the Second Vatican Council. He was even less enthusiastic about the preferential option for the poor that the Latin American bishops expressed at their conference in Medellín, Colombia, in 1968.

At Medellín, the bishops had urged Christians to go beyond superficial charity and become more involved in the lives of the poor by working beside them to free them. That stance had political implications in Latin America because of the huge gap between the rich and the poor. In El Salvador, about two percent of the population owned almost all of the arable land — much of which had been forcibly taken from peasants. While these landowners grew very rich, the vast majority suffered in extreme poverty. The bishops' statement at Medellín gave encouragement to priests, religious, and lay Catholic leaders who were already working with the peasants. The wealthy elite took a dim view of this activity, and repressed it through brutal, random violence.

Romero was suspicious of these ideas, but his thoughts began to change when he was named bishop of a rural diocese in 1974. Shortly after he arrived, the National Guard raided a village in the diocese, hacking people apart with machetes. Romero condemned this violence at the victims' funerals. His eyes had been opened to the people's suffering.

In 1977, Romero was named Archbishop of San Salvador, the country's capital. Soon thereafter, a priest who had supported the peasants' right to organize was gunned down, along with a seven-year-old boy and another man. Outraged by the loss of his friend, Romero buried the victims without seeking permission from the government; he excommunicated the perpetrators from the Church; and he cancelled all Masses in the archdiocese that Sunday, except for the Mass at the cathedral. Some 100,000 people attended to hear Romero condemn the government's violent oppression of the poor.

The violence grew worse. More Church leaders were killed and thousands of people "disappeared." Through all this, Romero stood with the poor and became defiantly vocal in his condemnation of the government. "The Political Dimension of the Faith from the Standpoint of the Option for the Poor" is a speech given at Louvain University in Belgium, and offers the thoughts that shaped his actions. A month after this address, he gave a homily in which he told the government's soldiers that they had no duty to obey immoral orders, and he ordered them, in the name of God, to stop the killing; the packed Cathedral erupted in thunderous applause. The next day, he was assassinated.

On the twenty-fifth anniversary of his assassination, the Vatican continued to investigate his canonization as a saint. But for the thirty-thousand people from around the world who gathered in San Salvador to celebrate his memory, he was already "Saint Romero."

Great Catholic Writings on Social Action
From "The Political Dimension of the Faith from the Standpoint of the Option for the Poor"

This has been a brief sketch of the situation, and of the stance, of the church in El Salvador. The political dimension of the faith is nothing other than the church's response to the demands made upon it by the de facto socio-political world in which it exists. What we have rediscovered is that this demand is a fundamental one for the faith, and that the church cannot ignore it. That is not to say that the church should regard itself as a political institution entering into competition with other political institutions, or that it has its own political processes. Nor, much less, is it to say that our church seeks political leadership. I am talking of something more profound, something more in keeping with the gospel. I am talking about an authentic option for the poor, of becoming incarnate in their world, of proclaiming the good news to them, of giving them hope, of encouraging them to engage in a liberating praxis, of defending their cause and of sharing their fate.

The church's option for the poor explains the political dimension of the faith in its fundamentals and in its basic outline. Because the church has opted for the truly poor, not for the fictitiously poor, because it has opted for those who really are oppressed and repressed, the church lives in a political world, and it fulfills itself as church also through politics. It cannot be otherwise if the church, like Jesus, is to turn itself toward the poor.

MAKING THE FAITH REAL IN THE WORLD OF THE POOR

The course taken by the archdiocese has clearly issued from its faith conviction. The transcendence of the gospel has guided us in our judgment and in our action. We have judged the social and political situation from the standpoint of the faith. But it is also true, to look at it another way, that the faith itself has been deepened, that hidden riches of the gospel have been opened, precisely by taking up this stance toward socio-political reality such as it is.

Now I should just like to put forward some short reflections on several fundamental aspects of the faith that we have seen enriched through this real incarnation in the socio-political world.

A CLEARER AWARENESS OF SIN

In the first place, we have a better knowledge of what sin is. We know that offending God is death for humans. We know that such a sin really is mortal, not only in the sense of the interior death of the person who commits the sin, but also because of the real, objective death the sin produces. Let us remind ourselves of a fundamental datum of our Christian faith: sin killed the Son of God, and sin is what goes on killing the children of God.

We see that basic truth of the Christian faith daily in the situation in our country. It is impossible to offend God without offending one's brother or sister. And the worst offense against God, the worst form of secularism, as one of our Salvadoran theologians has said, is: to turn children of God, temples of the Holy Spirit, the body of Christ in history, into victims of oppression and injustice, into slaves to economic greed, into fodder for political repression. The worst of these forms of secularism is the denial of grace by the objectivization of this world as an operative presence of the powers of evil, the visible presence of the denial of God.

It is not a matter of sheer routine that I insist once again on the existence in our country of structures of sin. They are sin because they produce the fruits of sin: the deaths of Salvadorans — the swift death brought by repression or the long, drawn out, but no less real, death from structural oppression. That is why we have denounced what in our country has become the idolatry of wealth, of the absolute right, within the capitalist system, of private property, of political power in national security regimes, in the name of which personal security is itself institutionalized.

No matter how tragic it may appear, the church through its entrance into the real socio-political world has learned how to recognize, and how to deepen its understanding of, the essence of sin. The fundamental essence of sin, in our world, is revealed in the death of Salvadorans.

GREATER CLARITY ON THE INCARNATION AND REDEMPTION

In the second place we now have a better understanding of what the incarnation means, what it means to say that Jesus really took human flesh and made himself one with his brothers and sisters in suffering, in tears and laments, in surrender. I am not speaking of a universal Incarnation. This is impossible. I am speaking of an incarnation that is preferential and partial: incarnation in the world of the poor. From that perspective the church will become a church for everybody. It will offer a service to the powerful, too, through the apostolate of conversion — but not the other way around, as has so often been the case in the past.

The world of the poor, with its very concrete social and political characteristics, teaches us where the church can incarnate itself in such a way that it will avoid the false universalism that inclines the church to associate itself with the powerful. The world of the poor teaches us what the nature of Christian love is, a love that certainly seeks peace but also unmasks false pacifism — the pacifism of resignation and inactivity. It is a love that should certainly be freely offered, but that seeks to be effective in history. The world of the poor teaches us that the sublimity of Christian love ought to be mediated through the overriding necessity of justice for the majority. It ought not to turn away from honorable conflict. The world of the poor teaches us that liberation will arrive only when the poor are not simply on the receiving end of handouts from governments or from the church, but when they themselves are the masters of, and protagonists in, their own struggle and liberation, thereby unmasking the root of false paternalism, including ecclesiastical paternalism.

The real world of the poor also teaches us about Christian hope. The church preaches a new heaven and a new earth. It knows, moreover, that no socio-political system can be exchanged for the final fullness that is given by God. But it has also learned that transcendent hope must be preserved by signs of hope in history, no matter how simple they may apparently be — such as those proclaimed by the Trito-Isaiah when he says "they will build houses and inhabit them, plant vineyards and eat their fruit" (Isa. 65:21). What in this is an authentically Christian hope — not reduced, as is so often said disparagingly, to what is merely of this world or purely human — is being learned daily through contact with those who have no houses and no vineyards, those who build for others to inhabit and work so that others may eat the fruits.

A Deeper Faith in God and in His Christ

In the third place, incarnation in the socio-political world is the locus for deepening faith in God and in his Christ. We believe in Jesus who came to bring the fullness of life, and we believe in a living God who gives life to men and women and wants them truly to live. These radical truths of the faith become really true and truly radical when the church enters into the heart of the life and death of its people. Then there is put before the faith of the church, as it is put before the faith of every individual, the most fundamental choice: to be in favor of life or to be in favor of death. We see, with great clarity, that here neutrality is impossible. Either we serve the life of Salvadorans, or we are accomplices in their death. And here what is most fundamental about the faith is given expression in history; either we believe in a God of life, or we serve the Idols of death.

In the name of Jesus we want and we work for, life in its fullness, a life that is not reduced to the frantic search for basic material needs, nor one reduced to the sphere of the socio-political. We know perfectly well that the superabundant fullness of life is to be achieved only in the kingdom of the Father. In human history this fullness is achieved through a worthy service of that kingdom, and total surrender to the Father. But we see with equal clarity that in the name of Jesus it would be sheer illusion, it would be an irony, and, at bottom, it would be the most profound blasphemy, to forget and to ignore the basic levels of life, the life that begins with bread, a roof, a job.

With the Apostle John we believe that Jesus is "the Word who is life" (1 John 1:1), and that God reveals himself wherever this life is to be found. Where the poor begin to really live, where the poor begin to free themselves, where persons are able to sit around a common table to share with one another—the God of life is there. When the church inserts itself into the socio-political world it does so in order to work with it so that from such cooperation life may be given to the poor in doing so, therefore, it is not distancing itself from its mission, nor is it doing something of secondary importance or something incidental to its mission. It is giving testimony to its faith in God; it is being the instrument of the Spirit, the Lord and giver of life.

This faith in the God of life is the explanation for what lies deepest in the Christian mystery. To give life to the poor one has to give of one's own life, even to give one's life itself. The greatest sign of faith in a God of life is the witness of those who are ready to give up their own life. "A man can have no greater love than to lay down his life for his friends" (John 15:13). And we see this daily in our country. Many Salvadorans, many Christians, are ready to give their lives so that the poor may have life. They are following Jesus and showing their faith in him. Living within the real world just as Jesus did, like him accused and threatened, like him laying down their lives, they are giving witness to the Word of life.

Our story, then, is a very old one, it is Jesus's story that we, in all modesty, are trying to follow. As church, we are not political experts, nor do we want to manipulate politics through its own internal mechanisms. But entrance into the socio-political world, into the world where the lives and deaths of the great mass of the population are decided upon, is necessary and urgent if we are to preserve, not only in word but in deed, faith in a God of life, and follow the lead of Jesus.

Review Questions

1. Why does Romero say that the Church fulfills its mission also through politics?

2. What better knowledge of sin did Romero acquire by being in relationship with the world of the poor?

3. How does Romero say liberation will arrive?

4. What makes the radical truths of the faith both radical and true?

5. What does Romero describe as "the most profound blasphemy"?

In-depth Questions

1. Romero describes an authentic option for the poor as entering into the world of the poor to offer hope in Jesus and in sharing their fate. What do you think these challenging words mean for the way you live?

2. The speech speaks of unmasking false pacifism and inactivity toward the poor. Name ways the following can be actively involved with the poor:
   • Your local church or parish
   • Your school
   • Your family
   • You

3. What do you think Romero means by the phrase "neutrality is impossible"?

4. Do you agree with this statement: "To give life to the poor, one has to give of one's own life, even to give one's life itself"? Please explain your answer.

"Poverty and Precarity"

Dorothy Day

Introduction

Some two hundred thousand workers paraded through the streets of New York City on May 1, 1933, many carrying the bright red banners of the Communist Party. The crowd was filled with desperate people who worked for poverty wages, in poor conditions—if they worked at all. It was the height of the Great Depression, and millions of families were hungry or homeless, and the government did little to help. Many people saw the Communist Party as the only group that cared about their plight.

Amid that crowd of Communists was an unlikely band of Catholics waving copies of a new paper called *The Catholic Worker*. Dorothy Day and her companions were harassed and jeered by the Communists, who believed that the Church contributed to the problems of the working class. Those who bothered to read the paper, though, might have been surprised to learn that the Church, led by its popes, challenged the practices that led to widespread poverty among the working class. Moreover, small groups of Catholics were trying to put into practice the Church's social teaching: the transformation of society so that everyone might live in dignity.

Dorothy Day was born on November 8, 1897, in New York City. Her marginally Protestant family was more concerned with great literature than with religion, but Dorothy absorbed some of the religious faith of her neighbors anyway. At the age of eighteen, she followed in the footsteps of her journalist father and began reporting for a socialist newspaper in New York. She covered strikes, bread riots, unemployment, and the suffragist movement.

She bought a cottage on the Staten Island beach, where she led a simple life with her common-law husband. Living amid the natural beauty of the seashore slowly reawakened her childhood faith in God. When she became pregnant she was filled with joy, and determined to have the baby, and herself, baptized into the Catholic Church. Doing so provoked her antireligious husband to leave her.

As a new Catholic, Day yearned to continue working for social change, but felt she could no longer do so among the Communists, who rejected God and religion. While covering a hunger march on Washington, Day prayed that God would show her the right way. The answer to her prayer came to her in the form of Peter Maurin, a deeply Catholic French immigrant who lived a life of voluntary poverty. He had a far-reaching vision for social change based on the Gospel, Church teaching, and French philosophers. Maurin shared that vision with Day, and convinced her to start a newspaper to promote it. *The Catholic Worker* was born.

As the circulation of *The Catholic Worker* skyrocketed, houses of hospitality in the spirit of the newspaper's program for social change were opened. Today there are about 190 self-identified Catholic Worker communities in the United States and ten foreign countries. In these communities, the faithful live much as the first Christians did.

The Catholic Worker movement that Day and Maurin founded provided an important example to Catholics everywhere, showing them how to translate the social teaching of the Gospel and the Church into reality. They influenced the development of the Catholic peace movement, as well as some of the changes of the Second Vatican Council. After Dorothy's death in 1980, the archbishop of New York began the process of advocating for her canonization as a saint.

GREAT CATHOLIC WRITINGS ON SOCIAL ACTION
"Poverty and Precarity"

It is hard to write about poverty.

We live in a slum neighborhood. It is becoming ever more crowded with Puerto Ricans, those who have the lowest wages in the city, who do the hardest work, who are small and undernourished from generations of privation and exploitation.

It is hard to write about poverty when the backyard at Chrystie Street still has the furniture piled to one side that was put out on the street in an eviction in a next-door tenement.

How can we say to these people, "Rejoice and be exceedingly glad, for great is your reward in heaven," when we are living comfortably in a warm house, sitting down to a good table, decently clothed? Maybe not so decently. I had occasion to visit the city shelter last month where homeless families are cared for. I sat there for a couple of hours, contemplating poverty and destitution—a family with two of the children asleep in the parents' arms and four others sprawling against them; another young couple, the mother pregnant.

I made myself known to a young man in charge. (I did not want to appear to be spying on them when all I wanted to know was the latest on the apartment situation for homeless families.) He apologized for making me wait, explaining that he had thought I was one of the clients.

We need always to be thinking and writing about poverty, for if we are not among its victims its reality fades from us. We must talk about poverty, because people insulated by their own comfort lose sight of it. So many decent people come in to visit and tell us how their families were brought up in poverty, and how, through hard work and cooperation, they managed to educate all the children—even raise up priests and nuns to the Church. They contend that healthful habits and a stable family situation enable people to escape from the poverty class, no matter how mean the slum they may once have been forced to live in. So why can't everybody do it? No, these people don't know about the poor. Their conception of poverty is of something neat and well ordered as a nun's cell.

And maybe no one can be told; maybe they will have to experience it. Or maybe it is a grace which they must pray for. We usually get what we pray for, and maybe we are afraid to pray for it. And yet I am convinced that it is the grace we most need in this age of crisis, this time when expenditures reach into the billions to defend "our American way of life." Maybe this defense itself will bring down upon us the poverty we are afraid to pray for.

I well remember our first efforts when we started publishing our paper. We had no office, no equipment but a typewriter which was pawned the first month. We wrote the paper on park benches and the kitchen table. In an effort to achieve a little of the destitution of our neighbors, we gave away our furniture and sat on boxes. But as fast as we gave things away people brought more. We gave blankets to needy families and when we started our first House of Hospitality people gathered together what blankets we needed. We gave away food and more food came in—exotic food, some of it: a haunch of venison from the Canadian Northwest, a can of oysters from Maryland, a container of honey from Illinois. Even now it comes in, a salmon from Seattle, flown across the continent; nothing is too good for the poor.

No one working with The Catholic Worker gets a salary, so our readers feel called upon to give and help us keep the work going. And then we experience a poverty of another kind, a poverty of reputation. It is said often and with some scorn, "Why don't they get jobs and help the poor that way? Why are they living off others, begging?"

I can only explain to such critics that it would complicate things to give a salary to Roger for his work of fourteen hours a day in the kitchen, clothes room, and office; to pay Jane a salary for running the women's house and Beth and Annabelle for giving out clothes, for making stencils all day and helping with the sick and the poor, and then have them all turn the money right back in to support the work. Or to make it more complicated, they might all go out and get jobs, and bring the money home to pay their board and room and the salaries of others to run the house. It is simpler just to be poor. It is simpler to beg. The main thing is not to hold on to anything.

But the tragedy is that we do, we all do hold on—to our books, our tools, such as typewriters, our clothes; and instead of rejoicing when they are taken from us we lament. We protest when people take our time or privacy. We are holding on to these "goods" too.

Occasionally, as we start thinking of poverty—often after reading the life of such a saint as Benedict Joseph Labre—we dream of going out on our own, living with the destitute, sleeping on park benches or in the city shelter, living in churches, sitting before the Blessed Sacrament as we see so many doing from the Municipal Lodging House around the corner. And when such thoughts come on warm spring days when the children are playing in the park, and it is good to be out on the city streets, we know that we are only deceiving ourselves, for we are only dreaming of a form of luxury. What we want is the warm sun, and rest, and time to think and read, and freedom from the people who press in on us from early morning until late at night. No, it is not simple, this business of poverty.

"Precarity," or precariousness, is an essential element in true voluntary poverty, a saintly priest from Martinique has written us. "True poverty is rare," he writes. "Nowadays religious communities are

Precarity and Precariousness

The root of these words comes from the Latin word *precarius*, which means to obtain something through prayer. To live a precarious life is to live by depending upon the will of another.

good, I am sure, but they are mistaken about poverty. They accept, admit, poverty on principle, but everything must be good and strong, buildings must be fireproof. Precarity is everywhere rejected, and precarity is an essential element of poverty. This has been forgotten. Here in our monastery we want precarity in everything except the church. These last days our refectory was near collapsing. We have put several supplementary beams in place and thus it will last maybe two or three years more. Someday it will fall on our heads and that will be funny. Precarity enables us better to help the poor. When a community is always building, enlarging, and embellishing, there is nothing left over for the poor. We have no right to do so as long as there are slums and breadlines somewhere."

Over and over again in the history of the Church the saints have emphasized poverty. Every religious community, begun in poverty and incredible hardship, but with a joyful acceptance of hardship by the rank-and-file priests, brothers, monks, or nuns who gave their youth and energy to good works, soon began to "thrive." Property was extended until holdings and buildings accumulated; and although there was still individual poverty in the community, there was corporate wealth. It is hard to remain poor.

One way to keep poor is not to accept money which is the result of defrauding the poor. Here is a story of St. Ignatius of Sardinia, a Capuchin recently canonized. Ignatius used to go out from his monastery with a sack to beg from the people of the town, but he would never go to a merchant who had built up his fortune by defrauding the poor. Franchino, the rich man, fumed every time the saint passed his door. His concern, however, was not the loss of the opportunity to give alms, but fear of public opinion. He complained at the friary, whereupon the Father Guardian ordered St. Ignatius to beg from the merchant the next time he went out.

"Very well," said Ignatius obediently. "If you wish it, Father, I will go, but I would not have the Capuchins dine on the blood of the poor."

The merchant received Ignatius with great flattery and gave him generous alms, asking him to come again in the future. But hardly had Ignatius left the house with his sack on his shoulder when drops of blood began oozing from the sack. They trickled down on Franchino's doorstep and ran down through the street to the monastery. Everywhere Ignatius went, a trickle of blood followed him. When he arrived at the friary, he laid the sack at the Father Guardian's feet. "What is this?" gasped the Guardian. "This," St. Ignatius said, "is the blood of the poor."

This story appeared in the last column written by a great Catholic layman, a worker for social justice, F. P. Kenkel, editor of *Social Justice Review* in St. Louis (and always a friend of Peter Maurin's).

Mr. Kenkel's last comment was that the universal crisis in the world today was created by love of money. "The Far East and the Near East [and he might have said all Africa and Latin America also] together constitute a great sack from which blood is oozing. The flow will not stop as long as our interests in those people are dominated largely by financial and economic considerations."

Voluntary poverty, Peter Maurin would say, is the answer. Through voluntary poverty we will have the means to help our brothers. We cannot even see our brothers in need without first stripping ourselves. It is the only way we have of showing our love.

—May 1952

Review Questions

1. Why must we always think, write, and talk about poverty?

2. What grace does Dorothy Day say is most needed during this age of crisis?

3. Why did the first publishers of *The Catholic Worker* give away their furniture?

4. What did Benedict Joseph Labre say was an essential element of poverty?

5. Why would Saint Ignatius of Sardinia never beg from Franchino, a wealthy man in his town?

In-depth Questions

1. Dorothy Day says that we are afraid to pray for poverty because we want to protect "our American way of life." Is America's financial status in the world something that concerns you? Please explain.

2. In telling of the exotic foods that have been donated, Dorothy Day says that "nothing is too good for the poor." Why do you think she made this statement?

3. Consider the definition of "precarious" and consider Matthew 6:26, 31: "Look at the birds of the air; they neither sow nor reap nor gather into barns, and yet your heavenly Father feeds them. Are you not of more value than they? . . . Therefore do not worry, saying, 'What will we eat?' or 'What will we drink?' or 'What will we wear?'" How do you think you can live precarious poverty?

4. A person is quoted in the reading as saying: "The universal crisis in the world today was created by the love of money." What do you think is the great crisis facing the world? Do you think it was created by the love of money? Please explain.

"My People Resurrect at Tepeyac"

Virgilio Elizondo

Introduction

Virgilio Elizondo hated his Catholic school as a child. Everything there seemed foreign to him: the language, people's mannerisms — even the way Mass was celebrated seemed strange. Although he had been born in the United States, the San Antonio, Texas, barrio where he grew up in the 1940s might as well have been located in the heart of Mexico. The son of Mexican immigrants, Elizondo felt like he was crossing the border of a foreign country when he crossed the street that separated the barrio from the rest of the city.

But by the time he entered high school, Elizondo had learned to see his daily "border crossings" between U.S. and Mexican culture as an adventure to be enjoyed, rather than as an ordeal. At his father's grocery store Elizondo relished his encounters with other cultures: the customers were Baptists, Jews, Catholics, Mexicans, whites, blacks — yet they mingled and laughed together easily. But as a young priest, he still struggled with the question of his identity; he felt too Mexican to be American and too American to be Mexican. It seemed that an ever-widening gap existed between the two cultures, and he was caught in no-man's land.

That changed in 1967 when a Mexican priest friend took him to the Plaza of the Three Cultures in Mexico City. A sign there commemorated the last battle between the Aztecs and the invading Spaniards. Although the battle marked the end of the Aztec culture, the sign noted that it ended not in victory or defeat, but in the birth of the Mexican people. He then visited the image of Our Lady of Guadalupe. In her, Elizondo's friend explained, the ancient Mexican soul had been united with the Spanish soul to produce the mestizo, "mixed," soul of Mexico. Elizondo realized that just as the Spanish and American Indian cultures had combined to produce a new mestizo culture in Mexico, a combination of Mexican and U.S. culture was giving birth to a new people in him and other Mexican-Americans.

Father Elizondo developed his insight into a revolutionary way of thinking about cross-cultural identity, and he called it "mestizo theology."

He drew parallels between the Mexican-American experience and Jesus's experience as a Galilean. Like Mexican-Americans, Jesus grew up in a border town that was considered backward and out of touch by most Jews. Like Mexican-Americans, Jesus experienced the violence, conflict, and rejection that people experience when they live on the border, the literal and metaphorical barrier that separates people when cultural differences are emphasized. But Jesus's presence on the border was transformative: he served the function of a bridge, uniting differing people and cultures. Mexican-Americans, Elizondo proposed, had the potential to follow Jesus's example by becoming a bridge to span the two cultures.

Father Elizondo applied his ideas to his work as rector of the San Fernando Cathedral, where he found ways to incorporate traditional Mexican ritual and symbolism into the worship. His bilingual Masses soon were broadcast on television networks around the world. He founded the Mexican-American Cultural Center and has written an avalanche of articles and books, including the essay, "My People Resurrect at Tepeyac."

Elizondo has been widely hailed for his groundbreaking work. *Time* magazine named him one of the world's most influential spiritual innovators of the twenty-first century and scholars around the world have begun applying his ideas about cross-cultural identity to other cross-cultural encounters internationally. In a world where religious differences are too often the cause of violence, this theology offers the hope of building bridges that transcend those differences.

GREAT CATHOLIC WRITINGS ON SOCIAL ACTION
"My People Resurrect at Tepeyac"

I do not know of any other event in the history of Christianity that stands at the very source of the birth of a people like the appearance of Our Lady of Guadalupe. One cannot know, understand, or appreciate the Mexican people without a deep appreciation of Guadalupe. Equally, one cannot appreciate the full salvific and redemptive force of Guadalupe without seeing it in the full context of the historical moment in which it took place. Guadalupe is not just an apparition, but a major intervention of God's liberating power in history. It is an Exodus and Resurrection event of an enslaved and dying people. The God of freedom liberates from the strongest possible government and this same God of life raises to new life what human beings seek to kill. Guadalupe is truly an epiphany of God's love at the precise moment when abandonment by God had been experienced by the people at large.

Were it not for Our Lady of Guadalupe, there would be no Mexican and no Mexican-American people today. The great Mexican nations had been defeated by the Spanish invasion that came to a violent and bloody climax in 1521. The native peoples, who had not been killed no longer wanted to live. Everything of value to them, including their religion, had been desecrated or destroyed. Nothing made sense any more. Nothing was worth living for. With this colossal catastrophe, their entire past became irrelevant. New diseases appeared and together with the trauma of the collective death wish of the people, the native population decreased drastically.

The Mexicans had been a well-developed and proud people. Now they were condemned to a subservient existence. The new masters had taken over and imposed a totally new system — new rulers, new ways of life, new language, and even a new religion. The missioners, kindly and saintly as they were, were nevertheless the ultimate legitimating agents of the new way of life. Hence, from the Mexican perspective, they were the ones to give the final blow of death to the Mexican way of life by seeking to uproot and kill their religion. Physical violence by the conquistadors destroyed their entire way of life, and religious violence through the activity of the missioners made life not only impossible but undesirable. It was better not to live at all. It was better to die.

It is in this climate of the stench and the cries of death that the new and unsuspected beginning would take place. Like the resurrection itself, it came at the moment when everything appeared to be finished. The old native ways had been crushed. There seemed to be no possibility whatsoever of future life. The Guadalupe story, like the stories of the Gospels, is very simple and child-like. Yet the full meaning of its imagery, movements, persons, and words is still to be discovered. I contend that it is the first real anthropological translation and proclamation of the gospel to the people of the Americas. That is why, upon seeing and hearing, millions responded in faith.

First "Evangelium" of the Americas

The elements of the Guadalupe story are as simple as they are beautiful. Early on the morning of December 9, 1531, a middle-aged Indian by the name of Juan Diego was on his way to mass at the church of Tlatelolco. As he passed by the edge of the small hill of Tepeyac, he was astounded to hear the most beautiful singing of precious birds. It was so beautiful that he thought he must be dreaming or be in paradise. Suddenly a beautiful lady, whose clothes radiated like the sun, appeared and called him by his name in a most endearing way.

She then spoke to him and made known her will:

Know and understand, you the dearest of my children, that I am the every holy Virgin Mary, mother of the true God through whom one lives, of the creator of heaven and earth. I have a living desire that there be built a temple, so that in it I can show and give forth all my love, compassion, help, and defense, because I am your loving mother: to you, to all who are with you, to all the inhabitants of this land and to all who love me, call upon me, and trust in me, I will hear their lamentations and will remedy all their miseries, pains, and sufferings.

In order to bring about what my mercy intends, go to the palace of the bishop and tell him how I have sent you to manifest to him what I very much desire, that here on this site below the hill, a temple be built to me.

Without hesitation, Juan Diego was immediately on his way. As could be expected he had difficulty in getting to see the bishop. When he finally got the desired audience, the bishop listened, but it was evident that he did not believe him.

Having been rejected by the bishop, Juan Diego returned to the lady with feelings of nothingness and unworthiness. He begged her to get someone better qualified and more trustworthy to be her messenger. But the lady insisted:

Listen, my son, the dearest of my children, I want you to understand that I have many servants and messengers to whom I can entrust this message, but in every aspect it is precisely my desire that you be my entrusted messenger, that through your mediation my wish may be fulfilled. Tomorrow, go to see the bishop and once again tell him that I personally, the very holy Virgin Mary, Mother of God, send you.

The next day, Juan Diego went as instructed. Once again he had difficulty getting to see the bishop. This time the bishop listened with more interest, but asked him to ask his lady from heaven for a sign that the bishop might believe. Juan Diego assured the bishop he would bring the sign and immediately set out to tell the lady. She assured him that tomorrow morning she would have the sign for him. However, when he arrived home, he discovered his uncle, Juan Bernardino, to be gravely ill. So the next morning, instead of going for the sign, he set out through a different route to find the priest that could come anoint his uncle. But the Lady appeared to him and assured him that his uncle was well and that he was to go to the top of the hill where he would find the sign the bishop asked for. He immediately ran to the top of the hill where he discovered beautiful roses of all colors.

He filled his *tilma,* or cloak, with the flowers and rushed to the bishop's palace with his great prize. When he was finally admitted into the bishop's office, in the presence of the bishop and his curia, Juan Diego unfolded his *tilma.* As all were admiring the beautiful roses, which were totally exceptional during December, the image of the Lady appeared on the *tilma* of Juan Diego and has remained there ever since. From that moment on, millions of Mexicans have come to the church through the mediation of the brown virgin of Tepeyac.

To appreciate the meaning of the story, it is necessary to see it through the categories of the ancient Nahuatl language—a language that expresses ultimate reality through image and poetry. The story begins with the *beautiful singing of the birds* and ends with *exquisite flowers.* For the native world, the expression for a divine message was precisely flower and song. Thus the entire story happens within the realm of a divine revelation: not from human beings but from God.

The lady hides *the sun* but does not extinguish it. This is most important, for the missionaries were trying to destroy everything of the native religion as diabolical. She is greater than the natives' greatest manifestation of the deity, the sun, but she does not destroy it. She will transcend, but not do away with. This is the assurance that their ancient way of life will continue, but now reinterpreted through something new and greater. She is standing upon *the moon* and therefore superior to their second greatest manifestation of the deity.

She wears the *turquoise* mantle. Turquoise was the color reserved for the supreme deity, who alone could bring harmonious unity out of the opposing forces that governed the universe. Her dress was the *pale red* of the blood sacrifices. She had assumed the blood sacrifices of her people and was now in turn offering herself to her people. She appears with hands folded over her heart and pointed in the direction of the people—the native sign of the offering of self to others.

She who was greater than all their divinities was herself not a goddess, for she wore no mask and *her eyes* were beautiful. In her eyes, the image of a person is easily discerned. In her eyes, every generation of Mexicans has seen themselves personally accepted, respected, loved, and valued. There is nothing more life-giving than to see ourselves reflected, accepted, and valued in the eyes of an important other. In the very gaze of the eye there is rebirth.

This beautiful lady who is truly from above and yet very much one of their own is pregnant, for she wears the *waist band of maternity.* Furthermore, over her womb, one finds the ancient Aztec glyph for the center of the universe. Thus she, according to ancient Nahuatl cosmology, has assumed the five previous ages—called suns—and is now the sign of the sixth age. What she offers to the world she carries within her womb: the new center of the universe about to be full born in the Americas. Through the lady millions would approach the church for Christian instruction and baptism.

BEGINNING OF THE NEW RACE

The natives who previously had wanted only to die now wanted to live; dances, songs, pilgrimages, and festivities resumed! A new life began. The immediate socio-political structure was not changed, but there was now an unsuspected foundation for a new future. In the beginning, the church opposed the new devotion, but the people promulgated and celebrated it. It spread like a wildfire propelled by high winds. Eventually the church joined, and in time even the pope came to venerate the new mother of all the inhabitants of the Americas.

At the end of an era, at the sanctuary of the ancient mother of this earth, arose the new mother of the *mestizo* generations to come. Races and nations had been opposed to each other, but as the mother of all the inhabitants of these lands, she would provide the basis for a new unity. It is not surprising that this event took place early in the morning, at the first signs of the new day, for it was the beginning of the New Day of the Americas. It was the sunrise service of the Americas.

She came from this soil. She did not come to undo the events of the past and return to "the good old days," for that never happens. But she did come to bring something new out of the chaotic events of the past. She is neither an Indian goddess nor a European Madonna; she is something new. She is neither Spanish nor Indian and yet she is both and more; she is inviting and not threatening; she unites what others strive to divide. She is the first truly American person and as such the mother of the new generations to come. In her children divisions of race and nationality will be overcome, the downtrodden will be uplifted, the marginated will be welcomed home, the cries of the silenced will be heard, and the dying will come to new life.

But beyond all my explanation and the pious or cynical interpretations of others, the power and force of the devotion continues to increase throughout the Americas. In any major city in the United States the 12th of December is celebrated each year with the greatest joy and solemnity. It is commemorated with processions, dances, songs, presentations of the original experience, masses, crownings. The impact of her presence attracts the masses of the faithful, but it equally attracts the attentions of theologians, historians, and scientists. It is not an event that happened only some 450 years ago, but an event that continues to transform millions of people throughout the Americas today. The full meaning of Guadalupe cannot be adequately explained, but it can be experienced.

Guadalupe has a magnetic power to attract diverse people from all walks of life and, in her, they can experience unity. The basis of this unity is not the feeling that one often has at large gatherings, that of being absorbed by the mob. The deepest basis of the humanism and unity is that regardless of the magnitude of the crowds, in her presence, each individual, experiences personal recognition. Each one is looked upon compassionately eye-to-eye and tenderly called by name. Thus Guadalupe is the experience (not the illusion) of family, of community and individuality, in the midst of a world of anonymity and division. In spite of the threats of death, Guadalupe is an experience and guarantee of life.

Review Questions

1. Why did the native people no longer want to live?

2. What sign did the lady provide for Juan Diego to take to the bishop?

3. For Mexican natives, what did the singing birds and the flowers signify?

4. At what time of day did the apparition occur and why is this important?

5. What can a diversity of people experience in the Virgin of Guadalupe?

In-depth Questions

1. The thesis statement of this reading is: "Guadalupe is not just an apparition, but a major intervention of God's liberating power in history." Do you agree with Elizondo's statement? Please explain.

2. Of the symbols that are mentioned and explained in the reading: the birds and flowers, the sun, the turquoise mantle, the red dress, her folded hands, and the waist band of maternity, which is your favorite? Why?

3. Please explain this statement: "She is neither an Indian goddess nor a European Madonna; she is something new. She is neither Spanish nor Indian and yet she is both and more. . . ."

4. Many people limit the significance of Our Lady of Guadalupe to Mexican peoples; however, Elizondo seems to indicate that she has significance for the entire continent. Do you think the Virgin of Guadalupe is an important symbol for our country? Please explain.

"Being a Black Catholic"

SR. THEA BOWMAN

Introduction

If the bishops who gathered at Seton Hall University in the spring of 1989 thought they were going to get a quiet speech from Sr. Thea Bowman, they were mistaken. True, this middle-aged African American nun was an academic, a professor of English, and an authority on the literature of fellow Mississippian William Faulkner. Bald and in a wheelchair, it was also painfully obvious that she was losing a five-year battle with cancer. But Sister Thea was anything but quiet, and anything but lukewarm. Dressed in colorful African robes, she was nothing less than ablaze with joy. In her talk, "Being a Black Catholic," she told the bishops what she told thousands of people across the United States and Africa: to be black is to be blessed, and black Catholics have many gifts to give the Church.

Thea Bowman was born as Bertha Bowman near Canton, Mississippi in 1937. Her father was a doctor; her mother, a teacher; her grandfather, a slave. As a girl, Bertha was shy but eager to learn. Unfortunately, racial segregation made learning difficult. Her mother discovered that Bertha could not read after attending public school for five years, and so enrolled her in a Catholic school. There, Bertha quickly learned to read and found inspiring role models in the religious sisters, brothers, and priests she met. She saw how they made a real difference in the world — feeding the hungry, sheltering the homeless, teaching children like herself — and she longed to join them. Although she was raised a Methodist, Bertha asked to be baptized into the Catholic Church at the age of ten, and at the age of sixteen she became a novice in the Order of the Franciscan Sisters of Perpetual Adoration. She took the name Thea, which means "of God."

The order sent her to its college in Wisconsin, where she majored in English and minored in speech and drama; later, she went on to earn a doctorate in English. For sixteen years, she taught English in Mississippi Catholic schools. Although the bishop granted her permission to teach in the diocese, he advised her to keep a low profile — it was 1961, after all, and racist attitudes were common even in Mississippi's churches.

Despite this advice, Sister Thea went on to become one of the most famous African American Catholics in the state, and eventually, the nation. In 1978, the bishop of Jackson, Mississippi, Joseph Brunini, invited her to become his consultant for intercultural awareness. That role opened the door for her to speak to audiences across the nation about the role of African Americans in the Church. Sister Thea was such a charismatic figure that longtime journalist Mike Wallace, who profiled her on television's *60 Minutes*, called her one of the most amazing people he had ever met.

Too often, she said, black Catholics were expected to conform to the styles of white Catholics. She rejected the idea that black Catholics—or any other group—should blend into the Church in a way that made them invisible. The experience of slavery and segregation had produced many gifts in the African American community, she said, gifts that should be shared rather than hidden: gospel hymns and spirituals, vibrant worship and poetic preaching, love of family and community, and identification with Jesus's redemptive suffering.

At the end of Sister Thea's speech to the U.S. bishops, she had them sing the spiritual, "We Shall Overcome." Her strong voice soared above the others. When she finished, the bishops gave her a standing ovation, and many of them wept. Sr. Thea Bowman died in 1990 at the age of 53. The Church, in 2003, began the process that could lead to her canonization as a saint.

GREAT CATHOLIC WRITINGS ON SOCIAL ACTION
"Being a Black Catholic"

BLACK AND CATHOLIC

What does it mean to be black and Catholic? For many of us it means having been evangelized, having been educated, having been given a chance through the work of the Catholic Church, through the Josephites or the Divine Word Fathers or the Holy Ghost Fathers or the Franciscans or the Edmundites or the Sisters of the Blessed Sacrament.

I'm from Mississippi. The first schools in Mississippi were started in the cathedral basement by diocesan priests and a group of lay women. For so many of us, being black and Catholic means having come into the church because education opened the door to evangelization. It means, in an age when black men and black women were systematically kept out of the priesthood and out of most religious communities, there were those who cared and who came and who worked with and for us and among us and helped us to help ourselves.

And now our black American bishops, in the name of the church universal, have publicly declared that we as a people of faith, as a Catholic people of God, have come of age. And it is time for us to be evangelizers of ourselves.

What does it mean to be black and Catholic? It means that I come to my church fully functioning. That doesn't frighten you, does it? I come to my church fully functioning. I bring myself, my black self, all that I am, all that I have, all that I hope to become, I bring my whole history, my traditions, my experience, my culture, my African-American song and dance and gesture and movement and teaching and preaching and healing and responsibility as gift to the church.

I bring a spirituality that our black American bishops told us — they just told us what everybody who knew, knew: that spirituality is contemplative and biblical and holistic, bringing to religion a totality of minds and imagination, of memory, of feeling and passion and emotion and intensity, of faith that is embodied, incarnate praise, a spirituality that knows how to find joy even in the time of sorrow, that steps out on faith, that leans on the Lord, a spirituality that is communal, that tries to walk and talk and work and pray and play together — even with the bishops. You know, when our bishop is around, we want him to be where we can find him, where we can reach out and touch him, where we can talk to him. Don't be too busy, you-all.

A spirituality that in the middle of your Mass or in the middle of your sermon just might have to shout out and say, "Amen, hallelujah, thank you Jesus." A faith that attempts to be Spirit-filled. The old ladies say that if you love the Lord your God with your whole heart, then your whole soul and your whole mind and all your strength, then you praise the Lord with your whole heart and soul and mind and strength and you don't bring him any feeble service.

If you get enough fully functioning black Catholics in your diocese, they are going to hold up the priest and they are going to hold up the bishop. We love our bishops, you-all. We love you-all too. But see, these bishops are our own, ordained for the church universal, ordained for the service of God's people, but they are ours; we raised them; they came from our community and in a unique way they can speak for us and to us. And that's what the church is talking about indigenous leadership. The leaders are supposed to look like their folks, ain't that what the church says?

To be black and Catholic means to realize that the work of the ordained ministers is not a threat to me and I'm no threat to that. The work of the ordained minister, of the professional minister, is to enable the people of God to do the work of the church. To feed us sacramentally, to enable us to preach and to teach, and I ain't necessarily talking about preaching in the pulpit.

You know as well as I do that some of the best preaching does not go on in the pulpit, but as a Catholic Christian I have a responsibility to preach and to teach, to worship and to pray. Black folk can't just come into church and depend on the preacher and say, "Let Father do it." And if Father doesn't do it right, then they walk out and they complain, you know, "That liturgy didn't do anything for me."

The question that we raise is. What did you do for the liturgy? And the church is calling us to be participatory and to be involved. The church is calling us to feed and to clothe and to shelter and to teach. Your job is to enable me, to enable God's people, black people, white people, brown people, all the people, to do the work of the church in the modern world. Teaching, preaching, witnessing, worshiping, serving, healing and reconciling in black, because wedded to the lived experience, to the history and the heritage of black people.

Getting in touch. To be black and Catholic means to get in touch with the world church, with my brothers and sisters in Rome, with my brothers and sisters in China, with my brothers and sisters in Europe and Asia and Latin America, with the church of Africa. Do your folk realize that there are more Catholic Christians in Africa than in North America, and then they run around talking about the minority? In Africa right now 300 people become Christian every day, and 75 percent of them are becoming Roman Catholics.

The Vatican central office reports that in Africa the number of students for the priesthood increased by 88 percent between 1970 and 1988, while in North America the number dropped by 43 percent.

To be black and Catholic means to be intensely aware of the changing complexion of the College of Cardinals. I picked up your Catholic newspaper and I saw the picture church, world church, and a lot of folk look like me. We've got to get the word out. To be black and Catholic still, though, often feels like being a second- or third-class citizen of the holy city.

BLACK LEADERSHIP IN THE CHURCH

You know, Bishop Jim Lyke said a long time ago that black Catholic Christians will be second-class citizens of the church until they take their places in leadership beside their brothers and sisters of whatever race or national origin. . . .

The majority of priests, religious and lay ministers who serve the black community in the United States still are not from the black community, and many of those people who attempt to serve among

BISHOP LYKE

Archbishop James Lyke was an African American bishop and a well-respected leader in the Church until his death in 1992. A native of Chicago, he served the Church as an auxiliary bishop for Cleveland and as the archbishop of Atlanta.

us . . . do not feel an obligation to learn or understand black history or spirituality or culture or life, black tradition or ritual. They work for the people, but they have not learned to share life and love and laughter with the people. They somehow insulate themselves from the real lives of the people because they don't feel comfortable with black people.

I travel all over the country, and I see it: black people within the church, black priests, sometimes even black bishops, who are invisible. And when I say that, I mean they are not consulted. They are not included. Sometimes decisions are made that affect the black community for generations, and they are made in rooms by white people behind closed doors.

Some of us are poor. Some of us have not had the advantages of education. But how can people still have a voice and a role in the work of the church? Isn't that what the church is calling us all to?

I see people who are well educated and experienced and willing to work. Sometimes they're religious; sometimes they're lay. They are not included in the initial stages of planning. They are not included in the decision making. Now, I know you are bishops and I'm not talking about somebody coming into your diocese and trying to tell you what to do. I'm talking about the normal, church-authorized consultative processes that attempt to enable the people of God to be about the work of the Catholic Church. If you know what I'm talking about, say Amen.

See, you-all talk about what you have to do if you want to be a multicultural church: Sometimes I do things your way; sometimes you do things mine. . . .

Black people who are still victims within the church of paternalism, of a patronizing attitude, black people who within the church have developed a mission mentality—they don't feel called, they don't feel responsible, they don't do anything. Let Father do it, let the sisters do it, let the friends and benefactors from outside do it. That's the mission mentality. And it kills us and it kills our churches. And so, within the church, how can we work together so that all of us have equal access to input, equal access to opportunity, equal access to participation?

Go into a room and look around and see who's missing and send some of your folks out to call them in so that the church can be what she claims to be — truly catholic.

They still talk about black folk in the church. You hear it, you know, you hear it over on the sidelines. They say we're lazy. They say we're loud. They say we're irresponsible. They say we lower the standards. So often we've been denied the opportunities to learn and to practice. You learned by trial and error; ain't that how you learned? And to grow.

Some black people don't approve of black religious expression in Catholic liturgy. They've been told that it's not properly Catholic. They've been told that it's not appropriately serious or dignified or solemn or controlled, that the European way is necessarily the better way.

How can we teach all the people what it means to be black and Catholic? The National Catechetical Directory says that all catechesis is supposed to be multicultural, but how little of it is. When we attempt to bring our black gifts to the church, people who do not know us say we're being non-Catholic or separatists or just plain uncouth.

CATHOLIC EDUCATION

I've got to say one more thing. You-all ain't going to like this but that's all right. Catholic schools have been a primary instrument of evangelization within the black community. The church has repeatedly asked black folk, what do you want, what can the church do for you? And black folk all over the country are saying, Help us to education. We need education. The way out of poverty is through education.

We can't be church without education, because ignorance cripples us and kills us. Black people are still asking the Catholic Church for education. Now, sometimes we don't have the money. Are we finding alternative ways to speak to the black community in a language that they understand? Bishop Brunini said a lot of Catholics spend time ministering to the saved and go out there and work with the church folks. A lot of black people out there are unchurched.

WE SHALL OVERCOME

We have come a long way in faith. Just look where we have come from. We as black people find ourselves at the threshold of a new age. And as I look about the room I know that many of you have walked and talked and worked and prayed and stood with us in society and in the church. And in the name of all black folk, I thank you.

Today we're called to walk together in a new way toward that land of promise and to celebrate who we are and whose we are. If we as church walk together, don't let nobody separate you. That's one thing black folk can teach you. Don't let folk divide you or put the lay folk over here and the clergy over here, put the bishops in one room and the clergy in the other room, put the women over here and the men over here.

The church teaches us that the church is a family. It is a family of families and the family got to stay together. We know that if we do stay together, if we walk and talk and work and play and stand together in Jesus's name, we'll be who we say we are, truly Catholic; and we shall overcome—overcome the poverty, overcome the loneliness, overcome the alienation and build together a holy city, a new Jerusalem, a city set apart where they'll know we are his because we love one another.

Review Questions

1. How does Sr. Thea Bowman describe her spirituality?

2. What does Sr. Thea Bowman believe the bishops' job is?

3. At the time that this speech was given, how many Africans became Christian on a daily basis and how many became Catholic?

4. What does Sr. Thea Bowman mean when she says black leaders in the Church are invisible?

5. What is meant by "mission mentality"?

6. What has been the primary evangelization instrument within the black community?

In-depth Questions

1. In many instances, Sister Thea uses the term *fully functioning* and expresses her desire to come to the Church "fully functioning." How do you define this term? Describe what your home church would be like if you came to it fully functioning.

2. What does Sister Thea mean when she says: "I ain't necessarily talking about preaching in the pulpit"? What are some real ways that you can "preach" in this way?

3. Sister Thea urges the Church to be multicultural in the way that it worships and in the way that it educates. Are you receptive or resistant to expressions from other cultures at worship? Please explain.

4. Sister Thea says that the Church is a family. How do you think you can help make the Church feel even more like a family?

Acknowledgments

The introductions for each chapter were written by Jerry Windley-Daoust.

The scriptural quotations contained herein are from the New Revised Standard Version of the Bible, Catholic Edition. Copyright © 1993 and 1989 by the Division of Christian Education of the National Council of the Churches of Christ in the United States of America. All rights reserved.

"The Five Ways" on pages 14–16 is from *Basic Writings of Saint Thomas Aquinas,* volume one, edited by Anton Pegis (New York: Random House, 1945), pages 22–23. Copyright © 1945 by Random House. Reprinted with permission of Hackett Publishing Company. All rights reserved.

Pensées on pages 20–22 is from *Pascal's Pensées,* by Blaise Pascal (New York: E. P. Dutton and Company, 1958), pages 66–69. Copyright © 1958 by Everyman's Library, at Northburgh House, 10 Northburgh St., London ECIV OAT. Used with permission.

"Message to the Pontifical Academy of Sciences: On Evolution" on pages 26–31 is from "Message to the Pontifical Academy of Sciences: On Evolution," by Pope John Paul II, at *www.ewtn.com/library/PAPALDOC/ JP961022.HTM,* accessed June 9, 2005.

"Leisure and Its Threefold Opposition" on pages 34–39 is from *Josef Pieper: An Anthology* (San Francisco: Ignatius Press, 1989), pages 137–143. Copyright © 1989 by Ignatius Press. Used with permission.

"The Prayer of the Church" on pages 42–47 is from "The Hidden Life: Hagiographic Essays, Meditations, Spiritual Texts," in *The Collected Works of Edith Stein,* volume four, edited by Dr. L. Gelber and Michael Linssen (Washington, DC: ICS Publications, 1992), pages 7–12. Copyright © by the Washington Province of Discalced Carmelites, ICS Publications, 2131 Lincoln Road, NE, Washington, DC 20002-1199, USA, *www.icspublications.org.* Used with permission.

"Is There Really Hope in the Young?" on pages 50–54 is from *Crossing the Threshold of Hope,* by His Holiness Pope John Paul II, translated by Vittorio Messori (New York: Alfred A. Knopf, 2001), pages 118–126. English translation copyright © 1994 by Alfred A Knopf, a division of Random House. Used with permission of Alfred A. Knopf, a division of Random House.

"Things in Their Identity" on pages 58–61 is from *New Seeds of Contemplation,* by Thomas Merton (New York: New Directions Books, 1972), pages 29–36. Copyright © 1961 by the Abbey of Gethsemani. Reprinted with permission of New Directions Publishing Corporation and Pollinger Limited and the proprietor.

"The Selfish Giant," by Oscar Wilde, on pages 66–69 is from *Stories of God: An Anthology of Literature for Catholic Schools*, edited by Br. Michel Bettigole (Dubuque, IA: Brown-Roa, 1992), pages 80–84. Copyright © 1992 by Brown-Roa.

"The Hint of an Explanation" on pages 72–81 is from *Collected Stories of Graham Greene*, by Graham Greene (New York: Viking Press, 1973), pages 361–375. Copyright © 1948 by Graham Greene. Used with permission of Viking Penguin, a division of Penguin Group (USA).

"God's Breath" on pages 84–90 is from *God's Breath and Other Stories*, by James A. Connor (Mahwah, NJ: Paulist Press, 1988), pages 92–101. Copyright © 1988 by James A. Connor. Used with permission of Paulist Press, *www.paulistpress.com*.

"Bad Friday" on pages 92–97 is from *Angel & Me: Stories by Sara Maitland*, by Sara Maitland (Harrisburg, PA: Morehouse Publishing, 1995), pages 135–142. Copyright © 1995 by Sara Maitland. Used with permission of the author.

The selections on pages 100–103 are from *The Diary of a Country Priest*, by Georges Bernanos (New York: Carroll and Graf Publishers, 2002), pages 291–298. Copyright © 1937, 1965 by the Macmillan Company. Used with permission of the publisher, Carroll and Graf Publishers, a division of Avalon Publishing Group.

"The Old Sailor" on pages 106–110 is from *The World, the Flesh, and Father Smith*, by Bruce Marshall (Boston: Houghton Mifflin, 1945), pages 16–22. Copyright © 1945, 1972 by Bruce Marshall. Used with permission of Houghton Mifflin Company. All rights reserved.

"The Beginnings of a Sin" on pages 114–122 is from *A Time to Dance and Other Stories*, by Bernard MacLaverty (New York: George Braziller, 1982), pages 135–147. Copyright © 1982 by Bernard MacLaverty. Used with permission of George Braziller, Inc.

The excerpts on pages 128–132 are from *The Sayings of the Desert Fathers: The Alphabetical Collection*, translated by Benedicta Ward (Kalamazoo, MI: Cistercian Publications, 1975), pages 4, 5, 6, 6–7, 13–18, 18, 18–19, 20, 193, and 196, respectively. Copyright © 1975 by Sr. Benedicta. Used with permission of Liturgical Press.

The Life of Brother Juniper on pages 134–141 is from *The Little Flowers of St. Francis of Assisi* (London: Catholic Truth Society, 1907), pages 170–185.

The excerpts from *The Cloud of Unknowing* on pages 144–149 are from "My Friend in God," in *The Cloud of Unknowing and Other Works*, translated by Clifton Wolters (New York: Penguin Classics, 1961), pages 59–66. Copyright © 1961, reprinted 1978 by Clifton Wolters. Used with permission of Penguin Books Ltd.

The excerpts from *The Story of a Soul* on pages 152–159 are from *The Autobiography of Saint Thérèse of Lisieux: The Story of a Soul,* translated by John Beevers (New York: Doubleday, 1957), pages 112–129. Copyright © 1957 by Doubleday, a division of Random House. Used with permission of Doubleday, a division of Random House.

The excerpts on pages 162–171 are from *Julian of Norwich: Showings,* The Classics of Western Spirituality, from the critical text with an introduction translated by Edmund Colledge and James Walsh (Mahwah, NJ: Paulist Press, 1978), pages 177–199. Copyright © 1978 by Paulist Press. Used with permission of Paulist Press, *www.paulistpress.com.*

Nican Mopohua on pages 174–186 is translated from the original Nahuatl text of *Nican Mopohua,* by Francisco Schulte.

"Day of a Stranger" on pages 190–196 is from *Thomas Merton: Spiritual Master: The Essential Writings,* edited by Lawrence Cunningham (Mahwah, NJ: Paulist Press, 1992), pages 215–222. Copyright © 1992 by Lawrence Cunningham. Used with permission of Paulist Press, *www.paulistpress.com.*

"A Hunger for God" on pages 200–204 is from *Finding God at Harvard: Spiritual Journeys of Thinking Christians,* edited by Kelly K. Monroe (Grand Rapids, MI: Zondervan Publishing House, 1996), pages 315–318. Copyright © 1996 by Kelly K. Monroe. Used with permission of the Zondervan Corporation.

The prayer on page 203 by John Cardinal Newman is from the Holistic-Online.com Web site, *www.1stholistic.com/Spl_prayers/ prayer_christ-radating-christ-newman.htm,* accessed June 22, 2005.

The excerpt on pages 208–213 is from *A Consistent Ethic of Life: An American-Catholic Dialogue,* (Gannon–Lecture) December 6, 1983, Box #44063.01, Folder #EXEC/C0500/1232, Joseph Cardinal Bernardin papers, Archdiocese of Chicago's Joseph Cardinal Bernardin Archives and Records Center, Chicago, (Kansas City, MO: Sheed and Ward, 1988), pages 5–9. Copyright © 1988 by Loyola University of Chicago. Used with permission.

"The Key to Union" on pages 217–223 is from *That All Men Be One: Origins and Life of the Focolare Movement,* by Chiara Lubich (New York: New City Press, 1969), pages 65–78. Copyright © 1969 by Città Nuova Editrice. Used with permission of the Focolare Movement.

Excerpts from "The Political Dimension of the Faith from the Standpoint of the Option for the Poor" on pages 226–230 is from *Voice of the Voiceless,* by Oscar Romero (Maryknoll, NY: Orbis Books, 1985), pages 182–186. Copyright © 1985 by Orbis Books. Used with permission.

"Poverty and Precarity" on pages 234–238 is from *Dorothy Day: Selected Writings: By Little and By Little,* edited by Robert Ellsberg (Maryknoll, NY: Orbis Books, 2005), pages 106–112. Copyright © 1983, 1992, and 2005 by Robert Ellsberg and Tamar Hennessey. Published in 2005 by Orbis Books, Maryknoll, New York, 10545. Used with permission.

"My People Resurrect at Tepeyac" on pages 240–245 is from *The Future is Mestizo: Life Where Cultures Meet,* by Virgil Elizondo (New York: Crossroad, 1992), pages 59–66. Copyright © 1988 by Virgil Elizondo. Used with permission of Chantal Galtier Roussel Agence Littéraire.

"Being a Black Catholic" on pages 248–253 is from the article "To Be Black and Catholic," by Sr. Thea Bowman, in *Origins,* July 6, 1989, pages 114–118. Copyright © 1989 by Catholic News Service.

To view copyright terms and conditions for Internet materials cited here, log on to the home pages for the referenced Web sites.

During this book's preparation, all citations, facts, figures, names, addresses, telephone numbers, Internet URLs, and other pieces of information cited within were verified for accuracy. The authors and Saint Mary's Press staff have made every attempt to reference current and valid sources, but we cannot guarantee the content of any source, and we are not responsible for any changes that may have occurred since our verification. If you find an error in, or have a question or concern about, any of the information or sources listed within, please contact Saint Mary's Press.

Photo Credits

Northwind Picture Archives: pages 11 and 63

Catholic News Service: pages 11, 125, and 197

Photography Collection, Harry Ransom Humanities Research Center, The University of Texas at Austin: page 63

Adam Lee: page 63

Erich Lessing/Art Resource, NY: page 125